WATCHING TV OFF THE BACK OF A FIRE TRUCK:
VOICES FROM THE FLOYD FLOOD IN EASTERN NORTH CAROLINA

We watched as the water slowly rose up one street to cover most of the stop sign nearest the river's edge. In the other street automobiles disappeared under the water. Suddenly it was like living in another world, maybe like Venice. The reflections in the water were everywhere, reflecting a world that had never watched itself before. It was a world of mirrors. It was a disaster and it was beautiful. I went into my studio and got my paints, my easel and set up in the street at the water's edge, which just touched the corner of my property.

Later several people commented that my paintings were too beautiful to be about the flood. To me they were honestly about the dark beauty I was seeing. When the flood waters began to recede, any beauty, illusion or otherwise, washed its way back down to the river, leaving in its wake an ugly, mucky, muddy, gray-brown groundcover, clinging to dead grass and tree bottoms.

Susan Luddeke
Greenville, North Carolina

North Carolina Humanities Council
Weaving Cultures and Communities

WATCHING TV OFF THE BACK OF A FIRE TRUCK:
VOICES FROM THE FLOYD FLOOD IN EASTERN NORTH CAROLINA

Edited by Julie Fay, Joyce Joines Newman and Harlan Joel Gradin
Assistant Editors: Ana Cowó, Sharon O'Neill, Gary Redding, Lois B. Watkins

Saturday night we stayed up watching the news with a portable
TV and a generator hooked on the back of a fire truck. We have
a new generator now. We burned out the old one. Have you ever
done that before? Watched TV off a generator on the back of a fire
truck camping out because you're homeless?

— Phyllis Adams
Belvoir, North Carolina

Photo on back cover courtesy of the City of Greenville.

Designed by Katherine M. Kubel, Chapel Hill, NC
Printed by Riverside Printing, Rocky Mount, NC

ISBN 0-9672180-1-2

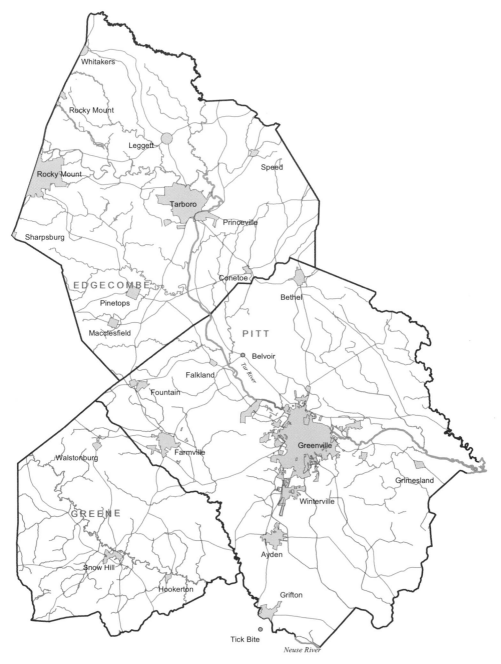

Whitakers

Rocky Mount

Leggett

Speed

Rocky Mount

Tarboro

Princeville

Sharpsburg

EDGECOMBE

Conetoe

Bethel

Pinetops

PITT

Macclesfield

Belvoir

Falkland

Tar River

Fountain

Greenville

Farmville

Walstonburg

Grimesland

GREENE

Winterville

Snow Hill

Ayden

Hookerton

Grifton

Tick Bite

Neuse River

Legend

▨	Towns
▢	Rivers
—	Streams
—	Primary Roads

Map: Michele Hayslett, State Library of North Carolina

CONTENTS

Editor's note:

Our collective editorial decision has been to keep the tone, style and local dialectic characteristics of the writings and interviews in their original forms. Therefore, we have not made significant changes in language use or grammar. For example, we have retained the word "wont" in place of "wasn't" and "weren't," or "going to go to the bad," as they are used in Eastern North Carolina dialect.

As you will note throughout the book, there are contradictions of fact and interpretation. This is true for the writings, interviews and recordings between individuals and groups and sometimes within the same person's own narrative. For example, the question of dams, dykes and flooding is mentioned several times in different workshop sites. In part, inconsistent reports of where and how the flood was exacerbated by opening dams occurs because of a lack of information available to residents in eastern North Carolina as well as the amount of misinformation present. We have chosen not to sort out and remove these points of difference. Although these editorial decisions may contribute to a sense of unevenness in the text as a whole, they preserve both voice and understanding as expressed at the workshops and interviews.

Finally, for Section III, "Someone to tell the story," we use only the first names of interview participants to protect individual identities. However, they are real people and we have not altered the contents of the interviews.

Prelude: WHO KNOWS THIS FLOOD'S MIND AND SOUL?

IT GOT ME THOUGH. IT HOLDS ME SO.

I can tell you about floods: Writing the flood of 1999

Harlan Joel Gradin, Ph.D.
Associate Director/Director of Programs and Publications
North Carolina Humanities Council

HOW TO BELIEVE WHAT WE SEE? PICTURES, TELEVISION AND RADIO REPORTS, newspaper articles, sound bytes—sometimes these media can capture and express people's core experiences during extraordinary moments in their lives. Other times, they are not enough to convey the power and depth of those experiences. The people who live through a particular time in a specific place need to tell their own stories in their own voices to make them real and understandable for others, and, often, to themselves.

"As long as there's no one to tell the story … it never happened," observed interviewer Ana Cowó. Making sure others know the great flood from hurricane Floyd happened in 1999 to real, individual North Carolinians was a primary motivation for the book that follows. Sponsored by an *ad hoc* group of flood survivors in the eastern part of the state, the After Floyd Up River (AFTUR) group, the documentary project on which this book is based was funded by the North Carolina Humanities Council (NCHC).

The Council sponsored writing workshops at four sites affected by the floods: Two were held in the town of Grifton (April and May 2000), two workshops were in the township of Belvoir (April and May 2000), three workshops were in African American communities of Rocky Mount (August 2000), and one workshop was at Pitt Community College in Greenville (October 2000). NCHC was very fortunate to have two extraordinary scholars facilitate these workshops: Ms. Julie Fay, an English professor at East Carolina University, led the Grifton, Belvoir and Greenville workshops, and Mr. Philip Shabazz, a writer, poet and teacher, led the workshops in Rocky Mount.

NCHC is a non-profit foundation and state affiliate of the National Endowment for the Humanities. Our primary goal is to fund free public education programs that enable North Carolinians to examine, interpret and discuss our shared history and traditions. These programs are opportunities for all state residents—across race, ethnic and class lines—to voice how they understand their experiences and how they are related to others.

NCHC believes that writing and telling our stories offers not only testimony but also an opportunity to reflect critically on one's experience and how that is intertwined with the lives of others. In this way, writing and storytelling became a process translating catastrophe and chaos into a form of grieving and healing. Moreover, writing and storytelling also can help stimulate empathy; they can offer an intimate glimpse of the hearts and minds of survivors in a way that other presentations (newscasts and sound bytes) just don't, and can't.

The workshops reinforced our convictions. Julie Fay explains that most people in the East now speak with a "common language" of "resigned acceptance of the reality that this could happen again, anywhere, anytime." At the same time, we hoped that a sense of common bonds would be underscored by more than language. By providing a vehicle through which victims who were culturally diverse could share their stories, the writing workshops also offered residents the opportunity to see their elemental connections with each other. Fay comments that, "a kinship of sorts was found as we wrote, and then read, our stories. We shared laughter and more than a few tears. We questioned our faith and were reminded of the tremendous strength of the human spirit, of our community. We complained and commiserated … [but] no matter how much we tried to get on with our lives, for some of us the anger was too fresh."

In a powerful way, the flood created a kind of community because it "reconfigured peoples' lives without regard to race, creed or religion," as Fay observes. For many, it leveled distinctions that traditionally have often separated individuals and pitted them against each other. Fay remembers, "In this moment, North Carolinians comforted the grieving, calmed the frightened, prayed together, clothed and fed strangers."

Yet, as Fay also notes, "trauma and hardship did not recede with the floodwaters." The apparent communal cohesiveness seemed to be quite fragile as people struggled with the hard day-to-day realities of rebuilding their personal lives. This proved true both in the language people used to describe and analyze their experiences, as well as in the difficulty of getting diverse groups at the same workshop. Workshops revealed the often contradictory senses of community that existed for some flood survivors, what that notion might mean and how it could be transformed. The range of frustrations people raised suggests how community worked or failed.

Many people were angry at encountering a bureaucratic maze in order to receive shelter, food, trailers and loans. This was especially true when victims who had lost everything were asked for their ownership and insurance papers. As one woman wrote, "going through all these steps before you get something … you've already seen my steps washed away from my door." People who had never before asked for help were treated as beggars who did not deserve the immediate materials for day-to-day life. Many continue to be angry at the evaporation of statewide concern for victims even as some still live in temporary housing, five years later.

In Rocky Mount, workshop participants conveyed particular bitterness about their experiences. One woman observed that in this disaster she felt "as before [Floyd] whites treated [African American] lives with less concern … [with] fewer resources and less help." Their writings and discussion questioned how forgiving a social system can be "regardless of mistakes that people made making drastic decisions after the flood." The sessions also demonstrated community leaders who rose, and still do, to organize local resources to assist the most vulnerable.

This project provides some insight into the key question of whether this flood event was transformative or transitory. A sense of dislocation existed simultaneously with actions of community connection. At first, the flood seemed to overwhelm all barriers of race, class, community identity; but even before the waters receded, people "started to retreat from each other back into their own circles and churches," as one workshop participant observes. What does it take for us to step back and see how we are all connected? In Belvoir, one man notes, "It's bad when in Greenville we're calling for help for two days, three days straight and they don't even know where Belvoir is. And most people go through it every day and still don't know."

Regardless of the workshop site, participants reflected a profound appreciation for contradictions in daily life and in the broadest terms of what it means to be human. "A situation like this will do one of two things," one person explains. "It will either bring out the very best in people or it will bring out the very worst in people. ... At the same time these good people were out trying to help one another, there was other people out trying to stab them in the back." This sober assessment seemed true regardless of whether barriers were economic, political, racial or gender. What does this experience say about our local areas and larger community, about culture change, about rebuilding the East and integrating it more fully into the civic and economic life of the rest of the state?

We weren't sure what would come from these workshops. Certainly, at a personal level I found it difficult to comprehend the scale of devastation from my own home in Durham. Although the media reports on the hurricane and flood made me feel sadness, fear, sympathy and disbelief, I didn't understand this life-changing disaster. I didn't really grasp what had happened until the first time I went to Grifton. It was overwhelming just to see the water marks high up the sides of structures still standing, let alone to imagine losing everything.

NCHC learned many things from these workshops, including reminders of how powerful place and home are to people. We also learned how challenging it is for anyone to write about traumatic experiences. The wider point is that it is both difficult and frightening for most people to write. This reluctance to write seems an intractable feature of our culture connected to how we take in, understand and express ourselves through language. Our society's major expressive mode continues to be oral. This characteristic has complex implications about the nature of language and differences in story organization between spoken and written narratives. Examining how this played out during all the workshops made us appreciate the importance of embracing a wide range of forms of expression.

In an effort to achieve the broadest possible participation, regardless of preference for or ability to write, we asked folklorist William Mansfield to conduct interviews in Grifton and Belvoir. Furthermore, we were struck by the power of people reading aloud what they had written. We decided to record future sessions beginning with the first one in Rocky Mount.

The workshops were very intense and moving. How rich to have a diverse group participate in the project, each with different tales that are at heart the same. Participants were eloquent. Their writings and their stories were wide ranging. Some are extraordinary tales, as you'll see reading this volume. Although not everyone had the same concerns, you will note that several themes kept emerging.

1   The overwhelming nature of the flood, human inability to control it and lack of preparation to respond to such cataclysmic disaster.

2   The incredulity of most who kept believing they would be back at their homes in just a day or two.

3   The fragmentation of time and experience often described as living "day to day," losing track of time.

4   The immediate and potential long-term impact of the flood on community relationships.

5   The difficulty of getting basic and consistent information. Indeed, that was still the case some time after the flood, and contributed to contradictions in fact and interpretation among workshop participants and in their own recollections. Several examples of these differences are reflected in the text.

6   Anger at the lack of organization of the institutions and organizations disbursing recovery aid. Most complained about the changing bureaucratic requirements that necessitated return visits to the same lines.

7   A perception that recovery agency personnel did not listen to the needs flood survivors were expressing.

8   Anger and disappointment at individuals and commercial institutions that seemed to be using the flood only as an opportunity to prosper at other people's expense.

9   The unfairness of response along racial lines perceived by many.

10 A sense of confusion about official pledges to help victims recover and whether survivors interpreted them to mean aid would restore people to their circumstances before the flood.

11 A religious sense that the flood was a warning and intervention by God.

12 The extraordinary and tireless help, dedication, generosity and courage of many local folks and people from outside the state.

13 The belief that even with the destruction caused by the flood, people had a lot to be thankful for since material things can be replaced.

14 "All I want to do is be [back] home."

By 2003, we had amassed over 600 pages of writings and interviews. The verbatim results took the reader through experiences expressed eloquently, touchingly, thoughtfully and sometimes distressingly; yet, the journey seemed overwhelming and unwieldy. It was our desire, especially Julie Fay's, to print as much as possible. These words had come at emotional cost to our remarkable participants and had unmediated and authentic power.

I wish it had been feasible to print everything, but it was not. We owe a great debt to everyone who participated as facilitator, writer and interviewee. That we could not include everyone's entry makes their participation no less significant; indeed, their stories and words helped us to understand those that appear in the following pages.

Selections come mostly from the workshop sites in which they were offered, though not necessarily in their formal or temporal order. In some instances, we have re-sequenced contributions to make it possible for readers to have a focused, thematic sense that conveys something of the whole experience without getting lost in one of the many stories of personal experiences of pain, satisfaction, wonder and confusion.

In developing the workshops with limited resources, we tried to be inclusive across race and class lines. Paradoxically, though, we ended up often being exclusive. In fact, that challenge mirrors our state's difficulties in integrating diversity. Coming together at the same workshop table was not enough to overcome people's hesitancy to share intimate, vulnerable experiences with strangers, even if they lived in close proximity.

Another factor contributing to the absence of racially diverse workshop groups was that we did not organize a bi-lingual component. We did not have the resources, linguistically and financially, to accomplish this goal. Unlike hurricanes in the past, Floyd's victims and survivors were not only white and African American, but included a large population of Latinos, a group affected like the others. Fortunately, AFTUR member Ana Cowó identified and interviewed some Latino families. Obviously, this is a part of the social history of the Floyd flood that has not received adequate attention.

We worked with long-time participants in Council programs, both individuals and organizations. That was how the workshops were organized in Rocky Mount. In Grifton and Belvoir, we met new people who worked hard to set the place and time of the events in as public and inviting a way as possible. Actually, the first workshop in Grifton turned out to be an ideal representation of who lives in eastern North Carolina. The large group was diverse by gender, race, occupation and class, life experience and local geography—from a contractor, to a town leader, to a local state legislator, to a person who was receiving public assistance.

The three-hour workshops were held in the old Grifton train depot, now used for community events. Sitting in folding chairs around tables, each person introduced him- or herself and told about his or her personal flood experiences. After the extraordinary beginning, Julie Fay led the group through writing exercises. These included "fast writing"—expressing immediate impulse without the mediating order that the grammar of formal writing tends to give our words—and extended writing exercises. Reading their writings aloud, participants recognized themselves in each other's stories. The issues this group raised turned out to be a prelude of the future workshops. Unfortunately, we did not collect the writings that evening, which is why Grifton does not have its own section in this book.

For a variety of reasons most people were not able to return for the second Grifton workshop. Given the vigor of community feeling of the first session, it is hard to explain why this happened beyond the usual logistical reasons of time, other commitments, travel and child care needs. Perhaps writing proved to be emotionally too scary after general introductions. In retrospect, one factor may have been that most of these people did not know each other very well. Local means more than the short distances between small towns. Some people were related and currently spend time together. However, even people in such groups were not necessarily connected personally to the rest of the participants. People may not have seen themselves as really forging one community despite proximity. Perhaps the remarkable fact is that so many different folks came to the first session.

In Rocky Mount, the situation was different. Most participants were connected in one way or another to each other and to the many community development organizations that sponsored and set up the workshops. Indeed, most of the same folks came to at least two of the three sessions. A similar situation occurred in Belvoir. We were fortunate enough to work with the central community institution for a large portion of the residents, the Belvoir Volunteer Fire Department. Again, most people were known to each other and to the organization hosting the workshops. It made the effort of those connected to embrace those on the outside of that institution all the more powerful and poignant. Yet, because the work necessitated a willingness to be emotionally intimate, this workshop, like others, did not attract people across racial lines, which reflects our state's fragmentation. Gender divisions also characterized the workshops: it was just as difficult to get both men and women to write together. As one person noted, "men tell stories" while women will write.

A critical key to reading this document is to appreciate it in the context of fluidity—no one person, neighborhood or group is static; there is always movement within and between. To make strong claims about the meaning of these together, though, requires the reader to make connections at a whole other, macro-level. Each section needs to be placed in dialogue with the rest, each illuminating the others and what is not present in them. These interconnected stories unfolded during the same time period, meaning that one must imagine them happening simultaneously. Tracking these experiences in the same moment reflects the real complexities and barriers on the ground that make it hard for people to forge public spaces in which all voices interact. Again, this raises questions about the notion of community, the contexts in which we use that word, and whether we have the political will to create and then sustain it.

By the first anniversary of the flood, many in the state, including NCHC, stopped focusing actively on rebuilding the eastern part of the state after the hurricane and flood. NCHC had hoped to sponsor more writing workshops and interviews. However, lack of funds and resources prevented us from following up with the kind and generous people who shared their incredible stories with us. We allowed too much time to pass before returning. In the spring of 2002, an *ad hoc* group of workshop participants and new folks decided it was time to bring closure to the project we had started together. The After Floyd Up River Ad Hoc Committee applied to the North Carolina Humanities Council for funds to collect the writings and interviews for publication in this volume. NCHC funded the project, one that we helped to begin, as one of our three special grants commemorating the 30th anniversary of the Council's work in the state.

NCHC owes special thanks to the wonderful people who gave their time and shared their stories at the workshops. Their gift is extraordinary. Scholars Julie Fay and Philip Shabazz were sensitive and probing. Many people helped to organize the workshops in each town. I'd especially like to thank Lois Watkins of Bridging the Gap as well as other organizations that acted as hosts in Rocky Mount, Phyllis

Adams in Belvoir and, again, Julie Fay and the AFTUR Committee including Joyce Joines Newman, Mike McClanahan, Sharon O'Neill, Katharine Blackburn, Ana Cowó, Gary Redding and Brandie Knox-Kirkman, who provided significant design assistance.

AFTUR journeyed far in this effort because of Julie Fay's remarkable efforts. Her passion, dedication and commitment undergirded the larger project in which her workshops took place. Fay did an exceptional job for NCHC and for the communities involved in the workshops. She has been assisted by several former workshop participants who also worked hard within their communities to repair the physical and psychological damages of the flood. As the work continued beyond anyone's time expectations, Fay recruited folklorist and artist Joyce Joines Newman (MA, University of North Carolina-Chapel Hill, MFA, East Carolina University) to become a full co-editor. Joyce's contribution is extraordinary: she transcribed the interviews, helped edit them, and helped develop the book. Equally important, she has worked hard to make sure the book got finished. I am grateful to them both.

I also want to thank our wonderful Assistant Editors Lois Watkins, Sharon O'Neill, Ana Cowó and Gary Redding. Ana Cowó and Antonio Ponce insured that members of the Latino community were not ignored. Sharon has helped track down details for the final version. William Mansfield deserves special thanks for his excellent oral history interviews in Belvoir, which has made the larger project richer and deeper.

I need to acknowledge the vision and commitment of present and former staff and members of NCHC who believed in this project in 1999, and who, again in 2002 and 2003, continued to invest financial, staff and other resources in it. In particular, I would like to thank Alice Barkley, Della Pollock, John Haley, Lucinda MacKethan, Peter Caulfield, Elizabeth Minnich, Bill Moore, Susan Levine, Janice P. Periquet, Genevieve Cole and Emily Dings, among many others. In particular, Della Pollock provided an insightful and passionate critique at an important moment in the process. Her careful reading reshaped how we edited the flow and narrative. Many thanks also to my NCHC colleagues: Genevieve Cole, Lynn Wright-Kernodle, Kelly Swindell, Doug Quin, Jennifer Edwards, Mary G. Holloway and Jacquie Smith. Katherine Kubel, who designs NCHC publications, came to our rescue by accepting the hard task of reformatting the book at the last moment. We appreciate her grace and warmth in helping us to finish. These colleagues have always been there for this project and for me. And, as always, thanks to Elise and Corey.

June 2004
Durham and Greensboro, North Carolina

Julie Fay and Anthony Dudley, Grifton Writing Workshop.

Photo by Jean-Henri White, courtesy of the Greenville *Daily Reflector*.

The book that follows

Julie Fay, MFA
Co-Editor and Workshop Leader

NO ONE WHO LIVED IN EASTERN NORTH CAROLINA WAS UNAFFECTED BY hurricane Floyd and the following flood. We are not the same people that we were *before* and some of us dealt with things *after* that we could never imagine. The rising water did not discriminate when it came into our homes; it dramatically reconfigured peoples' lives without regard to race, creed or religion. The AFTUR project is a way for us to examine what happened and how those events changed us to give our communal experience a voice and continue to try to heal.

The book that follows is part family album, part scrapbook, part memoir, part journal, part essay. Our aim has been to offer a place for members of the community to tell in their own voices their stories of what happened during and after the hurricane and floods.

In the spring, several months after the flood, I was contacted by the North Carolina Humanities Council and asked if I could recommend a local writer to lead writing workshops with flood victims. The Council and I saw this as a way of helping those people come to terms with the emotions and events that they had and were continuing to live through. After several days of asking myself if I wanted to put aside the book I was currently at work on to re-enter the emotional turmoil of the trauma of the flood, I called Harlan Gradin and said I would be willing to conduct the workshops.

The workshops that we held, along with the interviews, began in the spring of 2000. In the spring of 2002, we asked participants if they would be willing to tell us what their lives were like then, two years later, and several responded. Our goal was to record and witness these extraordinary days, to remember, to understand ourselves better as well as our definition of community, and, hopefully, to learn something from the events.

We began workshops with each attendee telling his or her story of the hurricane and the days that followed. We listened for as long as it took, going around the table, introducing ourselves, saying where we were during the storm and afterward. These were highly emotional introductions, with many people tearing up or openly weeping as they told their stories. After we had heard each person's story, we began to write. I suggested that people write without stopping to think too much about what they wrote, simply to let their ideas flow onto the page, not to revise or worry about spelling or grammar. I also handed out a list of questions which we read through together and asked them to circle ones they thought they'd be interested in answering or exploring in writing: What was the most surprising thing that happened to you during or after the flood? What does the word *community* mean to you? What was your community like before the flood? After? What are your feelings about the officials whose job it was to help people with flood-related issues? [*Editor's note: See the Appendix for a complete list of questions.*]

It is now the summer of 2004 as we bring closure on these events by completing this book. For many, closure continues to take place. Many flood survivors were given a small amount of money through state grants or FEMA, or received low-interest loans from the SBA to rebuild, repair, elevate, or relocate. Others had their flood-destroyed homes purchased under the federal buyout program. Where they once lived their lives there is now green space and empty air.

We are thankful to all of you who shared your stories. We thank you for sharing your loss, your sorrow, your grief, your bravery, your faith, your despair and your hope with the larger community of the state and with others who have lived through natural disasters. This book is offered to those of you who lived through the events described here, to your children, and to theirs.

There are many other people responsible for the making of this book. First, I would like to thank the North Carolina Humanities Council for its financial and philosophical commitment to the project over these past several years, most especially Harlan Gradin. I also want to recognize the substantial contribution from the Weyerhaeuser Corporation, who donated the paper you are holding in your hands and Walker-Ross Printers of Rocky Mount [*now Riverside Printing*], who donated the production of it. Walker-Ross, as you will see, was itself under water during the times of the flood and it has been very gratifying to work with them as they continue to recover from the losses they sustained. I also want to thank folklorist William Mansfield for the many hours he spent with the people whose voices are here, and Phyllis Adams of Belvoir for helping us to come into that community and pull up a chair to listen to stories.

For photographs, we thank members of the community, the North Carolina Forestry Service and Neil Moore, and Deborah S. Clark of the City of Greenville.

This book is the result of the hard and steadfast efforts of a wonderful team of people who made up the AFTUR Ad Hoc Committee: Katharine Blackburn, Ana Cowó, Brandie Knox-Kirkman, Mike McClanahan, Sharon O'Neill, Antonio Ponce, Gary Redding, and Lois Watkins. This group has kept the faith that we could achieve our goal of producing this book and each person has donated countless hours of time and effort. My co-editor Joyce Joines Newman, also a member of the AFTUR committee, has been especially helpful in the preparation of the book, keeping long hours and giving up weekends to meet our deadlines. And I want to thank my husband Henry Stindt and my daughter Zoe Fay-Stindt whose patience and support have sustained me during the project.

April 2004
Blounts Creek, North Carolina

❋　❋　❋

Walker-Ross Printing sustained heavy damage during the Floyd flood.

Photo courtesy of Walker-Ross Printing.

Ten years before Floyd

Joyce Joines Newman, MFA
Co-Editor and AFTUR Committee

TEN YEARS BEFORE FLOYD, I HAD MY FIRST HURRICANE EXPERIENCE WHEN hurricane Hugo hit the Appalachian Mountains. In comparison, Floyd and the ensuing flood were minor events for me.

Hugo roared across our hillside in the Brushy Mountains of Wilkes County on the morning of September 23, 1989. Hurricanes aren't supposed to go that far inland and not even Dan Rather predicted it, so my ex-husband and I were totally unprepared—no candles, drinking water, canned food, batteries for the radio, water to flush the commode.

When the sound of debris hitting the roof awakened us about 7 AM, the power was already out. During the first half of the storm we were busy closing windows, putting containers out to catch water, generally battening down the hatches. While the eye was passing, I went outdoors to look for our pets and found the cat on the side of the house protected from the wind, shaking. Our dog Betty was nowhere to be found. We discovered later that she had gone across to my mother's house on the sheltered side of the hill.

Before Hugo, the log cabin we had built ourselves sat in the middle of twenty acres of woods. The steep, rocky hillside would have been difficult to log, so the huge trees had escaped timbering for many years. There had been ground-soaking rain for several days before Hugo arrived, and the trees were still heavy with fall leaves. Conditions couldn't have been worse. The second half of Hugo blew the woods down.

Hugo sounded like a roaring train—a steady sound with no variation. I haven't heard anything like it before or since. Visibility was poor, not only from the rain and fog but also because the air was thick with thousands of shredded leaves. The trees didn't sway. Hundred-foot-tall oaks bent almost parallel to the ground from the force of the wind, their limbs and leaves all blowing in the same direction, upward along the trunk. They didn't fall with force. When they bent far enough over, their weight pulled the roots on one side from the sodden earth and the trees sank gently to the ground. The fallen trees were all parallel, laid out like matchsticks in a box. In all, Hugo blew down probably three thousand trees on the twenty acres around us. Eleven trees fell on our cabin and seventy-six across our drive.

The aftermath of Hugo was a huge ordeal. Ninety percent of the households in Wilkes County were without power. Falling trees had destroyed power lines everywhere. Volunteer power crews came to help from all over the East Coast— South Carolina, Virginia, Pennsylvania, Tennessee, New York—each in a convoy of trucks of a different color. On their front bumpers they placed handwritten signs: "Hugo Buster." To memorialize the event, one member of the team who came up our mountain clearing debris from under the power lines used the tip of his chainsaw to carve the following information into the fallen tree trunks along our drive:

> "Eddie Cole
> Kingsport, Tennessee
> September 27, 1999
> Opossuem" [*sic*]

The "tree man" who cut the maple from across the corner of our roof was a small taciturn man from Iowa. Power lines across the entire county had to be restrung, but instead of going across the hills and up the valleys like the old lines, the new lines followed the roads to make the restringing faster. We were without power for nine days, one of the last hundred houses in the county to have power restored because crews were concentrating on lines that affected multiple houses first and we were the only house on a spur line.

We lived in an area that was one of the worst hit places in North Carolina, with up to 100 percent tree loss, and our hillside had more damage than most. Our place became a destruction showcase for the Forestry Service, who brought carloads of FEMA officials and even the governor to see it to convince them to authorize emergency funds.

We never really recovered from Hugo. Where the woods had formed a deep rich canopy overhead we now had three tall trees left standing. It looked like someone had cleared a new ground. We signed up for the Forestry Service program where they would come and trim back debris for a hundred feet around a house to help reduce the fire hazard, although in the hot dry summer after Hugo a real forest fire would have jumped that space in no time. We tried to find someone who would log the fallen trees with a tractor, not wanting bulldozers to cut up the hillside, but they were all busy with timber that was easier to reach than our downed trees and no one would come. For several years we used the trees closest to the house for firewood but many are still rotting on the ground.

Hugo did almost no damage to anything we had put there. We replaced one piece of tin on the roof and a broken clay flowerpot. But the natural environment changed drastically. There was no shade for many years. The wildflower garden I had planted died in the sun. It was several years before the birds returned. There was no way to traverse what had been the forest floor; instead, we had to walk tree trunks to get to our spring box 400 feet down the hillside. In winter, there were tremendous ice storms. Even a small breeze would create a howling sound across the hillside. That hill with the wind blowing in minus-10-degree weather under a full moon was a desolate place.

The absence of things was disorienting. I missed the sound of water dripping from the trees after a rain. We built a rock wall and I planted rows of shrubs along the contour of the hill to counter the feeling caused by empty space that you might fall off. I planted white pines and Leyland cypress as a windbreak. I learned to find beauty in seeing yellow forsythia blossoms against the blue of the now visible mountains in the background, or in hoarfrost and fog on the hills around us.

I think I had Post Traumatic Stress Disorder. I no longer felt safe in the world. At home alone, I would go on crying jags. I had nightmares of being bombed by planes, my dreams coupling my anxiety with the sound of airplanes passing overhead, a sound that had been muffled by the woods before the storm.

I developed a healthy respect for the power of nature and the helplessness of human beings against it.

When I moved to eastern North Carolina to enter the MFA program in art at East Carolina University, I came to a place where hurricanes are frequent. They still make me nervous. When the wind starts blowing at a certain pace, the hairs on my neck rise and I develop a craving for Nutter Butters. I am hurricane savvy now and am always well prepared, although none of the hurricanes I've experienced here have been anything like Hugo. According to my scale, if there are ANY trees left standing afterwards, it wasn't a bad hurricane.

So as a hurricane Floyd seemed minor to me. The power in Winterville where I was living stayed on and so did the town water. But by Saturday, they were saying they might turn the water off and that the Greenville power plant was close to flooding which would put out the power. With the likelihood of having to deal with another post-hurricane ordeal a growing possibility, I opted for flight. I had paid my dues after Hugo. The moment the radio announcer said that Hwy. 264 was open to the west, I threw everything from my refrigerator in the trash can and some clothes in a duffle bag and drove across the state to refuge at my mother's.

The further west I went, the less news there was. All newscasts in the east were focused on the flood, but in the west there were only brief reports. I was amazed one day to see Sue Luddeke of the ECU School of Art on the nightly TV news from Charlotte; their reporter had spotted her out painting the flood from her front yard in Greenville.

When the university was scheduled to reopen and I came back east, the flood was over. Some students in the class I was teaching were affected and I had one acquaintance who had lived in an apartment beside the Tar River and had lost everything. I knew people who had volunteered to work in shelters. I donated some kitchen items to employees at the hospital where my neighbor was a nurse. Mostly, though, I kept the flood at a distance. My first encounter with it was transcribing some flood stories taped for a project by the public library in Rocky Mount, which eventually led to my involvement with the AFTUR project. It was only by listening to the stories we will present here that I began to realize some of what had happened.

15

After transcribing the Belvoir interviews by William Mansfield, I spent several hours in Belvoir with Phyllis Adams, who made the flood real to me. She drove me around and pointed out each house that had been flooded and each that hadn't. We stopped on a bridge over the Tar River and she showed me the power lines overhead where people in boats had reached out and tied ribbons to show how high the water rose. I still can't comprehend how much water it took to fill space and reach that height. Phyllis walked me through the house that she and her husband Mike are repairing. They've wisely raised it high off the ground in case of another flood.

Because of Hugo, I can empathize to some extent with those who experienced the Floyd flood. Even so, losing our woods was hard but our lives were still intact, unlike the lives of many of those who were flooded. The stories in this book fill me with immense admiration for the courage and strength of those who faced danger, met events with resourcefulness and resignation, and did what had to be done to survive. Many lost their homes, all their possessions, things that connected them to their family and history and sense of identity. Some lost their communities, uprooted after the flood to a new place. A few lost their lives or their loved ones. Many are still rebuilding their lives, often starting from scratch materially. Some will never be able to achieve the same kind of life they had before the flood. Some will never get over the loss.

Their stories show us what it was like to go through the flood and its aftermath. Perhaps more importantly, they show us people at their best. I cry at Mae Ricks' story of facing her own death as the waters rose to her chin. I laugh at Mike Adams' image of the next hurricane and everyone in Belvoir out on their porches with flashlights checking the water level. I gasp at Tammy Bullock's story of the return of her jewelry box. I smile at Earl Teel's dog who got his picture in the newspaper.

I'm grateful for the opportunity to help bring these stories to others, indebted to the people who shared their lives, and enriched by being part of the wonderful team that has worked to bring this book into being, including Harlan Gradin, Julie Fay, Brandie Knox-Kirkman, Katherine Kubel, Lois Watkins, Ana Cowó, Sharon O'Neill, the North Carolina Humanities Council, and many others. This is an important work. Others have looked at the Floyd flood from a disaster management perspective; now these stories add the voices of the people of eastern North Carolina who lived it.

What strikes me most is the importance of family and community, of people helping other people, of who can be counted on. Survival and recovery were not a matter of isolation, but of connection. For me, the most important lesson from the Floyd flood is that putting aside our differences—political, religious, racial, personal—is the path that might allow us all to survive in the long run.

May 2004
Fountain, North Carolina

The forest experts tell us

Katharine Blackburn
AFTUR Committee

The forest experts tell us that
a fire in a forest is a good thing,
a weeding out of underbrush allowing
the more prestigious hardwoods to grow.

The zoologists tell us the
delivery horses used by the
mighty department store giants
caught the epizootic and weeded
out the most sickly.

What did the flu epidemic
of 1918 weed out besides
my grandmother and other
relatives and friends that
I shall never know?

What did the flood weed out?

Was it a breath shared neighbor
to neighbor? A song breaking
over survey lines?

Was it time to dishevel
and toss trailers into
rivers while a large,
stuffed Barney sits
hitchhiking by the
side of the road?

Who knows this flood's
mind and soul?
It got me though.
It holds me so.

The black, inky waters
of the flood, devil moving
current, home to snakes
who would suck and
kill us. A stinking cesspool taking out
our cows, horses, all our
beautiful, if misunderstood
four-legged creatures.

What future ruinous
disaster did the flood
weed out by getting here first?

Friday, December 1, 2000 14:55

17

Start with the storm

Willa Peaden
Belvoir Writing Workshops

START WITH THE STORM THAT CAME THROUGH BEFORE THE FLOOD. THOUGHT the water was going away and we rode around looking at the water—places, access bridges we could not even cross. Woke up the next day Friday and water had come back in my garden and yard. I was, *What in the world?* Thought the water had gone. No electricity. Could not hear any news. No water to drink. Didn't know what to do, all the men were down on the river getting people out down there. Had no idea it would come up my way that deep.

But water kept rising and I kept moving things to higher ground. Got my potatoes from under the house and put them on the porch. By this time I was walking around in water about four feet deep. Looking out for snakes. Had a hoe in hand to balance myself because the current was very strong. It came up from the creek in the back yard so I was trying to put my chickens out of the hen house to higher ground. Never thought of putting them up there in the loft.

I met a lot of new people and learned how everybody joined together to help others and we actually enjoyed helping even though we knew we were in deep trouble at home.

After the floodwater was gone, we heard about all this help we could get. Some got a lot of help and some got very little. This I don't understand, but you know somehow with our families' and God's help we all made it through. We are not back to normal yet but we are getting there. It will take me another year to get my chickens back up and laying.

The saddest thing was going back home to all my dead hens. I think I wasn't myself for some time. I was beginning to wonder if I was going to get over this thing that had happened to all of us and how much each and every one had lost. But we all gained a lot when we realized how close it had brought Belvoir, our community, together and how far people came to feed us and help in many, many ways. Nobody was working. Water had just destroyed so much.

Julie Fay
Co-Editor and Workshop Leader

IT'S SEPTEMBER 14, 1999 AND WE'RE RUNNING AROUND IN OUR USUAL PRE-WORK pre-school morning frenzy and whirl of toothpaste, peanut butter and orange juice. Outside it's raining—again—raining hard. Raining like it's been raining all month. The lot in front of our house—the "beach lot" here on the Pamlico River at this small riverside community ten miles east of Chocowinity—looks like a lumberyard, piled with the remnants of neighbors' piers, 2 x 4s delivered the last week of August and the first week of September like pick-up sticks by Dennis I and Dennis II, the Sequel. "Dennis the Menace" as it was nicknamed, came, hit us, sat off the coast for a week, and returned to hit us again. My neighborhood's getting used to this seasonal picking up of huge chunks of their lives. One neighbor says, "You won't see *me* here next year." Hurricane waters, for the fourth time in three years, have washed through the ground floor of his two-story house. Another neighbor about 100 yards down the road in the other direction has finally, after three years, after hurricanes Bertha, Fran, Bonnie and now Dennis I and II, lost the foundation of his house and his entire yard. Ms. M., our eighty-year-old neighbor in front, has lost her entire yard and the waves this time were hitting the wall of her living room.

My husband, daughter and I leave for work/school, take off our shoes and socks and wade through the water running through our garage, and drive thirty miles "up river" to Greenville. In the late afternoon, I drag home from work, child picked up from the babysitter's, husband getting ready to teach his night class in Kinston and then spend the night in Greenville. My daughter and I will stay as usual out at the river. There is another hurricane, Floyd, bigger than Dennis, bigger than the state of Texas, headed slowly toward us. I see that nearly every one of my neighbors is in action. Moving boats, nailing up boards, bringing in deck furniture, birdfeeders, wind chimes. I run through all the things I need to do and curse my husband for holding his class. Tie the canoe to the maple with a rope long enough to let it float but not long enough to let it hit the garage or shed. Not a single one of the other four storms—for all the damage they did to this neighborhood—has been nearly as big as the one that's coming.

I go to the mailbox and get the bills. My neighbors are on the beach trotting up and down the piers with crab pots. "What's the latest report?" I ask. I've been in class all day and haven't seen the latest Doppler images.

"You see where you're standing?" asks Steve. "Ground zero."

That was Tuesday. Wednesday, we decided, given the massive size and force of Floyd, to evacuate. We boarded up the house, raised as much as we could off the floor, took a few of our valuables along with our insurance papers, and went to stay with friends in Greenville. Floyd passed through impressively Thursday at dawn and that evening we enjoyed the star-filled sky. Friday morning the phones were working again and I called my neighbor at the river to find out how our house had fared. "We're OK," Steve said.

While the waters were up, for some two to three weeks depending on where you were, I felt an enormous sense of survivor's guilt. When the Tar River had gone more or less back into its bed, I went to an area on the north side of the Tar River in Greenville, to Mumsford Road. The area was home for many African Americans, some whites, and to many Hispanics who had come to Pitt County for a better life. The homes were trailers, brick ranch-style houses, wood-frame bungalows. All of the houses now were covered with a putrid slime; all of them had the superfluous orange asterisk on the door, saying this house is uninhabitable.

Toward the end of my slow ride down Mumsford Road, I saw a woman sitting on the wide front porch of her home. She was staring into space past the mountain of furniture and clothes heaped at the curbside. I continued slowly past her house, then, just as slowly, turned around. I walked up to her and started talking. Her name is Lydia Graham. She and her husband lived in this three-bedroom house, raising their two grandchildren. She is a nurse at the hospital. On her lap, the slick little magazine published weekly by the Greenville Realtors association.

An hour later we were at the FEMA office. Two of the three computers there were "down." One of the FEMA housing staff said sarcastically to my new acquaintance, "Well, it's not our JOB to FIND you a house." Another FEMA worker told me later she'd been going home every night for the past two weeks and drinking. "Not a beer, not a glass of wine, but liquor," she said, "hard liquor." A lot of the inspectors had quit, she said, it got too depressing; they couldn't handle it. Some got in their cars with their field data computers and simply left. Lydia and I spent hours at the FEMA office that day and more the next day. Hours and hours spent trying to find housing. Trying to find out what help was available for Lydia, her husband, her grandkids. They'd been renting. Now they were staying in the small two-bedroom duplex of a friend across town. The FEMA office had the classified ads of apartments for rent in Greenville. We went—Lydia's husband, Lydia, the kids and I, to Courtney Square apartments. Lydia's husband went in, and in five minutes came back out, livid. They wanted him to pay $25 just to fill out the application. *And* they wanted them to sign a twelve-month lease. The Graham family didn't even know what was happening to them in the next twelve hours.

Two and a half weeks after the hurricane, when classes resumed at East Carolina University, I asked each of my students to jot down what had happened to them. Did they have housing? What, if anything, were they in need of? One student said, "I have not been affected by the hurricane or the flood." But even if, like that student, you were far away on the night of September 15th and the weeks that followed, you were, as a member of this community, affected by it.

Section I: IT WAS DOWN NEAR THE RIVER

Philip Shabazz with Shirley Myrick, Nellie Johnson Hunter and Doris Williams, Rocky Mount Writing Workshop, Opportunities Industrialization Center.

Photo courtesy of Lois B. Watkins, Bridging the Gap.

Harlan Joel Gradin
Co-Editor

IN AUGUST 2000, NCHC SPONSORED THREE WORKSHOPS IN THE EDGECOMBE County communities of Rocky Mount. Ms. Lois B. Watkins, Executive Director of Bridging the Gap, with whom the Council had partnered previously, did the hard task of organizing the workshops in collaboration with other local organizations. These hosts included the Rocky Mount Edgecombe Community Development Corporation (CDC), the Community Enrichment Organization, the Franklinton Center at Bricks, Visions Incorporated, NAACP and the Northeastern NC Association on the Affairs of Black People.

As in Grifton, each workshop lasted approximately three hours. The first was held in the sparse facilities of the Opportunities Industrialization Center, the second at Edgecombe Community College, and the final one downtown at the Harambee Center of the Rocky Mount Edgecombe CDC. The leader of all three workshops was Mr. Philip Shabazz. Based in Chapel Hill, Shabazz is a noted author, poet and educator. Participants were adults of a range of ages; no youth attended.

Shabazz began the first workshop by asking participants to examine why bad things happen. He designed an exercise which requested people to respond in one of four different ways: "One, we can write it like a letter to someone. Two, we could write it as if we're keeping a diary. They say guys don't keep diaries. I always kept a diary—well, a journal. Or, we could write it like a short story" or as a poem. He asked participants to write "about what happened to different people during the Floyd crisis, particularly about what happened to you."

In addition to having the participants write, we asked Lois Watkins to tape record the sessions. This turned out to be a significant aspect of the workshops. Each person read her/his writing aloud in her/his own voice; this helped make the sessions flow more conversationally and placed each piece in dialogue with the others. The recordings also gave a layered and complex sense of people's experiences as they discussed multiple issues at implicit and explicit levels.

The materials that follow are based on the workshop writings and transcripts.

WHAT IS FOR US
Nellie Johnson Hunter

Frank has been gone nine years. I remain in the home that we made for ourselves. I have nurtured and watched our children grow. When Frank passed, I was so hurt but I felt blessed that we had shared thirty-two years together. When Frank passed, our home, cars and furniture were all paid for. Our children had been given a college education. Then Floyd came and wiped away so much that we had built together. Frank was a man of faith, and he knew that God would not leave us alone. He knew that God giveth and He taketh away. He always praised God and blessed His name. Not only was he a staunch church member, a deacon and a pillar of society, he was a firm believer in the love of God. The boat that took us from our home would have been his way of saying, "God is trying to tell us something, Nellie." And what is for us, it's for us.

SURVIVAL
Melinda Belcher

I wasn't directly affected by the flood, but my two sisters—one who lived in Tarboro and one who lived in Princeville—they were both grateful to be alive as flood survivors because my nephew Ricky was rescued after being trapped in a house overnight. His experience entailed coming back to his mother's house to put some things on higher level. He fell asleep and when he awakened, water was at the level of the bed. He told how he managed to get in another bedroom to get a mattress and put it on top of the bed that he was on. He told how he heard the refrigerator falling over and objects floating in the room. How animals—cats and dogs and squirrels—floated by the window while he was waiting to be rescued.

WHAT TO DO?
Lois B. Watkins

What? When? How? I don't understand. What happened? When did all this water come? How did it fill the streets? I don't know. Lord, what to do? The roads are closed as I ride around. How do I get through this water that surrounds? It cuts me off from the east and the west. I can't allow this thing to defeat me. I must reach the leaders to determine what's the plan. We've got to get to the people and get them to understand.

WHAT IS "THE CRITERIA"?
Ida Boddie

I, Ida Boddie, am very angry with my country for the pain and stress that our flood victims are going through. I am not a direct flood victim; however, I am an indirect victim because I work hard trying to help those who are direct victims. During the flood there were so many homeless people, and there are still a lot of homeless people today, eleven months after the flood. It grieves my heart to see the evidence when they've worked so hard to make a comfortable home for themselves and they are without a home. Most of all, I'm angry with America because this is a rich country that sends money and aid to other countries but won't give proper aid to the taxpayers that made this country so rich and powerful, especially the black people who worked 200 years without pay. I also would like to know: What is "the criteria"? There was $800 million for the flood victims. However, the state is threatening to send back $600 million because the people don't meet "the criteria." What is "the criteria"? Is it something like the president's private affair which cost fifty-two million plus, or is it like the lighthouse which cost thirteen million to move? What is "the criteria"?

I GOT BURDENS
Shirley Myrick

I got burdens on me that I never had before. I got burdened since the flood.
I been under so much financial difficulty, I got burdens trying to keep a roof
over my head. I'd like to get back to where I was. According to where I was, I
got burdened. My sickness is worse. I'm not able to buy food like I was before.
I got burdened. My medication is too expensive for me. I lost my clothes. I got
burdens. If I could just get help. If I could just lift some of these burdens off of
me, I wouldn't have so much stress.

WHO ACTUALLY RESCUED ME FROM THE HIGH FLOOD WATER?
Mae Ricks

Around three AM September the 17th, 1999, two huge logs were filing across the
river, preventing me from reaching my friend's house who had promised to help me
with my generator. Turning my truck around, suddenly I looked back and I saw a
huge flood of water coming towards me. Then I attempted to back up, but suddenly
the flow of water overcame the truck and drowned the motor out. I was so scared
and frightened. I was paralyzed with fear. I could not move the truck. I got out and
attempted to walk out of the water. The water was too strong. I almost fell down.
My flashlight fell out of my pocket and it went down, down, down. That frightened
me, so I went back to the truck and sat back down and started praying and singing
and repeating every Bible verse that I remembered. The fear began to diminish.

I remained in the car for about two hours before anybody came. I started to
shiver. I thought about death. But something told me to clap my hands and pat my
feet and to shout around. I felt better. The water continued to rise until it came up
to my throat. I doubted then that I would live. I knew that I would die. And being
a nurse I knew how I would die—that the water would be in my mouth and that
my lungs would be overcome. I just kept saying, "Lord, don't let me struggle." And
I had given up everything and everybody.

A voice came in my right ear. It said, "Open your eyes." When I did, I saw
a small truck near the beginning of the water. I attempted to wipe the window
[*turned on the windshield wipers*] to let whoever was in the truck know that I was
alive. The truck turned around and it went out of sight.

Again I closed my eyes and returned to my prayers. Jesus just separated me
from all material things as I surrendered myself to the Lord. Then again a voice
came in my right ear and it said, "Open your eyes. Open your eyes." I opened my

eyes, and it was difficult this time because the water was near my mouth. And I saw the rescue squad truck already racing up and the police car with blue lights behind entering the water. I was so happy. I knew God had not planned to take me home that night.

So the driver came up to my car and said, "It's the lady. We have to lift her out." And all of a sudden I sprang up high from the water and said, "*I* can get out of here. Open this door." And they came over and opened the door. They said, "Don't take anything out." I had my briefcase with all my personal belongings on the back of my truck. I pulled it out, and I walked over to the rescue squad truck and I got on the back. They said, "You have to sit down." I said, "I'm just too happy to sit down. Let me hold on." And I held on to the truck and I was taken to the firehouse to wait for someone to take me home.

THE MOST UNBELIEVABLE TIME OF OUR LIVES
Sondra Williams

Floyd—the storm of the century. The first period of the storm was just like any other storm to me. I was thinking it would come and go without much or any damage to where I lived. Thinking that, I just kept watching what was going on, on the news. Finally, I decided to go to sleep. The first sign of day, I myself, my husband and child awoke and took a look outside. And it looked as if the storm had passed and went on its way. On September the 16th—the same day—in the afternoon, the water began to rise. But for the residents there was still no warning to get out. We went to sleep upstairs in the apartment. At three o'clock in the morning there was a knock on the door: "Leave now." As we began to leave, our car flooded. We got halfway through the water. It was about door high. So we sat there in the dark and began to pray. And about one hour later, the car started and God got us out.

DEVASTATION
Juanita Wright

I had never seen so much devastation in all my life when Floyd came. Water everywhere. Not able to get about the city. The thought is: *This could never have happened to us. This could never have happened to us. Someone else but not us.* People flooded out and nowhere to go. Going to the shelters and seeing all those people homeless, and some separated from families, even a list of names on a bulletin board of family members missing. Wondering about their future and where they will live. What about their jobs and cars? Needless to say, the material things were lost, and especially those things that couldn't be replaced like family pictures and mementos. For the elderly, having to start over again and rebuild their homes. Yet there seemed to be a lot of people assisting and helping out. No one actually realized the devastation of it all to each individual affected. Some even lost family members. Once upon a time you could look in people's faces and see a sign of contentment. But when this happened you'd look, you saw in their eyes hopelessness, fear, worry and anxiety. How will we ever begin to start over?

We had a crisis before the flood

Lois B. Watkins, the Reverend Richard Joyner and C. Michael Shaw
(with Harlan Joel Gradin and Joyce Joines Newman)

THE AFRICAN AMERICAN COMMUNITIES OF ROCKY MOUNT AND TARBORO, IN NASH and Edgecombe counties, were among areas devastated by the hurricane Floyd flood. Like many non-white communities in Eastern North Carolina, they were affected disproportionately because historically the only land black citizens had been able to purchase was often situated in low-lying swamplands that were more prone to flooding even in normal times.

Ms. Lois B. Watkins, Executive Director of Bridging the Gap, organized three writing workshops in Rocky Mount that included residents from nearby Tarboro and Princeville, a town founded by ex-slaves after the Civil War that is on the National Register of Historic Places. Watkins utilized a network of community development organizations already working together on social, economic and political issues. As opposed to the general call for participants for workshops in other locations, the Rocky Mount workshop participants focused more on an interconnected set of problems already in play before the flood—questions about race relations and local leadership, about fairness and justice, the political structure of local organizations and their relationships within the larger Rocky Mount area.

The tragedy of the flood heightened how these relationships played out for better and worse. The flood also offered an opportunity to accelerate initial efforts by citizen advocates and service providers to form a multi-faceted infrastructure addressing the connections among and consequences of racism, poverty, family stress, education, health care and economic development. This work, already in progress, was being organized by a group called People of Color.

Immediately after the flood, relief was provided through distribution centers at locations like Ebenezer Church and North End Church, set up by national organizations such as FEMA and the Red Cross, by individual black and white churches, or by other community groups. Leaders in some communities would go to a large distribution center, get supplies, and bring them back to a community site, where people from the community could come and get what they needed.

National relief efforts often were not channeled through the existing leadership in the community, which created tension among groups of people on both racial and social levels. In the Tarboro shelters set up in schools, for example, those in charge would not allow African American community leaders to have input into decisions. Instead, they presented themselves as experts who knew what to do and who did not need help from local leaders. This made local people very angry.

Relief and recovery efforts were also hindered by the fact that no one in the area had ever dealt with an event on this scale, so there was no system in place to handle such a crisis. Locally, individual groups and churches were assisting people, but their efforts were often limited to their own members or neighborhoods. No one knew where help was coming from, though many assumed it would come from the government. The consequence of the unexpectedness and immensity of the flood crisis left people feeling out of control, helpless and distrustful.

When the time came that national organizations such as the Red Cross were going to close their distribution sites, they wanted local churches, both black and white, to come together to continue the work of recovery. They invited the Reverend Richard Joyner to lead continuing efforts supported by People of Color. This direction was an important turnaround from the way previous relief efforts had been conducted. In this instance, African American representatives were asked on the front end to help establish the collaborative effort involving people from all communities, non-profit and for-profit groups, churches and other community organizations.

Local leaders such as Lois Watkins and Juanita Wright met with area ministers to plan how to pull Rocky Mount and Tarboro together. Ms. Andrea Bryant of VISIONS facilitated their discussions. An attorney with long-time family roots in Rocky Mount, Bryant helped them identify ways to break through racial and social barriers and provide recovery for the Twin County area. At the same time, they also realized they could leverage Twin County interfaith efforts in the future to sustain and strengthen the grassroots advocacy networks they were creating in response to the flood. They created the Twin County Interfaith Recovery Initiative (TCIRI). As of spring 2002, TCIRI had assisted some 1,116 families, including repairing 215 homes.

This network still continues to function. The confidence people gained provided new hope that their lives could change. Before the flood, many people had felt stymied, stuck, and powerless. The recovery process opened up the door to say, "You can go a lot further than this. Vision is not lost."

As told through the different writings and transcripts, the narrative outlining this process gave the Rocky Mount workshops an unusual thematic coherence. In particular, the following stories demonstrate a powerful example of how grassroots collaborations could help. Two central participants are Ms. Shirley Myrick, who fell through the cracks of an institutional network not fully in place, and Ms. Angela Bryant, who helped show Ms. Myrick how cooperative connections could assist her.

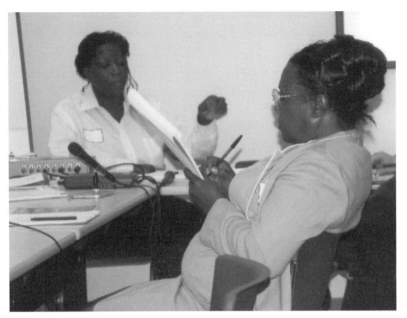

Lois B. Watkins with Ida Boddie, Rocky Mount Writing Workshop, Harambee Square.

Photo by courtesy of Lois B. Watkins, Bridging the Gap.

The water we got was not all sent by God

Rocky Mount Writing Workshops
Philip Shabazz with Nellie Johnson Hunter, Shirley Myrick,
Willie Harper, Lois B. Watkins, Ida Boddie, Lewis Turner,
Sondra Williams, Juanita Wright, Linda Virgil and Harlan Joel Gradin

PHILIP SHABAZZ: Let me ask you this question. Why do you think bad things happened to people who didn't bring it on themselves?

NELLIE JOHNSON HUNTER: It just happened. You know, they say that maybe we're in the flood's way, or flood zone, flood plain. I mean I can look at it in a different way.

PS: So you don't think it's bad luck?

NJH: I don't think it's a punishment for crime or for sin. But you know, it was not bad. There's no good and bad in it. It happens.

WILLIE HARPER: Well, that's true. These things will happen. Just like a lot of people didn't get caught in it, and a lot of them did. And that's what it's all about.

LOIS WATKINS: If you have an ounce of compassion and you didn't get in the water, you still got caught in it. We were all caught in it one way or another. You felt my pain. I felt your pain. We didn't escape. And you can't say, "Well then, they were so bad, they got caught." We didn't bring it on ourselves. It happened.

NJH: I didn't owe for a car. I didn't owe for a house. Everything had been paid for so long ago. But it shows: *Reduce the rubble,* you know. It's just stuff in the end. That's all it was. The most expensive thing you bought was the same as the man who had nothing. It was stuff. I taught thirty-seven years to get what I had—thirty-seven years I stayed in the classroom. But when Floyd came, it was reduced to stuff. That's all it was, you know. There's no real reason.

SHIRLEY MYRICK: I understand what you're saying, it's material things. When I moved here from Philadelphia I came here because of my health. I've been here five years. Everything I had worked thirty years for, was paid for, just like you. I don't feel bad that it happened right there. But I feel bad for so many of these senior citizens who don't have a chance to get back on their feet. I'm fifty-five; I do have a slight little chance if I live long enough to try and get something else back. But some of these senior citizens is not going to be able to get anything. And the people are not trying to help them to get what they need. And it's not right.

PS: Shirley, the night of the flood when you were in your apartment, what happened?

SM: The police came and they wanted us to get out, to go to the shelter. That was after twelve, maybe later. But I didn't hear them. I didn't even know what was going on. I was asleep and my son was there with me. And with the machines and things going, when the cops knocked I didn't hear them. My son heard it. He woke me up and he said, "The cops say for us to get out and go to a shelter because there's supposed to be a flood." And I said, "Oh, it ain't going to be nothing. Going to be like Fran." Fran came up to my back door, so I figured it was going to be another Fran, you know.

So he laid back down. And I laid down for a little while. Then I got up and I went to the door and opened the door, and I just seen all this water, right? My son got up, and I kept telling him, "Go move my car, go move my car." He moved my car three times. The third time he got up to go move it, he couldn't get out there to the car. He said, "Ain't no need to move it no more because it's past my knees now. It's in the car." I stood there in that door all night looking at this water rising and rising and rising. And the water was all up in my house, up over my knees, and I never felt it. And just so happened the water turned the trashcan over in the kitchen. That's when I realized it was water in the house. And he laying there on the couch asleep, the water all the way up to the couch. And then I said, "What are we going to do? We can't get out of here." And the lady next door to me she had two little kids, one of them maybe six months and the other one maybe a year, two years. They were just hollering and screaming, "Please help me get my babies out of here." Some of the people that live a little higher up on the hill thought it was me hollering because they knew I was on oxygen and everything. They come down there and they say,"Well, we're going to get you." So I told them, "No, leave me. Go get the people over there with the babies." So they got them out. They didn't come get us until the next day.

PS: Had the lights gone out?

SM: Everything was out. It was dark. We had flashlights and candles. And the lady next door, she lived by herself. And she said, "The furniture was floating around in the house when I'm in here asleep." The next morning we stood there in the water, and it had got up around waist high then.

PS: Did they come in with a boat?

SM: They had a little thing that kids play with that they put the kids on to take the kids out, and they pulled it up there. And the mother and the father, they walked up. But they had the kids on this little thing. Now when they did come get us, we couldn't bring nothing. And then the boat almost turned over. And I was screaming and crying and carrying on.

PS: How long did it take for the water to recede?

SM: You couldn't get into Leggett Road for over a week or two. They wont allowing nobody on Leggett Road. But it didn't take the water that long to recede because the second week, I think, my son went into the apartment to see how everything was.

PS: Were you on the first floor?

SM: All of them are one floor.

PS: How high did it get?

SM: Almost up to the shoulder in the apartment.

PS: Mr. Willie, how'd you get out?

WH: My neighbor kept calling. They had done got out. And they called me, and I said, "Well, that water ain't going to get that high. That water ain't never got that high before." I laid back down and went back to sleep. It was round about four or five o'clock in the morning. And next I heard from another one. She called and told me, said, "If y'all are going to get out of there, you better get up and come on or you ain't going to be able to get out." And that's when I went to the door and looked out. And I had my truck across the street in somebody else's yard because I didn't want the trees to blow the limbs down. I thought it was going to be a lot of wind. I didn't have no idea it was going to be all that much water. So I looked across the street at my truck, and the water had done got over my tires. So I run back in the house there and told my wife, I said, "Let's go. Let's go." I said, "That water is getting ready to come in the house here." When we walked out, the water had already got up to my second step.

So we went next door and helped some elderly people get out because they was sort of up in age. And we waited around there, and the lady was saying the same thing I was saying: "That water ain't never got this high before. I ain't going out of here tonight." I said, "Yeah, you're going to have to come out of here because that water is still rising." So when we left her house, we went on out to Leggett Road. And the neighbor's son and another fellow had to carry the father out. They had to tote him out. So me and my wife—I was on one side of this lady and she was on the other side and we got her out of there.

PS: What time was that?

WH: That was, I'd say, about seven to eight. Because it was seven o'clock when we left our house. By the time we got over there and helped them and waited on them—well I'd say about a quarter to eight when we left out. And her son had a mail truck out there on Leggett Road because that's as close as he could get it. So we went out there and got on that and took off. And then we went to his niece on Hill Street, and we stayed there three or four weeks. Had an apartment come open at Rolling Meadows Apartments, and that's where I stayed until about a month and a half ago when I moved back into my own house.

I think all that water brought a lot of things together. So many folk lost so much stuff. We were really helping one another. We seemed to be closer than we were before all this. We'd take enough time to let our neighbors know what's going on. We all need some help. This can happen to you as well as me. It makes a person start thinking.

PS: How did you get out, Miss Nellie?

NJH: Boat. A young man came, a boy named Chris Hill, and he said, "Miss Hunter, come on out." His daddy used to be a carrier for me for the *News and Observer*. He said, "Miss Hunter, come on." And I wasn't quite ready. I thought of something I could do. I saw these guys, twins, that walk Leggett Road a lot, and I said—I guess I had panicked—"Let's get this water out of my house." You know, my first impulse was to get that water out of there. Get this water out of this home, you know, it's not supposed to be here. Water had come up to the last step and water was up here.

When Stephanie and I looked in the family room, everything was swimming. We had turned the garage, years ago, into a family room. Everything in there was swimming. We walked down in that water and everything was plugged in the socket, you know, television and everything. But we were blessed. I think the lights had gone out maybe a half an hour or fifteen minutes before. But we didn't question that. We didn't know. And her brother was sitting in the back, and he said, "Mother, don't open that back door, because we'd be washed out. I think we'd better get ready to go." That was the river.

PS: Goodness gracious. What time was it when this was going on?

NJH: It was about seven something. Stephanie looked out the door and the cars were covered. She had a Toyota.

PS: Was it still raining?

NJH: A little, just a drizzle. And my late husband's Cadillac was almost covered.

PS: This is Leggett Road?

NJH: Leggett Road.

PS: Was it overflow of the river? Did a dam burst? Where did all this water come from?

LINDA VIRGIL: They said the dam was backed up and it had to be released.

HARLAN JOEL GRADIN: Folks in Belvoir talk about maybe they did something in Rocky Mount.

LV: They did.

LOIS WATKINS: And we got dumped on more.

LV: Because we live right across from the Tar River and we saw the water just rising, you know. You look at it, it's at your knees. Then the next thing you know it's up above your shoulders.

LW: Well, people from Princeville and Tarboro said the water came from Rocky Mount. Now they're saying it came from Raleigh.

LEWIS TURNER: The water we got was not all sent by God. In 1975 I was working with the city of Raleigh Engineering Department doing a survey with the fire chief. We did the flood study in Raleigh. They had to have a flood study in order to pass a flood plan ordinance. They had to have that before they could get national flood insurance. We got a topological map. And they told me that they were all white out there. Those people are moving out and selling to blacks now. They're in the flood plain out there. The reason they didn't get flooded no worse than they did, they turned the water loose and let the water go down to Princeville.

IDA BODDIE: And didn't give any warning.

LT: There ain't no doubt about that. And the assistant city manager, on TV—I didn't see him but they told me and I read it in the papers—admitted that they turned loose two feet of water. They had no idea it would do the damage it done. That's why everybody's telling about how fast the water was rising. That's right. They opened them floodgates, and they're responsible for all that damage.

IB: But they knew it was going on down to Princeville, see? And they've been trying to get rid of Princeville for years—or rather trying to take it over for years. You've been out on Raleigh Road, 97 going to Raleigh. You see they widened the creek. And I saw this in a plan—Interstate 95 is "Main Street, East Coast." Everybody wants to plant a factory near 95 because you can ship in and out so well. Hwy. 64 will be dual lane from Raleigh to the coast. Hwy. 97's the same, dual lanes. Princeville was in the way. They want to make a recreation area out of it, you know. We always said they wanted to put a Disney World down there.

LT: So they could cut the roads like they need them—or want them. But if you're sitting right in the way—and back then historical—they couldn't do this eminent domain thing, the government go in and take over if they show a need. Princeville was historical so they couldn't put Princeville out, you know?

IB: The original name of Princeville is "Freedom Hill." You see that on the signs, too. And the reason that all of the black people are in this area is because that was the onliest place they could go to after the Civil War. And they settled down near the river. And they called this "Freedom Hill." Because we were free, after the Civil War.

PS: And that's where they put them?

IB: No, they didn't *put* them there. They *went* there. That was the onliest place they could go. Down near the river. That was swampland, and the whites didn't want it. It was down near the river. That was the onliest place they could go—the black people.

NJH: People still believe they released that water.

SM: Oh, sure they did.

PS: Is someone working on a class action lawsuit? Because there was a handout about a class action suit, as far as the dam being opened. Does anybody know anything about that?

NJH: Yes, I have a copy here that I can share with everybody in here. A person in Tarboro gave it to me.

LW: I have consent forms. I have a copy of it and it's stating that there is a class action suit. And so they're saying for anyone who was affected somehow to complete the form. And once you fill it out, then you're added to that suit.

WH: Some fellow or other out of Tarboro brought me some of them.

NJH: That's where it came out of—Tarboro.

PS: And of course you know that for a class action suit to be successful, the more names the better. If you can get enough flood survivors, you can win that.

IB: Right. And most of the people don't even know anything about it.

NJH: I can get everybody down Leggett Road. My niece gave it to me. I gave my neighbors across the street copies. I shared it with everybody I could.

SM: This is what we need to do—get together. One person cannot do it.

LW: And what they did was just to build another higher dike. If there's another flood and the water comes over that dike, that dike won't be high enough. What's going to happen if there is another flood, is flood's going to wash them all away. That's what it's going to do. I'm serious. And did you notice where they put those other trailers down there? Right in the pathway of that dike. And the dike has just been put there. If another flood comes this far, that pile of dirt standing up there don't have a chance.

JUANITA WRIGHT: That's right.

IB: That water's going to wash them right on away.

LW: Tarboro fought against raising the dike because Main Street of Tarboro got flooded. If they raised the dike, all that water's going into Tarboro. That's right. It's going to hold it back into Tarboro to a certain point. It might be a little bit out here, but it wouldn't be as much out here. It's going to get them next turn.

PS: OK. Now this doesn't have to be the immediate after effects, but the impact of the flood and how it has affected your life. What's the thing that you happen to struggle with the most? What's the frustration? OK, let's go to you, Linda. If there's one thing that stands out in the aftermath of everything that's happened, what comes to your mind? What would that thing be?

LINDA VIRGIL: How powerful God still is, and awesome and how He kept us during the flood and after the flood. He still provides, and is still making a way. And sanity, you know—He still keeps me in the right frame of mind. I just praise Him and thank Him for just how good He is. Because it wasn't man—it couldn't be man because you didn't hardly see any the day when the flood come.

PS: Oh, my goodness.

LV: I'm serious, you know. Where we was, was a lot of people and there was help, but they wouldn't help us because—and I'm not a racist—but the thing about it is we were the only blacks where we lived. And they didn't give us a boat. About six boats came back there where we lived. And one of the next door neighbors said, "Don't you all have a circle?" See, they was out there in the highway in a circle getting their family members together, you know, getting them out. And my mama said, "You mean to tell me they're not going to help us?" I said, "Well, let's wait and see." I say, "God's going to send some

---

38

help." So we start singing songs, got the children to sing again, "The storm was passing over" [*a hymn*]. I've always believed in praising God, I don't care where I be. Singing a song or clapping my hands or doing something, you know. Letting the enemy know that he's not going to win. Because if you give up, you know, you're going under. So it wasn't a time to panic. And so, we saw them loading up and loading up. And the best thing I saw that day was that little boat, when my husband came home. It was rocking like this, you know, and he was waving his hands like that. And Mama said, "Yon he comes." Just like that, you know, "Yon he comes." She didn't say it, "Here he comes." She said, "Yon he comes."

PS: That's what your mother said?

LV: Yeah, that's what my mama said.

PS: "Yonder he comes."

LV: "Yon he comes." She said, "That's Clint. That's Clint." It took him four hours and a half to get to where we were, from Merita [*Bread*], and he saw a family drown before he got to us. Just seemed like to me, you didn't have time to think about who was left or what happened to who. All you knew, you had to survive. And then it would come to you, as things blew over, then you'd start thinking about it. One of my sons was missing. We was in the shelter and the people were calling out, getting information. We'd hear some screaming and hollering, you know. Everybody was trying to find out about their loved ones and what had happened.

PS: So you had a son missing temporarily?

LV: Yeah, temporarily, my next to oldest son. My oldest son said, "Mom, I don't know where Darryl is," said, "when we left, we left him and Travis at the apartment." We was at the church then. And I started asking who were some of the people at the apartment, phone numbers and things like that. So it was sort of like I did backtracking, and we finally got up with him. So, you know, it was just amazing how we were scattered but yet still God kept us all. There were ten of us at the house when my husband got there, and still two more of my sons, so really it was twelve. So I just say God did a wonderful thing. And even though I know some families lost family members, I'm just glad. Homes and all of that gone, you can get some more of that. But the ones that's left, He gave us another chance.

PS: Mr. Willie, anything in the aftermath of all this? Is it still affecting you in some kind of way, in the way that you live right now?

WH: Well, I'm back home now. And I had people from out of town come in and help me out getting my house back. Now, FEMA, they gave me $11,000. All that's been spent up. I bought all the materials and things, and the rest, the people that were coming in town bought. Those that were working on mine come out of New Haven and different areas. Some of them come from Philadelphia.

PS: New Haven, Connecticut?

WH: Yeah. They come out of different areas to work on people's houses. In fact, they're still doing that, down at my nextdoor neighbor's. And what was so bad about it, see, everything that I had got lost in water. Everything in there was lost. When we did get a chance to get back to the house and go in there, I didn't have nothing in there that you could save. The Red Cross gave me furniture. And I had the money that FEMA gave me. All that money's been spent. I had to take part of that and buy furniture and part of it to pay my house rent where I was living. Then I had to use part of it to pay on my house where it was damaged. So I had two mortgages going on at the same time.

PS: So it's never enough money?

WH: Never enough money. Never enough money. The electricity man come in there the other day and I had to pay him $750 for the work that he did. First he come in there and cut my lights off and took the wires loose so they could work on it. Gave him $760 to do that. Then he come back and put it back like it was supposed to have been. It was $750 to do that. And all that coming out of my money, because the FEMA money's gone. It's been difficult.

LV: Can I say something? What I've learned is that people are less concerned about what happened to you since the flood. It seems like their hearts would be more open now. If you know there's a need that they haven't been delivering and don't help. There's no compassion, you know, for what happened. Compassion. There has to be compassion, like "The Good Samaritan."

And going through all these steps before you get something. You've already seen my steps washed away from my door. You've already seen that I've got a need. Then why are you going to cause me this long wait? Why do you have to take me through another turmoil? And I say this for every person that was a flood victim or affected by the flood. Even if you didn't get flooded, you might have a loved one that was involved in the flood. So why is the heart stuck? Why is it so hard? And these people in need.

NJH: Some of my—well, I thought my best—friends looked the other way after the flood. They didn't come, didn't call any more. I had several people that I talked to almost on a daily basis—that I had worked with. I worked out here in Edgecombe County and Roanoke Rapids for a total of thirty-seven years. And some thought because my son was working and my daughter was working they would help me. My daughter couldn't help me. She's going to be kind to me, but I can't expect her to go into her pocket, you know? And I can't expect my son to, a man with a wife and two children. And so I had people who actually didn't speak to me any more, didn't call me any more. I had never asked anybody for anything. And I took people to distribution centers, those without cars, to get what they needed. I had to rent a car because all my cars went down in the flood. And my son said, "Mama, you know you're not going to a shelter. Come to my house." So I did, I went there. I could have stayed with them but I needed my space. I needed my space. I had lived thirty-seven years on Leggett Road.

PS: Did you go back home?

NJH: No, no, I'm in an apartment now.

PS: You're retired? Schoolteacher?

NJH: I'm retired, over five years ago. And they seemed to have thought, *Hey, you've worked, you've got some money saved somewhere.* I thought everything that I would ever buy would be a luxury from here on out at my age. Not necessities. But they put me in a position where everything was a necessity. That was for me to live on when I got old, when I got to my age. But then you're using it up. And then a good friend of mine who was a retired teacher from North Edgecombe, she carried me to Tarboro to some distribution center. And they said, "Well, let me come into your house and see what you have before we can see what we can help you with, like furniture, you know." Even though they knew everything had gone.

And the sad part about it—what affects me more when I think about it—was that out front [*of the flooded houses*] people were working fast as they could getting your furniture. We thought they were curiosity seekers, just coming by. And then they came back with vans. If they saw a couch they liked, they'd put it in their van. I know a woman right down the street from where I live on Leggett Road, she said, "Nellie, I was standing in your yard and my heart was breaking for all your stuff out there. And some guy came up and said, 'May I have this couch?'" She was so shocked. And then another guy came by that I had taught, "Miss Hunter, you're not going to get this bed?" I said, "Oh, go ahead and get it." Sometimes they asked. If you weren't there, they just took your furniture. And some had a way of drying it off and selling that stuff.

HJG: Were these things contaminated?

SM: Yeah.

HJG: So, people were picking up the contaminated stuff and selling it?

SM: And selling it.

NJH: That's why they asked us to throw it away—because it was so contaminated.

SONDRA WILLIAMS: Even one of the employees with the city picked up a lady's stuff. She had gone back to her apartment and cleaned up all her stuff. She had set it aside because they didn't have anywhere to carry it. She had set it aside and roped it off like the police said. The men from the city went and took her stuff, after it was roped off. They had a write-up in the paper about it. There were so many people backlashing, saying, "She shouldn't have put it out there." Well, this lady had been flooded out. She was on the river at those apartments. So they didn't have anywhere to put things. The apartment was already messed up. So they went out there and they put their stuff outside—cleaned their china and all their stuff up, roped it off. And the city came and took it all away.

WH: They grabbed the moment. You know, people grabbed the moment for themselves. They'd say, "What's she got?"

NJH: If they had gone in and gotten what belonged to those of us who were flooded and given it to relatives, that's the only way you can explain it. And then they'd throw their own furniture out. You'd see more areas where there was furniture everywhere, and the people didn't even know it rained there. They didn't get an inch of rain. They didn't get hardly anything.

LW: I think we all are connected, one to another. And whatever one does, it's like a chain reaction in terms of humanity. It's kind of like a chain. Each link, some are stronger, others are weaker. And when something happens and stress is pulling that chain, the weaker links break. For instance, in this flood those more vulnerable are the ones that suffered most. And the cause, I think, is what we've done to the earth all these years.

LV: I say it's a warning. God never does anything without a warning. And the preparation time that you had—there wasn't any. So it's sort of like car insurance—people take out car insurance in advance. They might never have an accident, but they pay it on and on. House insurance, and things like that. But for your own being, your soul, your spiritual side, where will that rest? To me it was like, *What if it was the great day that we should stand before Him? Would I be ready? Would you be ready?* Because there was no time to get ready. When we got ready to get on the boat, the man said, "You can't bring much." Don't that sound like the Word? I had bags packed, but he said, "You can't take them." All I could get was my children's asthma medicine. And it's just like the Word say, "He that is filthy, let him be filthy still. If he's on the housetop, let him stay on the housetop. There's no time, it's time to get out." So he said, "I can't take but five." There was ten of us. So everything was a countdown. Everything was limited, even at the time that it was happening, even though we all wanted to go. And it was just like we all can go to heaven, but it's our choice. It's the choices that we make. You can't blame each other. So that day it was your own fight, your own race. You've got to win your own race. You had to stay focused.

PS: Did the newspaper do a big exposé on some of the flood survivors and their stories, and the aftermath of this? I mean, with different people telling their stories just like we're doing here?

LV: They talked more so about the crest, the river cresting. And the Neuse River and all that. But they didn't get into a lot of details about people's lives. They kept naming a small number of people, like fifty-two people, that had drowned, knowing that it was more than that. I have newspapers all the way back, and I'm making a newsbook.

PS: OK. Good. Good. Good.

LV: I started working with the flood victims a little bit too, you know, to get my mind off things. Well, we were carrying our stuff upstairs. When I went upstairs and looked out the window and saw Merita Bread was underwater, I said, "No, we can't stay here." We thought about staying there, but when the water started coming up to the porch and to the dining area, and then you're just seeing things wash across the yard—you're seeing a brick walk floating across the yard and stuff like that. We were number 1001 at Red Cross. It took three days for us to get help and we was in six shelters. We was in this one church and they moved us from there because we was black. We went to the National Guard Armory and we couldn't use their phone; we couldn't leave till a certain time. We still hadn't had food, you know. Some lady out of the goodness of her heart had cooked some kind of meat that first night when we went to the church, but it wasn't enough to go around so we let the kids eat it. So we were eating chips, cookies things like that. Ice. These are real things that took place.

PS: How long did it take you to get a stable place to live?

LV: It was somewhere around the end of October because we were staying with family, with my daughter. I'd say round about a month.

PS: Mr. Willie, how about you? How long did it take you to get back home?

WH: Well, I just got back home a little better than a month ago.

PS: How long have you been out of your house, Miss Nellie?

NJH: Ever since the flood. That's a year. First, I went to live with my son. They made me welcome to stay there but, you know, you don't feel comfortable when you aren't in your own space. Then the people [FEMA] promised us this: They said for eighteen months, that they would pay up to five hundred and some dollars a month. They reneged on that.

PS: They reneged on it?

NJH: They didn't pay. They didn't pay for those apartments that long.

SM: They paid for my hotel room—800 and some dollars. After that the lady say, "Well, we're only supposed to pay one month—one month's security, one month's rent."

NJH: Where were we supposed to go?

SM: Now, that $858—they were giving me $225 a week in the hotel, yet they would go to these fast food places and pay $350 some a week for me to eat, and I couldn't get to the food because I had no transportation.

NJH: Plus you had to pay utilities, you know.

PS: Let's get some more stories about before, during or after—the impact that the flood had on you or your family. Lois, since you've been real patient with us and you've been doing all this work, maybe we should start with you. Is that OK?

LW: Well, I wasn't affected so much personally by the flood. We had hurricane damage to the house and so it took me a good month or more to realize that my family was really affected. I was kind of a caretaker, I'm always trying to take care of people, that's what I do in my work. So when I woke up that morning after the flood, I got in my car and went driving, trying to see how to get somewhere. I have a lot of family in Tarboro, east Tarboro, in Princeville, from that community. And so I wanted to get over there and I was trapped because all the roads were blocked. There was water everywhere, and I said—I had to tell someone—"God, what am I supposed to do? What do you want me to do?" And I kept wondering where to hear a response. And then Juanita—we work together—her and another sister, we went to Tarboro. And we had to go the backroads through the county and we were kind of worried about it. Should we be going? Because we were in fear. We were in fear, but we did it anyway. We went to Tarboro the day after the flood, went the backroads. We got over there and I was looking for my family. And we went to the shelter and I found some. Some I didn't, but I was encouraged that everybody was OK.

But my concern was, where are the leaders? What are we going to do? So when we got to Tarboro, first thing, you know, we just saw these white people who were in charge of running everything. And we finally got a black minister over there in Tarboro High School to a white shelter. And they started telling us about how white folks just came in and just took control. They would not allow the black leadership to even see or take care of their own people. So that was a big issue. And then they were pretty much working, trying to come together. Called a meeting together of the people from at least Tarboro and Princeville to try to rescue people they knew over there. Who was there? Well, it's not just Princeville and Tarboro; it's Rocky Mount, too. And if nothing else is going to bring East Tarboro and Rocky Mount together, this is it. So what you should do is to include the ministers from Rocky Mount as well as Princeville and Tarboro.

We were the only three women over there at St. Luke Church for the very first part of those meetings. We were standing up for the idea that, "You need to come together. You need to do this thing together." And they did hear us. And they said, "They're not going to come, because Rocky Mount thinks they're better than us. They're not going to come over here. If you think they're going to come, you can call them if you want to." And sure enough, that night we went home and started calling ministers. And they did go.

And it was good—all that had been summoned up for cooperation—but it hadn't been what I hoped to see. Because I hoped to see the gap bridged between blacks *with* and blacks *without*. Because we're all black and we're all without, really, if you look at it on a scale. But the way it affected me was—and the big thing for me to consider—was that this was an opportunity for us as people to really come together and bridge the gap and to close the door to our community. Because it just showed me how they were in control of all the resources. They chose who did what for our people. And we as leaders had no say-so. We had no resources. We had nothing we could go and give our people. We had to go to the whites for everything. And they didn't even respect our leaders enough to even come to them and say, "How can we help?" They went directly to our people. That's the way they do all the time. It's like the door to our house is wide open and they just come and go right to your children, to your people, without even coming to the head of the house. And that's how it is to me, because our men are the head of our community, and *they* are outsiders.

IB: Supposed to be.

LW: They're supposed to come in to your community and go to your leadership, but they don't. But they don't. They don't. Because we don't have our doors closed. And so that's how it affects me. And so we have all been working together to get a coalition built among leaders trying to bridge that gap and build relationships. Working with Angela and reconstruction. We meet here every Thursday morning. But that's my heart cry, is to see our community— East Tarboro, Princeville and Rocky Mount, the counties—just so closed, so tight that even though the whites have the money, they can't come in and say, "This is what we're going to do. This is who's going to do it." They must come to us and say, "How can we be of help?"

PS: Come to the leadership?

LW: They must come to the leadership, that's what I want to see. And I hope that's something that's going to come out of this flood.

IB: What I see is, this so-called "leadership" of ours will not cooperate with the so-called little persons.

LW: Exactly.

IB: That's the way I see it. Because during that flood all these big and rich churches we black people have—the biggest churches there is in Rocky Mount, we have them—they did not open the doors and say, "All my people come in." They didn't do it. The church was too good for their own people.

LW: There was one church, it was just a huge church, and the minister was only going to open the door for their own congregation. But the congregation compelled him. They started calling him and going to see him. They compelled him to open the door. That made me feel real good.

IB: Sure did. But there was no reason for no one being in a shelter in a school in Rocky Mount with all these big fine churches here. The churches were too good for their own people to go in. And that's where I have a problem with our so-called leaders. That's what I'm saying. And they are calling themselves "leaders." That's what I'm saying.

LW: And that's why the whites come in with money and they tell us what we got to do. We have to go to them.

IB: Right. We have to take what they dish out, because our so-called leaders are too good for us. You see what I'm saying?

PS: Go ahead, Mr. Lewis.

LEWIS TURNER: During one of our Thursday morning meetings here we had a minister, an activist minister in Tarboro. I don't remember what triggered it but that particular morning we got to talking about the "Willie Lynch syndrome" and being taught to work against your own people. And this person said, "Yeah," say, "they came to me and gave me a bill of goods, and I worked against and helped them defeat Thomas Walker. And as soon as we got him out, then they went and turned my deacons against me and they turned me out of my church."

IB: To work against each other.

LT: Now that we have recognized how foolish we have been lead to act, we still didn't rise up and say, "I'm not gonna do this no more. I'm gonna turn about-face and do the right things." Our so-called leadership ain't our leaders, folks. I can remember the modern Civil Rights movement. I know a couple of those boys at the sit-in at Woolworth's—when that movement exploded across the country, the system tried to slow the person in head of it down. They tried to appoint your leaders for you. "This is your leader, who speaks for the Negro."

PS: Because *you* ain't got sense enough to say who your own leader is.

LT: Right. Right. No. We're all leaders. We're all leaders.

PS: Let's get back to the flood. Anybody want to talk about before, during or after? Something about this flood? Sondra, you live in Princeville, right? Tell us a little bit of what happened—when it first hit, what you had to do to get out, and that kind of thing. Did you believe it was going to happen?

SONDRA WILLIAMS: No, because earlier that day they were just saying it was like rain—it's going to go away. Well, we were just like chilling, just waiting for the lights to come back on. And so we rode it out for a while, and the water was coming high like. And my sister that came to my house, she was like, "Y'all better get out of here." I said, "We ain't going nowhere. It ain't in my house." And so I went in my house without lights and I started cleaning up, you know. Clean up. Let's clean up this stuff till the lights are back on. Three o'clock came, my neighbor was knocking on the door. She said, "Y'all get up." We was upstairs laying down asleep then.

PS: This was three o'clock in the morning?

SW: Yes, on September 17th. She was saying, "Y'all get up." I'm like, "Get up for what?" She says, "Y'all leave, leave now. Get a pillow for your head, that's all y'all can get. Let's go." And so we went outside. I'm like, "What in the world is going on?" It was pitch dark. So we left. And we got out of the driveway right down there in front of my son's school and the car flooded. So the policeman that came and knocked on the door to get us out, he said, "Well, we're going around checking, making sure everybody's out. When we come back through, if y'all's car don't start, we'll leave your car and y'all can come with us." We was already in the middle of the water and he already had people on the car. My husband's name is Joe, and I'm like, "Joe, we've got to pray and believe God for this right now. I'm not getting on that car with these people. It's already full. Where are we going to sit?"

PS: Dark?

SW: Dark. And so a truck driver came up, and he was like, "What's wrong with your car? Don't pedal it. Let's let it sit here for a few minutes and let the water die back down out of it, because that's why it flooded." So we sat in the car, and my baby was sitting in the back. It was kind of funny to him, but he didn't know what was really going on. He thought it was a joke. And I was scared. So we just sat in the car and we prayed. And my husband, he was getting all frustrated. I said, "Baby, it ain't the time to get frustrated. You've just got to pray. You need to pray now." And so, God be my witness, the car started and we got halfway through. We got to the end at the stop sign coming out of Princeville by the school. The water was over the car, and I was like, "Oh, my God." We couldn't go from downtown Princeville to Tarboro, we had to go over the railroad track into Tarboro. So that night we got to my sister's house and we stayed there.

The next morning the police came over there and said, "Y'all got to leave from here." And I'm like, "God, where we going now?" Because I knew we couldn't get out of town, no way. Couldn't get out of Tarboro no way. Couldn't go to Rocky Mount. So we went to my other sister's house and stayed in Tarboro. We got over there, and there was my brother. He was already there from Rocky Mount. He came from Rocky Mount and stayed. He was there, I was there, and my sister and her children, they were there. And then there was my nephew and my niece and her friends. It was like twenty people in one apartment, and two bedrooms, with no lights. We stayed there for about three or four days.

And you know when a bunch of people get in a house all that chaos starts going on. So I was like, "Oh my God. God, I don't know what's going on, but we have got to get out of this situation." So we left from Tarboro after about three or four days and went to Plymouth. And when we got halfway through Chocowinity, there was water in the road there. And I'm like, "OK. I ain't going through no more water today, God. I ain't going through more water." And I was sitting there and my leg was jumping up like, "Just get out and let me drive." I can't get out because I'm scared, and I can't move. So we're just going to sit here and wait till our turn and go through this line. So when we got ready to go through the water, you could feel the water pouring in the car; the current was so close to the ditch you could feel the current. And I'm like, "Jesus God." And I knew that on the side there was cars covered with water. But it just so happened that God made a way. We made it through the water.

And we came back a couple of days later to Princeville. It was still chaos. You couldn't get no help from people. The people that you thought would help you, the black people that was handling things, it was like they had turned against you. You could stand in line for hours just to get help, and then would be told, "Well, let me see your FEMA number" or whatever. Or, "You can't get this." Or, "We're closing down for an hour so come back then." And it was just chaotic. And even now, we're still trying to get help to get back into a home because we lost everything too.

PS: Lost everything?

SW: Yes, we lost everything. And they go, "You guys are overqualified. You

FEMA Disaster Application Center and FEMA trailers.

Photo by Neil Moore.

don't fit with this program. You don't fit with that program." And I'm like, "Overqualified for what? What in the hell are you going to qualify with?"

LT: You know, the tragedy wasn't the water. The tragedy was the way the system treated the people.

IB: That's true.

LOIS WATKINS: And in some ways they're punishing Princeville because they would not go for that buyout.

IB: They would not build any low-income homes in Tarboro. Had the money to do it with but they refused to build.

LW: And because at Bridging the Gap we work with some other programs, I met these other families like yours. We have families from Princeville and East Tarboro, and they weren't homeowners, they were renters. And a lot of them were in public housing. They haven't even begun to rebuild public housing. And most of those people left out there in that FEMA trailer park that they're writing these negative stories about in the paper are people who were living in those public housing homes. And they haven't done anything to replace their homes. And now because they gave them that money, people are saying, "They had theirs."

IB: Some of them. Some of them. All of them didn't get it.

LW: Some of them did not get that much money. And then about the ones that got money, they're saying, "Well, they should have took the money and went and bought something." But if they had, they couldn't have afforded to keep it. They would be back on the street or back in the FEMA park by now, because their rent doubled. Even if they got $10,000, that would have been gone by now. They couldn't have afforded to keep it. They would have been out on the street anyway.

IB: Some of the homeowners was paying a mortgage on a home in Princeville and then paying rent over here. How long is $10,000 going to last?

LT: Ten months.

IB: Plus some of the businesses was washed out. All the cars was gone. What are you going to do?

LW: And then lots that were selling at $5,000 are now $20,000 for a lot.

IB: Everything went up and doubled.

LW: And your income did not change.

IB: We had a high rate of unemployment, eleven percent, before the flood even came, so we had a crisis before the flood. All these programs gone—the welfare reform, they called it. So we had a crisis before the flood.

LW: The empowerment zone, we live in the empowerment zone.

IB: And then along came the flood.

LW: Made matters worse.

SW: Yeah. Because the homes they're building now, for people to afford them they should be $200, $300 a month rent. But they got them from $600 up.

LT: And the income level does not allow anybody to live in them. Hey, if you're on minimum wage, how are you going to pay that? You can work four jobs and you won't have enough.

LW: And another thing is that the papers always spread these stories about this amount of money came, that amount of money came. But the dollars have yet to be deposited in the bank. It's going somewhere else. It's not helping those that deserved it. They didn't get it. They haven't got it yet.

IB: It's not trickling down where it belongs.

LT: That $10,000 thing they talk about that a few of them did get, they came as a thief in the night and got people to sign their rights away and gave them this little bit of money. There was nowhere for them to go. There wasn't even land for sale. There wasn't nothing to do with the money. The only thing they could have done with that money was you take it and be gone in sixty days. That means you had to leave eastern North Carolina, because there wont nowhere to go, no permanent housing in eastern North Carolina. Nowhere. If you take

$10,000 and go find permanent housing, you've got to go either out of state or west from here, way west from here. Only way it could be done.

LW: They set people up to fail because they baited people with these rent-to-own, make-a-down-payment deals. Take part of your FEMA money and you put $3,000 on this home and you pay $750 a month mortgage.

IB: For their SBA loan. I haven't seen anybody yet that got that $13,600 grant. You got to go through that loan before you get any type of grant. They push you through that loan.

LW: It's just wrong. It's just wrong, what they're doing. It's wrong.

LT: It's criminal. Criminal.

PS: I did want to hear from Miss Mae and Juanita.

MAE RICKS: This is worse than when it was mostly blacks against blacks.

PS: And that was a big problem, probably.

MR: Yeah. This lady asked me to come and help, because I had been helping in the community a lot. And she asked me to come help. She said, "Come here, Ricks, and help me with this food." The Sears man was coming to my house to do something to the chicken house. And I said, "Well, I can help you till I see the Sears truck go past." And I went in there and helped her get the stuff out of the truck, all them boxes. We got them in and then we started stuffing—emptying boxes and setting up what we thought a family would use. So it would be fifty or sixty packages in a box. And we divided it all up. I think it was on a Thursday. So then we got all the names of the people who really didn't have anything. And then Friday they say we're going to give it out Saturday morning. She said, "You come at eight o'clock."

So I get up early and do my chickens and run up there—why, there's nothing in the building. Everything was gone. Not a package was in there. And I said, "What happened?" So I called the lady that had asked me to help, and she said, "Oh, they came at one o'clock yesterday and they gave out everything." I said, "Well, my own neighbors didn't get anything." Because I always see they get something. I had given them some of my food because I always have chicken and stuff. But I said, "I'm going up here and get y'all some other stuff in my truck."

What actually happened was they got people from Charlottesville, from Rocky Mount, from all around. And they called up all their cousins and relatives and everybody and got in there Friday evening and took all the food. That's the way people did each other. That's the way we did each other. Now this was really blacks as far as I know. I don't know whether the white folks told them to do it, or who told them.

LT: They did that several places.

MR: All the food. All the food. Because we made boxes, you know, with a certain amount, and we divided it so people wouldn't take a big container. We told them to bring the containers to put the soap powder and the other stuff in, so that everybody would get enough to wash their clothes and stuff. But they didn't. They didn't.

LT: Well, now, I can't say that was deliberate, but in my heart I believe that was deliberate, to get you fighting among yourselves.

MR: That's right. I don't know why they did it like that. There was no reason for it. And then they'd dribble out a little bit, you know, a little something. And it was just really like the people who were supposed to have been in charge never were. People still got great big containers of soap and cooking oils, stacks of toilet tissue. That's what they say, they'll have this for the next three or four years.

PS: Well, the people who were supposed to have been distributing didn't do what they were supposed to.

MR: The lady wasn't even there who had brought the truck.

IB: Another thing too that made me sick, I coordinated the distribution center down there on Atlantic Avenue, and we couldn't get any men to help. We got Stokes Funeral Home's truck, went out to the distribution place and picked up stuff. Picked up water, water, water. And we had so much water and foodstuff in that center down there it was full. Then we started putting it on the outside of the building. When the women got all this water sitting down there we'd say, "Well, thank God, we got some more water here." And all of a sudden the men would come up in a drove, putting all this water in their trucks. But you couldn't get them to go get none to save your life. Couldn't get them up there. Looked like they were standing back behind the corners watching.

LT: If you beat me one time, that's your fault. But if I let you beat me another time, that's my fault. There comes a time when you put your foot down. If you don't come to help, don't let me see you. Don't even ask. Don't even ask. Don't even ask.

Mae Ricks and Sondra Williams at Rocky Mount Writing Workshop, Harambee Square.

Photo courtesy of Lois B. Watkins, Bridging the Gap.

Fallen through the gap

Rocky Mount Writing Workshops
Philip Shabazz with Shirley Myrick, Nellie Johnson Hunter,
Lois B. Watkins, Ida Boddie, Lewis Turner, Juanita Wright

PHILIP SHABAZZ: Do you think these local politicians in Rocky Mount make a difference for people's lives here?

SHIRLEY MYRICK: No. No, they don't. They make a difference for the people in their clique. Reason why I say this is because this was different for everybody, when this flood happened. Nobody knew it was going to be a flood. This is something that just happened, right? And from what I understood Governor Hunt got on the TV and said everybody would be put back in the position that they were—not above what they were, but where they were prior to the flood. If you lost a microwave, they would replace that microwave. If you lost this, they replaced it. I haven't got none of these things that he said that he would replace. There's people I know that got furniture vouchers. I never got one. They got food stamps. I never got none. They got food vouchers. They got furniture. I got none of that stuff.

PS: How did that happen?

SM: I don't know what happened. I went the same places they went—Red Cross and everything else. But they got these things that I didn't. Why, I don't know.

PS: So the principle is that if Governor Hunt said that people would have what they had prior to the flood they should have it, no matter what the politics is?

SM: No matter what the politics were. I'm not asking nobody to put me above where I was—but put me back where I was. Just give me the things that I had when that flood came. When that flood came, I was able to pay my rent, pay my bills, and live comfortable. Now I'm not able to even buy my medicine.

PS: So it's costing you too much to live?

SM: To live now, and I don't think it's fair. And there's other people out here who was in the same flood I was in, and they're living on "High Street."

PS: Talk to us about how your lifestyle was before Floyd.

SM: Before Floyd? I was comfortable, living happy. Had my own car. It was paid for. All my furniture was paid for. All my bills was paid up. Everything was in place. I had a hundred to two hundred dollars a month left out of my check that I could buy my medicine and go to my doctor, and do the things that I wanted to do in life. Buy me a piece of clothes here and there, you know. I could go to Philadelphia and stay with my grandkids for a week or two, a month. No problems whatsoever. Didn't have to ask nobody for nothing. Now I can't even go to the corner store and buy a loaf of bread without asking somebody to loan me a dollar or two.

PS: Because your whole situation has changed?

SM: I'm back like when I was a teenager, when I was raising my kids by myself. I'm back down to that. Cook a pot that lasts me two or three days. I shouldn't have to live like this. I worked two jobs until six years ago. I always worked two jobs. I paid tax. I feel as though I should be able to get some help. I don't understand this system at all. I don't want to beat the system, I want to be a part of the system, you know. I want to be where I can get up in the morning, go in the kitchen, see something in there that I want to eat, and eat. Not worry about what am I going to eat today?

PS: How did you get jammed in this situation after Floyd?

SM: My biggest problem is I had a Section 8 apartment. I lost that. And then I went in debt for a trailer that I'll never be able to pay for. With the trailer fee, the mortgage, the light fee, and all my utilities—I don't get enough money to pay for that. Right now I'm scuffling so hard, I'm under so much stress. I get my check on the first, and by the third or fourth I ain't got a dime left in the bank and I ain't covered all my bills because it's not enough.

PS: So you're stuck with a trailer?

SM: I'm stuck with a thirty-year mortgage. I was from day one trying to get rid of it. Nobody wants to buy it. I went there and I signed a lease for that lot, you know. I can't just walk away and leave that trailer on that man's lot. That's not right. Even though at my age I'm not planning on ever buying anything else, but I don't want to do something where I'll have no credit or nothing. Bad enough now.

PS: Were there people telling you that you should do this, you should get the trailer?

SM: Yeah. I'm on Home Health Care, you know. And Red Cross put me in a hotel. The social worker from Home Health was trying to get me a trailer from FEMA. They never put me in a trailer from FEMA. I stayed in a hotel until I couldn't pay no more.

PS: How long did you stay in a hotel?

SM: Almost two months

PS: How was that?

SM: It was terrible. They gave me a food voucher for the fast food place, which was about a half a mile from where I was staying. There was no place for me to get food. And I just had that one room, so there was everything stacked all around, all these boxes. It was like I was in prison. Nowhere to go, just sit down all day and watch TV.

PS: So then that's when you made the trailer deal?

SM: Yeah. I used the money that FEMA gave me, which was $4,536, for a down payment on a trailer. It took them almost two months to process me. And on December the 20th they put the trailer out there and I moved in.

PS: So it's costing you too much to live in this trailer? What did they give you? A ten-, twenty-year mortgage on it?

SM: Thirty-year mortgage.

PS: On a trailer?

SM: On a trailer, singlewide trailer. Thirty-year mortgage. With my mortgage and my lot fee—just my rent and lot fee alone is $464 a month. I only get $877. By the time I pay my electric bill, water and sewer, cable bill, telephone bill—I can't pay my other bills. I don't have anything left for anything else. I can't buy my medicine. I don't feel as though a human being should have to live like this.

PS: Are there other people that you know who after the flood are just having a total lifestyle change? They can't go back to the way that they lived, and it's just a total hardship on them now?

SM: A few people I know. But a lot of them I know, they're doing better than they were before the flood. And I sit around and I look and I look and I say,

"Lord, why did this happen to me? Why can't I bounce back like the other people?" I don't think it's right either that because I was trying to do what I thought was best for me—because I had nowhere to go and because I made a mistake and bought the trailer—now that I want to try and get back into the apartment that I was in, they cut off my Section 8.

NELLIE JOHNSON HUNTER: Somebody needs to do something. I think that something needs to be done. Somebody needs to do something.

SM: It was as if they was telling me that because I was renting, I wasn't important. You know what I'm saying? Because I didn't own nothing, I wasn't important. Like I didn't really lose anything because I wasn't owning anything, just because I was renting.

PS: Yeah, but you owned your lifestyle, you had a standard of living. You had things worked out. That's what you owned.

SM: But the way that I'm living now—I cannot live for three days and be stressed out the whole month. The first, second, third and fourth, I'm happy because that's how long that check lasts. Then it's gone. Then I have nothing for the whole month. If it wasn't for my sister, I don't know what I would do. She comes by and she gives me a few dollars here and there to keep me going, you know, to tide me over. If it wasn't for my sister, I don't know what I would do.

PS: So they don't honor the people who were on Section 8 before the flood?

SM: They did honor them. They said you could go back into your apartment.

PS: Oh, there was a time period?

SM: Yeah. But at the time I bought the trailer, I went back and got my security for the apartment. If I had left my security there, I would have been guaranteed to be on Section 8 and back in the apartment. But at the time I had got in a trailer, so why let them hold my security? I could use that money. And this is what I did. So that's how I lost out on everything. Now I don't know what to do. And then you've got people out here who have gotten so many things from this flood that didn't even have water damage. I've seen a lot of them down to the Red Cross. They were just giving to people who come in there and ask for it. That's how come so many people didn't get what they need, because it wasn't done properly.

LOIS WATKINS: And now they think everybody's lying.

SM: And now they think everybody's lying about what they need. They're cutting everything off.

PS: Is it dried up?

LW: No, it's not dried up. The people with the resources are acting like Social Service providers, not being advocates for the public. That's the problem.

PS: Now I don't want to try to start signifying anything, but as far as the black preachers, are they running interference for people who are in need? Or what's their role?

SM: My pastor's doing pretty good about me. He comes and checks on me to see what can he do for me, or what the church can do for me—my church.

PS: But that doesn't take you back to your lifestyle that you had. They can't get that for you.

SM: I don't look for them to do that for me, you know. Because if it's a government problem, then let the government put me back where I was, not my church. It wasn't my church's problem. This was a statewide thing. This wasn't just me. When the flood first came a lot of ministers did help me. That's how I really got started. The churches gave me money, and food and clothes and things.

  I can't bounce back and I don't understand why. I've never been where I couldn't get my foothold back down again. I've been down and out many a time, but I've always been able to bounce back. I guess since I'm not able to work and get the things that I really need, I can't bounce back. And so, I'm about ready to give up now. I really am.

PS: It seems to me that there should be somebody working on behalf of flood survivors, particularly when it comes to Section 8. Going back to Governor Hunt's statement about getting people back to where they were, regardless of mistakes that the people made when making drastic decisions after the flood. There should be a group of people that would go into that Section 8 office or anywhere and get them to work in emergency situations. Are there any advocates in the community? I mean, it seems like that there's an inequality here. You've got a whole lot of flood survivors who are not getting back to the lifestyle that they enjoyed before all this. Are there any advocates to help people get back?

LW: Oh, the United Way "Recover with Dignity." I was with them before I started working with legal services, and what we did, we contacted a lot of the flood victims first, and then worked with other issues, you know, like maybe eyeglasses or something like that. Food. But the main issue was to see what their needs were after the flood. And medically. And we just stayed with them. There were two or three people that I worked with real closely. I did home assessments and follow through. There are some other advocates working in Princeville, but there are so many people. And in the headlines they say X amount of dollars given here and here, but the funds haven't been released in a lot of instances. The actual dollars haven't come in. That's a real big problem. One thing too is that there was no flood readiness plan. I mean no one was prepared. No one was trained and there was nothing in place to deal with a disaster.

PS: No agency?

LW: Nothing. I mean we have Red Cross, but . . .

PS: They're more hands on.

LW: So what was happening, and probably part of the problem, was just getting volunteers. And people coming and trying to practice and learn at the same time. So a lot of mistakes have been made, and a lot of them probably weren't intentional.

IDA BODDIE: Documentation is so complicated, even the FEMA representatives didn't understand their own documentations. They turned around then and they changed them again, which was complicated. Then the FEMA people had to write their own documentation all over again. In the meantime the first group that had been to FEMA got to turn around and all go back again. And they were asking questions wrong. Because one particular question they had been asking was, "Did you have any insurance?" Naturally, anybody would think that was homeowner's insurance. "Yes, I had insurance." But you get this paper back and they say, "Well, you said you had flood insurance." I didn't say I had flood insurance, I said I had home insurance. They should have asked, "Did you have any flood insurance?"

LEWIS TURNER: Nobody had flood insurance. Nobody had it. Not flood insurance.

LW: But the other thing was asking for documentation in places where the whole house was underwater and you had come out on a boat. What kind of documentation would you have?

IB: No one had any type of documentation. Nothing.

LT: Because it was all underwater.

IB: Right.

JUANITA WRIGHT: That's right. All underwater.

IB: I mean they had a time. You got to run around here and run around there. You're trying to prove this, then you're trying to prove that.

LT: There was a lady that went to some session they had at Coastal Plains, at the mental health place. They asked this lady, "How much damage did you have?" And she said, "Well, I don't know. I have no way of knowing." She was from Princeville. She goes through that. She couldn't tell them how much damage or whatever. Asked a stupid question, she couldn't answer. Her house is still underwater. And they turned her down. Didn't even start taking more data because she couldn't tell them how much damage she had or what she lost. And there was another young man there said, "Now, what happened with you?" And she told him. He said, "You go back in there. You done lost everything. Your house is still underwater. You don't know how much damage. You haven't been home. Can't get home."

LW: And then too they were using local whites who already were racist. And I've heard people say, going to Red Cross, "I'm sitting here with this white person in front of me examining me. Sitting next to me is another white person being examined by a white person. And I'm listening to the information that they're sharing and the resources they're hooking this person up with, and over here I'm not getting that kind of help, not the same."

[*several people talking at once*]: Sure. Um hmm. Right. That's it. That's it exactly.

IB: I also heard that even in the beginning they didn't have many bunks in the shelters, and if a black person had a bunk and a white person came in they would make that black person get out of that bunk and give it to this white person.

PS: No!

IB: I heard that.

LW: There was some crazy stuff going on.

We'll come up with something

Rocky Mount Writing Workshops
Philip Shabazz with Shirley Myrick and Angela Bryant

Editor's note: At a later point, Philip Shabazz brought Shirley Myrick together with Angela Bryant, an important worker in the pre-flood community development efforts and in flood recovery work in Rocky Mount.

ANGELA BRYANT: Where are you living now? Are you in one of the parks?

SHIRLEY MYRICK: No, I was never offered a trailer.

AB: Are you with family?

SM: No. I went out and went into debt and bought a trailer. Now I've got to try and get rid of it because with my income I cannot afford it. Now, there's another headache on me. I've got to try and get somebody to buy this trailer. I've got to keep paying lot rent until somebody buys that trailer. And it's just too much. It's too much. I don't want anybody giving me anything. Just show me how to get back on my feet. Because since this flood I have been down, really down. And I don't know where to go anymore.

AB: Well, do you know what is the most important thing that you need?

SM: Housing, somewhere to go.

AB: And what is wrong with the trailer? Is it the affordability of it? You can't afford the payments?

SM: No.

AB: And did you get any other relief in order to get the trailer, like the $10,000 grant?

SM: They didn't give me that.

AB: And did you lose a house you owned?

SM: I didn't own. I was renting.

AB: Yeah, and that's hard, you were renting.

PHILIP SHABAZZ: She was on Section 8.

AB: You were on Section 8 and you were renting. And that's the big gap. They haven't done as much for renters. Have you talked to the people at the Twin County Interfaith Initiative?

SM: Where's that?

AB: I'll have to write that down for you. They do have money. It wouldn't be long-term assistance, but it would be short-term assistance with the payments. At the Twin County Recovery Interfaith Initiative. And they would know what other options are. And have you talked to a housing counselor? At Harambee Square, across the street.

SM: I talked to them over there. They sent me to another place on Grace Street.

AB: That was the Twin County Interfaith. What did they say at Grace Street?

SM: Nothing. They did nothing. They just took the information from me.

AB: OK. I can take care of that. Are you living by yourself?

SM: Yeah.

PS: One of the serious problems that Shirley has is that before Floyd she was on Section 8. After the crisis she bought a trailer. Now she can't afford the trailer, but now she's having to go back through the application process with the Section 8.

AB: Section 8. Yeah, and get a line. Yeah.

PS: And she can't go back to the kind of stability and lifestyle that she had before the crisis.

AB: Because there's no subsidy in this arrangement as it stands right now. Well, I can tell you this. On Thursday mornings at eight o'clock we do a meeting every week over at Harambee Square. And a lot of the people working in flood recovery are coming. There are a couple of important things that can happen there. One is that we might get more resources, which can help you out temporarily, but this is a problem that needs a long-term solution. You are a very important example of the person who has fallen through the gap. There have not been any significant arrangements made for people who were renting. Most all of the monies are for people who own houses, or again who want to buy, but you've got to buy in this process that they have created. The person who did something on their own without any assistance got lost. You see what I'm saying?

SM: Yeah. I understand what you're saying.

AB: Because if you were now interested in buying there might be something. But I don't know. It seems like there was a gap with the people who rented, and the people who went on their own and solved their problems, then got left out of the forms of assistance. But it would be helpful if you come and the others there hear your situation and we're clear that we have a live person that is an example. We know we have live people, but I mean if a person present was an example of this gap, it may help us be able to make the case for some solutions for the gap.

SM: I'll be there. I'm one of the people that got lost in the system. I feel this way.

AB: I'm not saying we have a fast solution. And it makes me think that what we might need to do at this point, because it didn't seem like we needed that before, is maybe we need to run a piece in the paper saying if there are folks who feel like they have fallen through the gap or they're looking for support and they've been everywhere else, that they might come to this meeting. It may be time that we do that. We haven't done it because that meeting had been for the folks working in the relief, who lead the relief. But it may be that we need to make a shift at this point.

PS: Right. And also be an advocacy group.

AB: Yeah. Basically coming after us for people who have fallen through the gap. Yeah, it may be what we need to do, or at least temporarily—to see.

SM: Well, you're the first one that has really sat down and talked about what could be done. You have uplifted me because you're telling me things that I can do, where this wasn't happening before. Since this flood, I've been so stressed out I've been thinking about committing suicide. There are days I don't have food to eat. You know?

AB: And you're driving yourself around, right? You've got transportation?

SM: Yeah.

AB: Because another option I can give you is—again just a temporary solution, but it might turn into a different kind of solution—is that if you just want to eat a meal, one of the things our project we run at the Wright Center is … Have you ever heard of the Wright Center?

SM: Over on Raleigh Road?

AB: Over on the corner of Raleigh Road and Grace Street. It's an adult day health center for elderly and disabled adults. Even though you may not need the complete day of care—at least you might not feel like you do at this point. And what county do you live in?

SM: Nash County.

AB: Nash County. Perfect. OK. It might be worth your stopping by there. I will make arrangements for you to come and eat lunch, at least. And you might want to look at enrolling and coming a couple of days a week. The reason I'm saying you might want to enroll is we can get paid for it if you enroll. You may not see yourself as, quote, "needing the service," even though you fit the description of the people we are designed to serve. Well, I don't know your age either. Do you mind?

SM: Fifty-five.

AB: Perfect. That's right in that age range. You're just there, you know.

SM: Yeah, because a social worker was trying to get me in that.

AB: It might be over sixty. You might be a little young, but we can still work it out.

SM: She said fifty-five, I could get in at fifty-five. I couldn't go there under fifty-five.

AB: You might need to be over sixty, but don't worry about it. We'll come up with something. You know, some kind of way. And this is the card. And this is the number of the Wright Center. I'm going to underline it. And I will let them know you will be coming to eat lunch and for them to make arrangements for that. And then we have to go from there to figure out how to get it paid for. You don't have to just be hungry any particular day. And you'll have company. So if you're depressed there'll be enough people there that you'll have to talk to.

SM: I've never been like this and I don't know what to think because it's so devastating to me that I had to go back to being this way. And I was doing so good before this flood.

AB: Yeah. I understand. And, you know, it's going to take years to get back to that point. Unfortunately. It's just that this kind of disaster—that's why it's a 500-year flood, you know—is the worst disaster in the history of [this area].

There's just no way you could turn your back

Rocky Mount Writing Workshops
Philip Shabazz and Angela Bryant

PHILIP SHABAZZ: Angela, when you talked about the flood impacting you indirectly, would you talk a little bit about that?

ANGELA BRYANT: Yeah. Well it impacted me personally in that two particular people in my life were affected by it. One was my ex-husband, whose family flooded out, and it was sort of ironic in the sense that I was not here. I was out of town. I have a mother who's eighty-nine and who is an amputee, a diabetic, moderate Alzheimer's, quite frail. We had floodwaters coming into the house, so our initial concern was what we were going to do with her. Because evacuating somebody with her level of disability—we weren't optimistic about how helpful that would be. We didn't know. And water was coming into the lower level of the house at the time. And I was out of town.

So the people caring for my mother contacted my ex-husband who is generally the person they would call under that kind of circumstance for advice or support or to figure out what to do. And he was calling around trying to find a place for her to go. As you can imagine by that time all the hotels were filled, and it was unclear where was a good place to go. And then they were concerned about people coming to them, because they didn't know their situation. I mean, anywhere you went at that point could have been a potential problem. We weren't clear where was safe.

And in our talking back and forth about that—there was like a thirty-nine-minute span between when they were consulting with the Fire Department about what potentially to do with my mother—and in a thirty-nine-minute span his house had filled with water and he was evacuating his family and neighbors. And I couldn't even reach him. So in the meantime the water stayed stable in our house and then receded. You know, not immediately, but in that same period. So it was like in a thirty-nine-minute span that the whole scenario flipped.

And I was away and could not do everything. And then ultimately could not get back because all the roads were flooded. There was no way to get back, say for ten days. It was seven or eight days before there was a way to get in through Hwy. 97. But it was a long time before you could get in on 64, 301—all of those were closed off. So eventually I was able to get back.

So one way it affected me is that he moved back, which is a sort of ironic situation. He ended up moving back in with me as a result of being flooded out. Just because of the flood, not because we decided to get back together. We're divorced. So that was one way it affected me. It was like the whole nullification of the marriage became irrelevant in the context of the flood.

PS: How long had you been divorced?

AB: I'd say two or three years. You know, it wouldn't have been twenty. I don't even remember, but it had been awhile. I'd say three at least. And it surely was logical. At that point I needed him to come back because I wasn't there. Somebody needed to be there to take care of my mother. And surely you wouldn't turn anybody away that you loved and cared about, because people were taking in all kinds of people that they had hated for years. You know, love was no factor, or a relationship. I mean, everybody had to have somewhere to go or you had to go to a shelter.

PS: Right.

AB: So that was one piece. The second piece was that one of the women who had been very close to my mother who was part of the team of people that took care of her got flooded out. So that completely discombobulated the whole network that we had for her care. And then she struggled for a while. That was all irrelevant for a short amount of time because people were all involved with the flood and in some instances they couldn't even get around. Once everything kind of got back to normal, eventually she came back to work. But she then became depressed and despondent, so much so that it was surely difficult to do the work of caring for somebody else in that kind of situation. Her energy appropriately needed to be on her own situation. So that not only it took a caregiver away, at some level an employee but at another level an important companion who had been there a long time for my mother. And she had moderate Alzheimer's, so for her it was hard.

PS: The caretaker did?

AB: No, my mother. With Alzheimer's it's hard to compute all of the details of what is happening, but emotionally you respond. You know that somebody you care about is upset. You have all of that working, but you don't have the wherewithal to make sense out of it and to keep it whole. She could understand there was a flood and all of that, but couldn't keep all that in a complicated fashion over hours and days and to make sense out of it as it unfolds.

PS: So what ended up with the situation?

AB: Now, some nine months later my ex is just moving on to making a different arrangement for himself. And again, he was living with his mother and their family. He and his brother had gone in to buy a house for her. And as they went through this new arrangement, it didn't make sense for him to stay involved in that as they rehabilitated it. And of course the benefits came to the brother who owned the house. And the family decided, appropriately, it needed to go to secure the mother's arrangements.

PS: So that left him to deal with a bare minimum, right?

AB: He got some immediate assistance after the flood and some money for his personal property, but there was no program for somebody like him, which is similar to Miss Myrick, you know—an adult who was in some kind of living arrangement where you didn't own the house or whatever. So he has to reconfigure himself in a market that doesn't have a lot to offer, in that pretty much the owners and landlords can dictate the market. It's not like there's a lot of competition.

The woman who was caring for my mother seems to be one of those people who came out better, after a lot of pain and despondency and depression. She lived out there in the Leggett Road area in a home that she was renting and paying her own way, unsubsidized as far as I know. She was a renter, which ought to put her in a similar situation, but she was able to use the various connections of churches and getting adopted and basically getting all the resources out there. She's happier. She's lost weight. She's done some traveling to kind of occupy herself while things were in limbo. So she looks like she's doing better. Now I don't know the inside story. You know what I mean? I don't know what her whole financial situation looks like. I don't know what her debt situation is.

PS: Who's with your mother now?

AB: I live with my mother, which we always did. And now there's a new person taking her place with my mother, but who also was a flood victim, interestingly enough. A younger woman who is sort of making her way through the cracks but hasn't chosen to deal with any of the systems at all, of resources that she could get.

PS: Where did you stay for ten days?

AB: I was traveling. I was out of the state.

PS: So by the time you got here, the water had receded?

AB: Right. And I ended up staying wherever I was. I stayed a couple more days until I could get back.

PS: Where does your mother live now?

AB: We're still over there in the same place. So that's one part of how it affected me in terms of these people. But there's another impact in that my work was multiculturalism consulting and community development work and diversity consulting—which is what I was doing when the flood came. I was away working on various contracts we have out of state. And I was on an extended road trip anyway, but it got more extended, you know, because I couldn't get back. In some ways it was fortunate I had something to do and at least I was getting paid most of the time while I was away. But the whole shift of my work—I had a whole plan for my life and for my work that involved our organization. The Wright Center had received an award, an international award, to provide community development work around aging issues here. So that was my focus, one of my focuses. And my other job was to hire a director for the Wright Center, which I was doing as a volunteer so that I could work on this community project. And then I was going to put my energy in the other consulting work that we do and the traveling that I just described. And kind of stabilize my life where I was trying to do two or three jobs and wasn't getting paid but for about one and a half of them.

The flood just shifted all of that in terms of my work life. Which meant because I'm the kind of person as the community activist that I am, I'm not going to *NOT* work in the flood, you know, with these people affected. So that meant trying to shift everything I was going to do to that. So it delayed everything. Like, there was no way to start this grant. Who cared about community education for elderly and disabled adults in the middle of the flood? I mean, it was just sort of stupid, you know. I would have looked foolish. So that meant it delayed that. It delayed me hiring the director because there just was no way to focus on that. Meanwhile, here was work to be done in the community. So I then got busy scuffling, trying to get funding to pay myself and my organization and to support the work that needed to be done to provide support for the community leaders and other people working in flood recovery for Princeville and that kind of thing. So I spent nine months working—consulting to Princeville, doing this Thursday morning group, consulting to the folks who were leading these programs. Trying to make sure it's no worse. It's still not great.

PS: Out of the Wright Center?

AB: Well, through VISIONS. It's two organizations—VISIONS and the Wright Center. VISIONS was the parent organization and the Wright Center was the aging program. In some ways I was both. I shifted my work for that whole period to supporting folks doing flood recovery work, basically trying to keep us from self-destructing in the black community in the face of the disaster. You know, letting our internalized oppression, if you will, play out and keep us from doing the coalition building we need to do to maximize our opportunities. And so I think I have helped and others of us have helped to make it no worse. Clearly there are ways we're falling through the gaps, as Miss Myrick shows. People are falling through the gaps.

PS: Would you speak about the response of politicians relative to black people in this disaster? And you can be frank, too.

AB: Yeah, I'll be frank. It's a mixed response. In some ways we have gotten more attention and focus than we otherwise would have because of the numbers we have in terms of flood damage, you know, not only in this area but in the region. So that's good news. But it's not like they're paying attention to us—like looking Miss Myrick in the eye or Angela Bryant in the eye and really resonating with what I'm telling them. It's not that kind of attention. But in terms of getting some funding and being listened to about what needs are and getting some ear time and some response from a policy perspective, I think we've surely got some of that. But some kind of genuine understanding and transformation—we haven't got that.

PS: Are you banking on them to support an advocacy group for people like Miss Myrick? Would they do that? Would they support or endorse an advocacy group?

AB: Well, now the issue is what politicians are you talking about? I think the politicians that have saved our behind on the line are the black ones. I mean we've got Eva Clayton. We have local elected officials here on the city council and the county commissioners. We got key city officials in place. You got the Princeville leaders. You got the Edgecombe County Commissioners. You got the black folks on the town council in Tarboro. You got the black caucus, you know, in the Legislature. So it's primarily the black elected officials.

And the white ones have been supportive. And our local white elected officials have been supportive. But I'm saying the backbone of our being looked after is because of the black elected officials that we've had the foresight to have there at this particular time, along with the whites who have been responsive to their constituents. I can't think of any elected official we've had that hasn't been responsive, you know, at some point. They'd be a fool. There's just no way you could turn your back. You know, in this situation not to be responsive would be career ending, I think—to NOT be responsive. So we haven't had anyone that hasn't been. I'm talking about the Republicans. The Conservative Republicans have been responsive, so in that sense we have to say it's better than we've ever had.

PS: Is there a politics of this kind of response in the sense that maybe some of the politicians are playing politics to give themselves leverage as they respond? Are they doing it genuinely?

AB: I think it's been too devastating. No, I just think it was too devastating.

PS: To play games like that?

AB: No, I haven't seen anybody, you know, unless you say Bill Clinton. I don't even think with him coming down here to go to Tarboro. I mean, there's some people who are cynical and say, "Yeah." But, I mean, he's put his money where his mouth is. He's created a Princeville Commission, you know. So he's returned payment on his visit. So I don't think there's anybody. And Governor Hunt did a whole package, put his money where his mouth is. So I don't think you could just say—while you might be cynical, you know, about politicians—I don't feel like anybody could really legitimately say that any of the efforts have been hollow. I think there's just too much devastation and too many losses.

PS: And it's good to hear that coming from a community organizer. Because you're on the front lines and you can see.

AB: Yeah, that's my opinion. But that's not to say we don't need more money, or we didn't need more. But they have delivered in a lot of ways. Now there clearly are more needs. And if the gaps have been there, they haven't been necessarily willing to help.

And some of this is the way the infrastructure of recovery is. First of all, the whole disaster stuff is built for owners—business owners and homeowners. It doesn't have in mind a, quote, "community economic development" component. You know, it doesn't have in mind having people come out better. It's basically just kind of to put you back so you're not devastated but it's really not designed to help you come out better. And I think, frankly, we had folks who just needed to be helped before the flood. And it's stupid and it would be a waste of resources to put them back where they were. It would be crazy.

And some of that's hard to get across, you know, and to get support for. And at some level the state can't. We have to do it at a local level. In some ways it can't be done by other people. You hear what I'm saying? There's no politician that can really do that. We have to do that.

PS: Right. Locally? On the community organizing level, practice level?

AB: Right. Yeah.

PS: In your work is there any particular case that stands out of how Floyd impacted young people? Nothing comes to mind?

AB: No particular individual. I mean I just know that kids' lives have been changed because of the disruption, you know, living in those trailers, living with relatives. Heck, some people who lived in Tarboro's families were living over here in Rocky Mount. People were coming back and forth, you know. I don't even know if the kids got back to the same school. In some ways sometimes it wasn't practical to have the same day care arrangements.

People's lives were disrupted. So I don't know. I can't think of an immediate story that jumps out at me but I know that children's lives have definitely been disrupted. We know that. It appears that school-based problems have been worse. We can't document the causes of each and every case, but the numbers of problems with kids at school have gone up.

 PS: Thank you, Angela Bryant.

Politics

Sharon O'Neill

Plastic pandering politicians
appear with perfectly coiffed hair
professing, while sipping Evian,
to understand how we feel.
From the comfort of their homes
built with our tax dollars
they promise that they will help
with low interest loans
if our credit is good
and think that we should
kiss their feet in gratitude.
In the FEMA office
Michelle swears under her breath . . .
"Damn, I can't even pay the loan
on what I don't have any more
and now they want
to give me another loan?
How is that supposed to help?"
Living on minimum wage
with her six-year-old daughter,
barely able to afford
the meager payments
to live in a trailer
built next to a river
that was bound to flood and
is bound to flood again
and they want to give her
another mortgage?
How are we supposed to
survive after this?
Harold lost his crops
and all his equipment
when the water came, and now
his unpicked crops
stand rotting in a field
of stagnant water
while he stands helplessly
rooted in the FEMA office
drowning in red tape.
Litter of our lost lives
left behind by the receding river,

a reminder to us all,
a wake-up call.
See the devastation.
See the lost hope
in the eyes of our neighbors
who toiled their whole lives
to build what little they had
only to lose it in a blink.
Now they wade, chest deep
in the wreckage,
trying to salvage their lives.
See the total destruction
in the bloated bodies of wildlife
forced onto the roads
only to be washed into the ditches
to drown in the black water
that once gave them life.
See the pain in the eyes
of once proud people
begging for subsidies,
forced to stand in endless lines
only to be told there is nothing left
and they should try again tomorrow.
Moving mouths hoping for re-election
say they feel our pain.
Live in this war zone, we say,
and you will know our pain.
Reach into your pockets
and give of yourselves,
give until it hurts,
and then you may know
redemption.
We just want our pride back,
our homes, our lives,
a soft bed to rest in
after a day of mucking through
what the river left behind.
Is that too much to ask?

September 30, 1999

Section II: BELVOIR IS A SMALL COMMUNITY

Belvoir crossroads under water.

Photo courtesy of N.C. Forestry Service.

Belvoir became an island

Joyce Joines Newman with Phyllis Adams and Derrick Moore

ONE OF THE PITT COUNTY AREAS HIT HARDEST BY THE FLOOD THAT FOLLOWED hurricane Floyd was the small farming community of Belvoir, which lies northwest of Greenville along the Tar River on Hwy. 33 West near the Edgecombe County line. Belvoir is a community of white, African American and Hispanic families, many of whom still farm crops such as tobacco, cotton and soybeans. A small mercantile center sits at the crossroads of 33 West and 222 North and consists of several gas station/convenience stores, churches, and the Belvoir Volunteer Fire Department.

Like many small rural North Carolina communities, Belvoir doesn't have the financial base to pay permanent full-time firemen but instead depends on local volunteers who respond to an emergency whistle when needed. These volunteer firemen and their families played an extremely important role in rescue and relief efforts for their community during the Floyd flood.

While most other communities in northeast North Carolina had at least one transportation route that remained open and became an avenue for relief efforts, Belvoir was cut off in all directions and became an island. For several days flood refugees were dependent for safety and support on the efforts of their fellow residents and of members of the North Carolina Forestry Service. The combined experience of these two organizations in handling both local and widespread emergency situations such as fires or forest fires formed the basis for their immediate, efficient and effective response.

The Belvoir Volunteer Fire Department had long been the source of assistance to residents of the Belvoir community, and many flood refugees now looked to it as a safe haven after fleeing the floodwaters that quickly inundated much of the community. Operating in familiar surroundings allowed the volunteer firemen to focus on the work they needed to do. Volunteer firemen who were not flooded joined those who were to provide aid for the displaced.

Altogether, floodwaters stranded some 600 to 800 people in Belvoir, hundreds of them displaced from their homes. Some were lifted by helicopter to community shelters in the area. Many of those who remained found refuge in the homes of relatives, friends or even strangers. Some homes sheltered as many as thirty-two flood refugees. About forty people congregated at the Belvoir Fire Department.

An important factor in rescue and relief efforts for the Belvoir community was the presence of several members of the North Carolina Division of Forest Resources (NCDFR), particularly Pitt County Ranger Tom Harris, Assistant County Ranger Derrick Moore, and Ray Peaden, the forest fire equipment operator. Harris and Peaden responded to a call from Emergency Management at 3 AM Friday morning that several people needed rescuing from their homes in Belvoir. By the time Peaden reached Belvoir on his fishing boat, people were climbing to their rooftops to escape the rising water. Harris and Peaden spent the day Friday evacuating people from their homes, while Derrick Moore and the volunteer firemen organized a staging area and temporary shelter for refugees at the Fire Department building.

Volunteers boated to deserted homes to gather food from refrigerators and cooked it on the Fire Department's pig cooker. By Saturday many of those who had planned to remain in their homes were forced to call for rescue. Flood currents had become so swift that boat rescues were difficult. The National Guard managed to get a two-ton truck with some medical supplies through the floodwaters to Belvoir.

When rising floodwaters also threatened the Fire Department building, refugees and Fire Department equipment moved up the road to higher ground at the Gum Swamp Free Will Baptist Church. The group relocated first to the churchyard, which was littered with fallen limbs and debris from the hurricane. In the graveyard beside the church, a recently-buried casket had been forced to ground level. The refugees left it undisturbed but cleared away other debris and repaired the broken water line to the church. Soon someone unlocked the church fellowship hall and the group moved inside.

Derrick Moore, who spent his wedding anniversary in Belvoir, and Phillip Wall, another Assistant County Ranger, oversaw efforts for Forest Service helicopters to bring in supplies and evacuate some refugees to shelters in surrounding areas. Residents of Belvoir nicknamed the Forest Service "Santa Claus" for the gifts they were bringing. By Sunday, helicopters were beginning to bring in much-needed food, water and medical supplies.

As floodwaters began to recede, the relief staging area moved back to the Fire Department building. Area churches and businesses began sending food to Belvoir and portable showers arrived. After over a week of being displaced from their flooded homes, residents of Belvoir faced the long ordeal of recovery, many returning to their homes to find overwhelming destruction or nothing left at all. Many homes were condemned; hundreds more needed extensive repairs.

The Forest Service continued to help with the cleanup, retrieving coffins that had been washed from cemeteries, operating incinerators to dispose of dead farm animals and pets, and removing debris from the highways.

Belvoir Writing Workshops

Harlan Joel Gradin

WITH ASSISTANCE FROM LOCAL LEADERS, INCLUDING PITT COUNTY COMMISSIONER Eugene James, NCHC sponsored two three-hour workshops in Belvoir in April and May 2000. Held at the Belvoir Volunteer Fire Department building, the workshops were led by Ms. Julie Fay. Participants included a diverse range of residents in terms of age, occupation, and role in the community. Fortunately, the second workshop met at the same time the Fire Department was meeting in the adjoining engine room. Although the men were reluctant to join the writing group, Phyllis Adams, a workshop participant whose husband and brother are members of Fire Department, persuaded the firemen to become important project participants by agreeing to be interviewed at a later time. Folklorist William Mansfield conducted seventeen interviews in the summer of 2000. The following section is based on the workshop writings and interview transcripts.

Belvoir Volunteer Fire Department.

Photo by Joyce Joines Newman.

Sandra Warren
Belvoir Writing Workshop

ON SEPTEMBER 15 AT WORK WE WERE HEARING REPORTS OF THE HURRICANE expected to hit Greenville that night. Everyone was very anxious and concerned about the possible danger to their homes and family. All of us had been to the grocery store for staple items. As we left early that afternoon we all hugged each other and with tears in our eyes we went home.

Upon arriving home, I packed the last few items and my family left to go to our church fellowship building in our community. We stayed throughout the night listening to a small television we had carried with us. We also tried to sleep. The next morning, Thursday, the wind was very strong. Water was everywhere in the churchyard, inches deep. My husband and son left to go home and check on things. While they were gone I was packing up things. When they returned the first question I asked was, "Is the house OK?" The answer was yes, but water was everywhere. A few minutes later we heard a soft brushing of a tree branch on the roof of the building. A tree had fallen on top of the church fellowship building. We left to go home and I felt relieved that our house was safe.

During the flood our church was turned into a distribution center. Lots of food was brought in by helicopter. I stopped at the church on Saturday morning and found people distributing food items. We all pitched in and helped. Others in the community that do not attend our church stopped to help. They walked in and said, "Tell me what to do." While I was working one day, a man appeared that I had not seen before. He assisted me in lifting heavy boxes of canned items. As we worked we started talking. I learned he lived on Old River Road and was able to stay in his house. He walked from his home for several days and worked six to eight hours per day. I also met other people that have lived in Belvoir for many years that I did not know.

I believe the flood did bring us closer as a community. People were willing to give of their time and energy to help others that were less fortunate. It shows there is still good in the world when all we seem to hear on TV and read in the newspaper is evil and violence. It lets you know exactly what you can do to help others. Just carrying a box of groceries to someone's car was a help. Many of the teenagers were able to walk in and start to work organizing items to be given away. It was not a matter of, *Should I help?* but of, *What can I do?* I worked harder during the days following Floyd than I am used to, but it was some of the most rewarding work I have ever done. To see people so grateful for whatever you could give them; no matter how much or how little, they were grateful. At night, going to bed, all my muscles would ache.

Tom Harris, Ray Peaden, Phyllis Adams from Belvoir VFD, Phillip Wall, and Derrick Moore.

Photo courtesy of N.C. Forestry Service.

Forestry kept us busy

Interviews with William Mansfield
William Mansfield with Phyllis and Mike Adams;
Doug, Tammy and Chad Bullock; Henry Foskey and Doug Everette

Shortly after the Belvoir writing workshops were held, the North Carolina Humanities Council asked folklorist William Mansfield to interview members of the Belvoir community. Interviews were held at the Belvoir Volunteer Fire Department.

Among those who played key roles in the Belvoir community were Phyllis Adams and her husband Mike, her brother Assistant Fire Chief Doug Bullock, Doug's teenage son Chad, and volunteer firemen Henry Foskey and Daniel Everette. During the flood, Doug's wife Tammy was keeping vigil at the intensive care unit of Pitt County Memorial Hospital where her mother was a patient.

Mike Adams owns a body shop in Ayden, south of Greenville, and his wife Phyllis is a nurse at the Ambulatory Surgery Center at Pitt County Memorial Hospital. Mike and Phyllis live in the family home built in 1913. Phyllis's mother, Mattie Ruth Bullock, built a new brick house beside the original home and Phyllis's brother Doug lives in a doublewide trailer with his family on the other side.

PHYLLIS ADAMS: I remember late that afternoon it started raining, and raining and raining and raining and raining, and it rained and rained. Mike, my husband, went home early to check out things, secure things. And it just kept raining.

CHAD BULLOCK: We had just got out of school when the hurricane was coming in and I had gotten someone to take me out to where my dad works and drop me off.

WILLIAM MANSFIELD: Were you glad to be out of school?

CB: Yeah. And I was out there helping him and it just kept right on raining and raining and raining. So we came on home because he had to work late to help get generators out to people.

PA: We went to bed that night and it was still pouring down rain. And when we got up the next morning, we noticed that our lights were kind of flickering and we knew we were going to lose power, so we fixed breakfast real fast. And it was sort of strange. It was all this water everywhere around our house from the hurricane. And there was things laying beside our house, like landscaping timbers from other people's yards.

WM: They had floated up?

PA: Um hmmm, because there was so much water. It was water where we'd never seen water stand before, but I wasn't upset because I knew the hurricane was gone. It had gone on to Elizabeth City or wherever. So my brother, Chad, Mike and I got in the truck and we were going to go out and see what kind of damage was done. We rode around that Thursday morning, and we managed to get to Belvoir. We had to go around power lines down, and trees. And we get down to our friend's, and that's when our deputy sheriff told us, "You do know there's a curfew?" So after that we went back home, and we just thought it was kind of different that we had so much water from the hurricane that we were, like, fishing.

MIKE ADAMS: The water in the back yard was what? A foot deep or more?

DOUG BULLOCK: It was almost up to my waist.

CB: We were just walking around out there having fun in the water before the flood, the actual flood, hit.

MA: Walking around in the water making jokes, "We always wanted beach front property," and that kind of stuff. And what was so strange about it was that after the hurricane had gone through we knew we had a lot of water on the ground, but by that afternoon the water had receded probably four foot, not in depth but I mean length, you know. It left a trash line along the edge, and you could see that it was going away. So when we went to bed we just assumed everything was fine. If the water level had been a gradual, steady increase, then everybody would have known that we needed to do something. But when you see the water going away then that gives you the illusion that everything's going to be OK.

79

PA: We didn't have any power from about 9:30 that Thursday morning on, and we had just bought a brand new gas grill about two weeks before that. So Chad and my mom and Doug and Mike and I cooked out on the grill. But there was one thing now that we can remember that we really were not paying a lot of attention to—the helicopters up and down the river. We were not tuned in to that.

MA: Well, we assumed they were flying up and down the river and checking, and if there was a problem they would probably let somebody know, because at that time my phones were still working and we still had current.

CB: They had flood warnings out for Greenville, but nothing out here.

PA: Not out in the country.

MA: So we didn't get any warnings. The first warning I got was my dog at three o'clock in the morning, whining. That was the morning after the afternoon that the water started going away. It was unusual. He wasn't barking; he was whining. And when I got up, the water was to the first doorstep. So that was a pretty strange feeling at three o'clock in the morning. You think the water's going away, and then it's coming back on you.

WM: What did you think when you saw it?

MA: Well, since Phyllis, my wife, was familiar with Emergency Services and knew some people over there, my first thought was, *How many people on this road are still asleep and do not know that this water's coming back?* So I got her up and told her she needed to get on the telephone and call Emergency Services and let them know what was going on out here because there was probably a lot of people still asleep who didn't realize the water was coming back. We always had the feeling that they had those dams backed up and then they got so much water in them they couldn't hold. They couldn't contain it. And they had to release it or they broke or whatever happened. And then all that water at once started coming back on us, and we weren't aware of that. And there was no warning. Or we weren't getting any warning.

HENRY FOSKEY: I had heard on the radio one time that there was a wall of water coming from Rocky Mount and it would be there within an hour or a couple of hours. I had heard that, where I don't know.

MA: I don't even know who would be in charge of something like that, but the people who were supposed to have the knowledge or education or whatever … This was something that was of such a magnitude that even the weather people didn't know. You'd keep listening to them. When's the water supposed to crest? They would tell you it's going to crest tomorrow morning at nine o'clock. Well, tomorrow morning at nine o'clock, you'd get up and you'd watch the news and then they'd changed it. It would be this afternoon at four o'clock. You know, they were speculating. They were giving educated guesses. But they still weren't comprehending what it was. Finally I just said, "Well, they don't know when the crap it's going to quit." And they didn't.

PA: That's right.

MA: They said the flood stage in Tarboro was nineteen foot. And it was twenty-four foot above the nineteen foot in Tarboro. So that's a lot of water.

PA: But also we feel that since we worked that entire time with Forestry so strong, they knew. Because we'd get up in the mornings and say, "Is the water going down today?" And they'd have this long face and they'd go, "No." And then the next day, we'd say, "Is the water going down today?" Or, "Is everything OK today?" "No." They wouldn't tell you a whole lot but I felt like they were being fed the information but didn't really share all that much.

DB: They knew what was going on.

MA: Well, so the first thing that morning, Phyllis called Emergency Services and they told her that the water could possibly be eight foot deep in a few hours.

PA: And I got Doug and Chad up. And at that time Tammy, Doug's wife, was at Pitt County Memorial Hospital in the intensive care waiting room, so she wasn't even home to experience any of this with us.

DB: Phyllis called and woke me up and I walked to the front and looked out the front door and water was fixing to come in the door then. It was already up to the door.

MA: And when the sun started coming up, it was like looking across the ocean because you could see that red glare from the sun on the water.

PA: Like on a boat. And the strangest thing was watching people's stuff floating by. Here comes a cooler, a gas grill, a barrel, a bucket.

MA: Because the current was so strong.

PA: It was just like at the river front.

CB: There was a fish swimming all around.

MA: And I had my dog in the dog pen and I turned him out. And I propped the back porch door open. We had a freezer on the porch. And I said, "Well, I don't know how high the water's going to get, but I assume that if I leave this door propped open and if the water comes, then maybe he'll get on top of the freezer, you know. Hopefully, it won't get that high." I had no comprehension that all that stuff was going to float.

PA: By the time I waded out to Doug and Chad's home, the water was starting to come up in their vent some, had already gotten into their air conditioning system. And when we got my mom up, the first thing she did was drive her car over in my yard to a spot where you could see a little bit of dry land, and she was out there dipping water out of the car. She was thinking, *I got to get the water out of my car, got to dry my carpet.* And I said, "Mom, stop, stop." And she kept going. I said, "Mom, stop." I said, "The water's coming. There's no need to keep dipping it out." And she said, "Well, I almost got it dry." So that was her logical thinking. And I'm thinking, *We got to get the heck out of Dodge.*

MA: That's when we told her it was going to be eight foot deep in a few hours and dipping water out of the car wouldn't make no difference.

PA: So I called 911 and talked to Eddie and said, "Somebody needs to get us out. What are we supposed to do?" We already had a lot of water then. It was at our first doorstep by the time we got up and next thing you knew it was our second door step. And it just kept coming.

MA: Somebody said at that time when it was first coming in on us it was rising about six inches an hour. And it really was rising pretty fast because we woke up at three o'clock and at seven o'clock we got on a boat to leave the house. And by seven o'clock the water was just before coming in our house. And our house at that time was off the ground probably about three foot. So it was rising pretty quick.

PA: Eddie said get a couple of changes of clothes. Well, when somebody tells me a couple, that means two. And get non-perishable foods and get all your medications. Get all my family at one address. And they were going to send out a boat. They already had the boats out and they would put our name on a list. And I got to thinking, *Oh boy, the county's a little slow. And if they've got to get everybody out, they might not get to us in time.* Well, that made me uncomfortable so I said, "Look, there's somebody in our Fire Department, some of our neighbors—somebody's got to have a boat."

DANIEL EVERETTE: Doug called me about 3:30, and I laid there till four o'clock wondering what in the world he was saying. Because he asked me, "Do you have a boat?" I said, "I can get one." He said, "Well, go down to the Fire Department and see if the Fire Department's flooded and call me back." And I said, "All right." I laid there till about four o'clock. My fiancée had stayed over that night. She was worried and everything so she stayed over that night. And she asked me, "Who was that?" And I said, "It was Doug and he wanted to know if I had a boat and wanted me to ride down to the Fire Department to see if it was flooded." She said, "What's he talking about?" I said, "I don't know." So I come down to the Fire Department and rode all the way around it and I called him back. I said, "It ain't flooded." I said, "You still need me to get a boat?" He said, "Yeah, I got water coming inside my house." I said, "All right, I'll see what I can do." And I started calling around trying to get a boat.

Actually—I ain't told them this—but I dosed back off because I thought it was a dream.

PA: You feel better now, don't you, since you shared that?

DE: I actually dosed back off. But he had told me that they were coming to get him, and, you know, I didn't know what was going on.

DB: We wanted the first one that could get to us.

DE: We thought the hurricane was going to be like Bertha or Fran, you know, some trees down and everything. But we didn't realize it was going to be twenty-five foot of water.

PA: So we called Scott who's on the Fire Department and asked him did he or one of his neighbors have a boat. He said, "I'll come and get you. We'll find a boat. We'll come and get you." They couldn't get to us until the sun came up because there was power lines still down. But the problem was they could come a certain way with a boat and then hit dry land. They couldn't get the boat down past the dry land to the water where we were.

MA: Scott called and asked me if I could possibly get there with the truck.

PA: So Mike and Doug took Mike's pickup truck, a short bed Silverado Chevrolet, and drove his truck in the water like *it* was a boat to go get the boat. Leaves Chad and my mom and me sitting on the porch watching them as far as we could see them.

MA: The water literally came over the hood, and I was afraid that the water would drown the engine out. There was two places in the highway that was pretty low. And as we were going down in those, the water started coming over the edge of the hood. And Doug and myself, we was setting in the truck and we could feel the truck—it felt like it was trying to . . .

DB: It was floating.

MA: You could tell it was getting light. It was getting real light. You could feel it raising up. As long as the truck was moving, the water was splitting just like you were in a boat. You couldn't go fast, had to go slow, but it was still splitting the water. Water never came in the floorboard of the truck but it was rolling up over the edge of the hood. And my biggest fear was that when we were in those low places near the canals it would really get a lot deeper there and the truck would cut off and the water would just wash us in the canal. In one of those canals the water probably was ten foot deep.

And we finally went through the second low spot, and there was a person in a truck setting on the dry land right at the edge of the water and he saw me coming through. And when we finally came out on the other side, he said, "I never thought you'd make it through that water." He said, "I was looking for you to quit any time." I told him, "Evidently, the Lord was back there pushing it, because there was no way that the truck was pushing up that water."

And if we hadn't left at that time on the truck we probably never would have got there. But we just luckily did get to where the boat was, put the boat in the back of the truck, and then we drove back as far as we could on the highway and then unloaded the boat. And me and Doug stayed with the truck and three guys went with the boat. And at that time it was hard to maneuver the boat because there was still places in the road where one spot would be high and one spot would be low. So what they had to do was to put the boat on the edge of the road in the ditch and walk along with the boat until they got to where it got real deep in certain places and then they'd ride in the boat. That's the way they got to the house. And my wife said that when they come up they just stopped the boat right up beside the porch.

PA: It was real funny. We could hear the three guys coming in the boat laughing and talking. I was thinking, *Oh, here comes the boat.* They drove right over the top of our shrubs, went right up to the side of the house to the porch. We had to step up into the boat because the water was already so high.

WM: Did your truck come through the flood OK?

MA: Yeah. Just as I went across there was a, I guess, a point of no return. You make a decision of whether you're going to stay or you're going to go. So I decided I was going to go with my family. But I couldn't carry my truck. So one of our neighbors who was on pretty high ground decided to stay, and he told me, said, "You can park your truck in my yard." And it just so happened where I parked it, it didn't get flooded. So I was lucky on the truck. Still driving it right now.

WM: All those ads for the Silverado!

MA: Doug used a few choice words. He said, "I'll tell you one thing, that's the toughest damn truck I've ever seen." He said, "I never thought it would go through that water." It's tense when you're in there.

PA: But you know what I found? You were having to make quick decisions. You were having to think real fast, you know? And you were hoping whatever decision you were making was a good one.

DB: It was split-minute decisions.

MA: Well, you really didn't have time to set down and think about it. If we had been warned earlier, we probably could have thought of something. But Doug, where his house was it was a little bit lower than it was at our house. And he was asleep and he gets up and there's no water in the floor at that time. Within an hour the water was coming in.

DB: Before we left out, we opened the front door and water was coming in the front door. When I was looking out first thing in the morning when the sun started coming up, it was just like a lake. It looked like it ought to be Louisiana or Mississippi.

MA: Another thing, you take it for granted that when you look at the road, because you can see the road, you know where the road is. But when the water is totally covering everything, the only way you've got to judge where the road is, is the light poles or mailboxes. And in some places you couldn't see the mailboxes. All you had was light poles. And you were wondering, "Am I in the middle of the road or am I on the edge of the road?" You're kind of trying to judge that distance to make sure you're running the middle of the road.

Hwy. 33 near Belvoir under water.

Photo courtesy of Phyllis Adams.

HENRY FOSKEY: You pretty much could get lost. You could know exactly where you were and get lost on the boat. You'd know the area, and you're on water and you're looking around and you'd say, "Whose house is that?" Because you couldn't tell. When I rode the boat, I put in above Parker Road and I rode the boat all the way down from above Parker Road, hit 33, took 33 all the way down to Penny Hill Road, and took a right on Penny Hill. And there was some people staying back up in there who'd never left. They were on this island. We took food for the horses. We took food for them and they said they had plenty, so we turned around and came back for that day. To see that—to ride a boat down Hwy. 33 as far as I did and not have to get out and walk but twice. And this was a seventeen-foot boat with a 35 Johnson on the back. I mean we could pretty much open it up, you know, just like we were on the river.

MA: It was very strange coming out on the boat. When we came across the bridge, the water was maybe three inches or four inches from the top of the road sign. The only thing I seen was "Old River Road" on the sign.

DB: I think we took a picture of that because it said Old River Road and there wasn't nothing but water.

MA: One of the guys who was on the Fire Department with us had recently gone to Greenville Fire and Rescue and he was in Greenville. When it started flooding in Greenville, he said they'd be on the rescue boat getting people out of houses and you could hear the propeller go "ting, ting, ting, ting, ting." And he said they were trying to figure out what it was and they finally figured out it was the antennas sticking up on cars. He said when they were driving over the top of the cars, you know, the water was so deep they couldn't tell if there was a car there or not. And the propeller would hit an antenna and it was making a tinging noise.

PA: I don't know what kept us going considering what we went through. Like I said, Eddie said get a couple of changes of clothes. To me that means two. But we didn't go home for eight days. We left Friday and didn't go back home until Saturday. Once we got down to the fire station there was a mob of folks down here. I mean people were coming out. They were swimming with children on their shoulders to get out. Stokes Road, Old River Road. They came here, it was like a destination point. "If I can get to Belvoir Fire Department, somebody can help me." Well, before we could turn around, Doug and Mike and Chad and Henry and whoever else was here, we ended up working with the Forestry Service, rescuing people. We went out on fire trucks to pick people up. For the next probably five to seven days we were so busy helping with rescue, shelters, Forestry, we didn't really concentrate on our loss.

MA: Well, Doug is the Assistant Fire Chief, so he's been knowing the Forestry guys a long time. Tom Harris is the head one in this area. I knew when the woods caught on fire they'd call out the Forestry Service and they'd take a plow and plow, you know. I thought that's all they done—and maybe count trees in the woods or something. That's what I thought up until that time. Well, there were no doctors in the area, and my wife's a nurse. So naturally people were coming up excited, needing their blood pressure checked. Then the Forestry people found out that Phyllis was a nurse, and then we just kind of knitted together and everybody just tried to help one another.

PA: Teamwork.

MA: And there was several neighbors that had boats and they were up here. We just carried the Forestry Service out. And the Forestry Service had some of its own boats. And some of the deputy sheriffs were up here. It was almost like you were watching one of these disaster movies or something. That's the way it really was. It was, I guess, organized chaos around the Fire Department. How many nights did we stay down here?

PA: We came down here Friday morning. We stayed Friday night. We had to evacuate here about five o'clock Saturday afternoon.

MA: Well, I remember staying here that night, and the water. We would keep going to the back door, looking out. And you could see the water rushing by. And you could see all the cans and trash and all this kind of stuff. We were trying to figure out at what rate it was rising and was it ever going to stop? What were we going to do with the fire trucks? We had just recently got a new fire truck, and we definitely didn't want this stuff to float. So I got a stick and measured it off in one-inch marks and stuck it in the ground out there, and we kept watching that stick to see how fast the water was rising.

PA: That was on Saturday.

MA: We watched it all that day. The rising had slowed down, but I think it rose about six inches that day, and it was still rising. So finally the water came within probably two or three inches of the roll-up doors in the Fire Department. We didn't plan making a shelter. We were just doing what we had to do to survive. Doug and Bugsy [*Daniel Everette*] and me and Chad and Scott—we were all together. We had to pick a place to put the fire trucks so we come up with Gum Swamp Church.

PA: I think Doug and Tom went out riding to find us a safe place.

MA: The preacher happened to be out of town at that time, so the only person that we could think of asking was somebody who went to the church, and that was David and Sam Warren. So we stopped and talked to them, and we said, "Look, we got to put the fire trucks somewhere. Will it be OK if we park them at the church?" They said, " Sure, we don't see any problem with it. Go ahead." So we moved all the fire trucks and stuff to Gum Swamp Church because that was the highest peak of ground that we could find at the time. And we hooked up the generator and the coffee pot and sat out there and drank coffee and watched the water rise.

PA: And cleaned up the churchyard and built a bonfire.

MA: And then finally Sunday morning somebody came and unlocked the church so we could get in there and sleep. The Forestry Service had some cots flown in so they'd have something to sleep on. And finally some of the deputy sheriffs in there kept calling the sheriff and telling him, "Look, we need some food. We need some help." And they said, "Well, we've got a shelter set up at Wellcome Middle School." They thought that we could just get in a car and drive to Wellcome Middle School, but we couldn't do it because we were cut off by water. We were isolated. We just had a small area here where we could move around. They didn't comprehend the situation that we were in. And the news media wasn't able to get in because the military helicopters wouldn't let the news media helicopters fly in the same territory that the military helicopters were flying in. So people wont really seeing what was going on.

WM: Did you listen to the news and what was reported on TV and the radio?

PA: The only thing we were hearing was a radio. But what you were hearing was that some of Greenville was being flooded. But nothing about out in the country.

MA: Well, see, for some reason it seems like Greenville was getting a lot of publicity that they were having a problem. Princeville and Tarboro, they were getting a lot of publicity that they were having a problem. We were stuck out here in the middle, but we were kind of unknown. Nobody really knew what we were going through.

TAMMY BULLOCK: I was sitting at the hospital and every time the newscast came on, I was like, "Be quiet. Be quiet. Let me see if they're saying anything about this area." They never said anything. And then [the reporter] come on and she said, "I've just been to Belvoir." And I was like, "Y'all have got to be quiet. I've got to hear this." Because I didn't know what was going on. And then when they showed Old River Road I started looking for my home. And I couldn't really see anything because everything was underwater. And then my cousin that lives on Papa's place down here on Porter Road called me and said, "All I can tell you is I've talked to Doug and Chad. They are fine. They're with the fire station." Then the fire station got flooded and she called me back and she said, "They've moved. They're at the Gum Swamp Church. They're doing fine. I'm staying in contact. I'll let you know." That's all I got. I was hoping that everything was OK. But by me being at the hospital, I just had no idea what was going on out here. We had the hardest time because my grandmother had passed and we were supposed to bury her the day of the hurricane. We had to wait another week to bury her. The ground was so saturated that they couldn't dig the hole until after all the family members had gone home. I had uncles in Virginia that couldn't even make it to the funeral of their own mama because of the storm. There was no road passage between Norfolk to get to the funeral. And they had to dig the hole and put the vault and the casket in all at once within an hour's time. That's how saturated the ground was.

MA: So people wont really seeing what was going on. We started getting stuff flown in to us. The way that happened was we were at the church and there were some neighbors close to the church, you know. They come up and they said, "Have you got any food? Or any drinks or diapers or anything? We've got small children. We don't have any food. We don't have any milk." So the people around was just trying to help one another the best they could. Forestry Service saw what was going on. Tom Harris finally started having stuff flown in by the Forestry Service helicopter. If it hadn't been for them to start with, we wouldn't have had nothing.

PA: The Forestry Service played a big role here. And I know that you've heard Mr. and Mrs. James's story? [*Pitt County commissioner for the Belvoir district*] He was airlifted to Edgecombe County. We had already got the shelter started before he even got here.

MA: We didn't plan it. We didn't think of it. It just kind of happened. And we already had a shelter and everything was already going. And then these other people come in and they just got the fame and glory and all this stuff. It ain't nothing that nobody needs fame and glory for either.

DB: Not a bit.

PA: No, it was teamwork. Community.

MA: But I like to see the proper people recognized as the ones that actually done something.

PA: Daniel did not get flooded but he was our best buddy. He was there with us. He did not leave us.

WM: What did you do?

DE: Anything they asked. I knew it was part of my Fire Department family down here so I brought them a cooler so we could fill it up with ice. And brought them some pillows and bed linens and stuff like that. I knew they were down here sleeping and stuff.

PA: And support.

DB: Coffee, with lots of sugar.

MA: Lot of love.

PA: Lot of hugs.

WM: Did you work with the fire station pretty much throughout the whole time?

DE: I cut out one time before the flood for about two hours. I had to go to Greenville before the water got too high to get a generator for the Fire Department. And then about four hours later I had to cut out and go to Greenville again to get my grandmother out of her house. She lives on East Jackson Avenue right behind the fairgrounds. All the Marine people had scared her to death with the helicopters and everything. I got a grandma and a great-grandma. My great-grandma had just turned a hundred years old. So they didn't want to go up on the helicopter and they didn't want to be put in a truck. So me and my brother took a boat. We was going to try to paddle through it, but the current down there was a whole lot stronger than it was down here.

WM: So you didn't make it with the boat?

DE: Yeah, we made it. We tied the rope around us and we walked through it. Towed the boat about half a mile. We got up there and the water wasn't in their house yet but it was probably two inches from going in.

TB: I have friends that also live over there. And if the sheriff had come to your door and you refused to leave one time, they would not go back. I had a friend whose aunt lives over there. The deputies came to the door but her family wasn't ready to go out because they wouldn't allow them to pack anything before leaving. So the deputies took the grandchild out and left them there. And they refused to go back when the family called them.

WM: The Sheriff's Department refused to go back?

TB: The Sheriff's Department refused because they claimed that her family had refused to leave. But they were not refusing to leave, they were saying, "Give me a chance to get some clothes." That's all they were asking, was to get some clothes. And the Sheriff's Department denied them that.

PA: That was not the situation here. We tried to get some people out and they decided to stay. And then they were calling to get out and the Forestry and Sheriff went back in to get these people, even airlifted them off the roof.

MA: We got the call here at the Fire Department there was some people at the church on River Road and they needed to get on a flight out. So one of the deputies went out with his personal boat to go pick them up. And while he was out he had a problem with the boat motor and he was running the motor with his hand. And the Sheriff's Department called him, because he was a deputy sheriff, and they said, "You're not supposed to be in the water. Get out of the water." And he said, "I've got a call that there's people need help and I'm going to help them." And they paged him on the pager and they put a message on there, "Don't backtalk on the radio."

PA: While he's trying to use his hand to hold the throttle and drive the boat and get people to safety. So that's why we say it brings out the bad in some people.

WM: You said you got your grandmother and your great-grandmother. Were they pretty agitated when you got there?

DE: No, they weren't agitated. By the time we got there we were already about waist high in water. I mean there wont really nothing we could tote out. Her car was already submerged, and there wont nothing that we could go in there and pick up and put on top of anything to try to save it. In her house it didn't get but about a foot deep. So it didn't really mess up clothes. And what it did, you know, the smell and everything, we washed it out.

MA: What do you think when we got back to our house? Or Doug's house? Well, you see, nine days—all the refrigerators and freezers had flipped over and all that food was stinking. Plus Doug had two dogs that were dead and decaying in the bathroom. And I told him, I said, "Man, we're going to have to have an air pack to go in and get them." He said, "No, I'm a farmer. I'm used to burying dead cows and stuff." He said, "I can get in there and get them." I said, "Well, I can't do it." So I made a break for it. He went in there and he drug the two dogs out and their paws and the meat was falling right off, feet and legs, when he was dragging them down the steps. Man, I couldn't hardly stand it.

DE: You smelled it before you seen it.

MA: All that was mixed, mingled together with the smell of all that rotten food in the refrigerator.

DB: And a lot of the flood water, too.

DE: Yeah, the flood water stunk, too. Yes.

MA: That was a tough smell.

PA: What I saw about Bugsy during all that, he was very quiet. Even though he was there, he was very quiet. And we would joke with him and, you know, punch him and hug him and stuff like that. But I knew in my heart, you know, that I had lost everything that he hadn't and I knew he probably didn't know what to say or how to approach us.

WM: When did you know that you weren't going to get flooded out?

DE: I didn't know until the water went down because it was rising in my back yard just as fast as it was rising in anybody else's.

WM: When you found out that your house wasn't flooded and that other people you knew lost everything how did you feel?

DE: I had some—I wouldn't call it guilt. I just wanted to know what I could do to help them out. Just try to help people out the best I could. I was sorry for them.

WM: How do you think you've changed after the flood?

DE: I don't like water too much.

WM: Any other ways you think you look at the world differently?

DE: Well, you've got some corrupt people in this world. It's bad when in Greenville we're calling for help for two days, three days straight and they don't even know where Belvoir is. And most people go through it every day and still don't know where Belvoir is. That's the thing that I hated about it.

WM: When you were talking about what was happening, did you get angry?

DE: Yeah.

DB: Yep.

TB: Irritated.

PA: Frustrated.

DE: When you're going around to stores and trying to feed thirty-five, forty folks that are down here at the Fire Department and they're hungry—trying to feed folks that were flooded that the Forestry Service and Sheriff's Department had rescued and brought down here to the Fire Department. And you go to a store or something and try to round up some food to feed them—it kind of gets aggravating.

MA: The first day we were here, Billy that ran the store over there—finally the current went off so all the food he had was going to go to the bad—so he brought it over here and started cooking on a pig cooker. Just started cooking.

DE: And there was a lot of people that were flooded and came out on boats and they said, "Go get the food out of my freezer and cook it," you know. That didn't last but a couple of days.

DB: We went three days and three nights without sleeping before we finally slept some.

DE: Saturday night we stayed up watching the news.

PA: With a portable TV and a generator hooked on the back of a fire truck. We have a new generator now. We burned out the old one. Have you ever done that before? Watched TV off a generator on the back of a fire truck camping out because you're homeless?

DE: Sunday me and Doug and Mike and Chad and Scott built a little campfire and we sat out there and roasted marshmallows until Chad went to sleep. And Scott went to sleep. And me and Doug stayed up, watched the sun rise and the crows croak. And then Monday night we were going to build another campfire but the water started coming.

PA: Our days did not have names. And now when we're trying to think back … Every day I would get up and I'd say, "What is today?" "What is the date?" Because it was like we just lived a day and it just was another day with no name.

DB: The regular routine was broken.

MA: I lost track of time.

DB: Took me three days to wind down.

DE: Doug got about a three-hour nap and it was the best time I ever had, watching him sleep.

WM: Did you sleep yourself?

DE: I slept after that, but I was making sure. I just wanted somebody to be up. And I was inside the fellowship hall with the sheriffs and all that, just clowning around with them.

PA: Forestry guys.

DB: Forestry kept us busy, didn't they?

DE: Oh, yeah.

DB: Forestry kept us on the road.

PA: You know what we did with them? I was thinking back. We were very instrumental for them because this is our home and we live here. And if they would say, "Do you know so and so on such and such road?," I'd look around and say, "Henry, you're 33 West. Tell him where so and so lives." Then they would say something about Porter Road. I'd say, "Bugsy, Porter Road. Help him find these people so they know where to go pick these people up." And we worked like that all the time. You know, everybody has their strengths, and we tried to pull together and to use everybody's strength at that time.

WM: Did you know these strengths beforehand or did they just kind of emerge?

PA: Well, I knew some of the strengths but we learned a lot about other people's strengths too. And you know some people really surprised me.

WM: How so?

PA: Well, let's talk about this one individual. You know, I wasn't real sure about this person that's on our department. You know, he talks kind of rough—well, I don't mean rough, but, you know, he just says what he thinks. It's not sugar coated. You know exactly where he's coming from. Sometimes it's not perfect. But for this person to invite us into his home and show the concern for us and checking on us later and stuff like that. It changed your way of looking at people. So my idea of that person before the flood and then my idea of that person after the flood are entirely different.

MA: You don't really know who your friends are until you're in a situation like we were in. A lot of times the ones that you really wouldn't expect are going to be there will be, and the ones that you expect to be there won't.

PA: Several of us have been friends being on the department, but I just think the flood pulled these people even closer.

MA: Well, you know everybody's personality is different. And everybody has their own way of tolerating stress or their own humor level or whatever. But when you get in a bad situation and you need some help, it don't matter what somebody's personality is. It's, Who can you count on? Who's willing to do the job to help you survive or whatever it takes to get it done?

PA: We ended up taking Holly Hill Free Will Baptist Church right down here almost in the crossroads to be the helipad to land the helicopters. Because the area around Gum Swamp Church had tobacco fields and when those helicopters came down they were slinging tobacco stalks everywhere. So this was on pavement and it made it real easy. And then they used those big Army trucks to bring the stuff up to the church. But we had to airlift. One thing we were running into was patients who didn't have medications. And Tom Harris told me, he says, "Phyllis, if you can get the prescription bottles for me, I will get them airlifted to Pitt County Memorial Hospital and I will get these people their medicines. But it may be tomorrow. It'll be a twenty-four-hour turnaround." So I ended up at Gum Swamp fellowship hall with a composition notebook writing down medications and sending out bottles in a Food Lion bag.

And then on Wednesday they finally sent in teams of doctors and nurses to give me a break because I was exhausted. I was doing house calls at twelve o'clock midnight. The Forestry guys would come and get me where I was staying and take me to people's houses to see if I needed to get them airlifted to the hospital. We ended up getting a little child's fever back down who had pneumonia, who could see the doctor next morning when they flew in.

PA: And what we were running into was people getting hit by fire ants, people without medications. We airlifted, what? About five patients?

MA: Several patients, yeah.

DB: Some people over that way were bringing ice and stuff this way. This is before we actually started getting stuff flown in on the helicopters. And there was a signpost beside the road where they brought the boat up. And the fire ants were just wrapped around that signpost, you know. Because those fire ants, you could see them, they were all grouped together in a huddle. It's like they were all holding on to one another, and you'd just see a mass of them and they'd be floating in the water. That's how they floated. And if they could get up to a tree or a post or something like that, they would attach to it. And you had to be very careful propping on trees and posts because they would get you. And one deputy sheriff, he said it didn't take him but one time. He said that he realized that you don't prop on light poles and signposts.

DE: I had this certain woman [*Phyllis*] who wanted me to go to a doctor while we were down there.

PA: I had some sick people staying up all night, sleeping outside, getting laryngitis, sinus infections, colds.

WM: So you recommended that he go to a doctor?

PA: Because he couldn't talk. Got laryngitis. He was sick. We had doctors flown in by then, when I finally made all of them go.

DE: What did the doctor say?

PA: Voice rest and go home and get in the bed and go to sleep. Get some good sleep.

WM: Well, did he follow the doctor's orders?

DE: About five days later.

PA: But it was just, there were so many helicopters flying, landing. So much military equipment. I know now how it feels to be in a combat war zone or something, kind of, without the bombing. Because at night you heard helicopters, and it was like a dream that you were not waking up from and you just kept living that dream over and over. I really don't know who I was during the flood that week. I don't remember me. I felt like I was living a dream.

DE: Who didn't feel like they were living a dream?

PA: I mean, I don't remember me. But I lost nineteen pounds.

DE: Four million gallons of water, two hundred bags of ice, and no telling how many cans of food—you probably gained some muscle too.

PA: Yeah, we lifted and moved. But we met some people in our neighborhood that you knew were in your neighborhood but now you know them on a first-name basis.

MA: I think all of us who were together, it was almost, I guess—well, I've never been in the military but I would assume in a stressful situation you either get close to one another or you get where you can't stand one another. But I think most of us got along very well. Everybody was pulling together. A lot of people like Forestry Service and some of the different sheriffs, we got to be good friends, almost like family. And one of the deputy sheriffs, his boss called him and told him it was time for him to leave, that we were OK over here. And he said, "I'm not leaving." He said, "These people still need me." His boss said, "Are you disobeying a direct order?" He said, "Call it what the hell you want. You can fire me if you want to. I'm not leaving." That's what he told him. But you see at that time when he told him that, they still didn't realize what we were going through. They still didn't realize that we were isolated. And when the message did get across and they finally figured out that we weren't able to get to the shelters, then supplies just started coming in by the truckload.

95

PA: By Tuesday or Wednesday. Tuesday we started to get some in. And see, we didn't have bottled water. And then all of sudden they said, "Oh, don't drink the water. Boil the water." And I'm thinking, *Oh boy. We've been drinking it now how many days? It's not going to kill us now.* But we had no idea. And here we are, drinking it for four days. And finally then we started boiling, and then we ended up getting bottled water. But it was rationed because we didn't have much and you could give a bottle per person a day.

WM: A gallon?

PA: No, a little bottle. That's all we had because we didn't have many supplies to go around. And what happened was, people sent a lot of food that you have to cook but we didn't have any power so we couldn't cook. You needed something that you could pop the top off of or whatever and eat right then. And then we had some people come out of Robersonville—because once the water started going away on a couple of roads we could get to Williamston, Robersonville, that way. And some ladies came in and started serving soup and lasagna, you know, things that they could make in bulk. Then we started getting mass supplies. There were so many supplies coming in that we ended up making the Fire Department a warehouse. But it was only … When did the Red Cross get to us? Tuesday or Wednesday? It was a few days later. At first, Red Cross was nowhere to be found, and we were doing the best we could. We were winging it on our own. And then the Salvation Army finally got down here. But we have to recognize the church, Cedar Grove. Those people raised money from their community, they raised thousands. And this man who has a catering business came out here and set up a tent and fed us some of the best food I've ever had.

MA: Wasn't the Forestry Service—when this first started, when we weren't getting any food—weren't they cooking plates?

PA: Yes and airlifting them over. They brought us barbecued chicken. That's all we had was barbecued chicken and bread, which was fine. Anything was good then.

MA: They were cooking it and putting it on plates and flying them over in helicopters themselves.

DB: You could see, people pulled together. A lot of people pulled together.

MA: In some ways I think that people who didn't get flooded, they had this, I don't know, sense of guilt or wishing they could help or not knowing what to do. It affected different people different ways. But I saw a few of the highway patrols, they stopped by our house and they almost had tears in their eyes because they felt sorry for you and they didn't know what to do. And they'd see you taking all your stuff out of your house, throwing it in a pile, and it made me feel bad to look at some of them. The way they were looking at me, you knew they were having a tough time handling it. And *you* didn't know how to handle it.

PA: And you were having a tough time because it was you.

MA: You didn't know how to answer people. It's just one of those things you don't know how to answer. You just do what you've got to do and you keep on going.

I'm just thankful that we had friends and family that could help us because as helpless feeling as we were, it would have to be worse on somebody that was new to this area with no friends and no family. It really would. And I'm assuming there's quite a few people probably still in those FEMA campers. I know that's got to be one tight place. People who can't take stress and pressure and get ill, you know. I'd hate to combine it cram-packed in there in a small area like that, especially when it gets hot, you know. Then you got stress too.

PA: Henry stayed in a home that had how many people in there? Fourteen? They had a different experience. They didn't have milk and we had to have milk flown in. And then they didn't have anywhere to put it to cool it.

HF: There was either fourteen or seventeen and three babies. When I say babies, I mean infants.

PA: Tiny, tiny.

HF: I think there was three. One of the mothers worked for Social Services and she was over there at Pitt County away from the child. And then we had my brother-in-law's baby, his wife. My other brother-in-law's baby and his wife. It was just a lot of people. I think it was three beds in the whole house.

WM: Were people tense? Were tempers getting short with all these folks in a house? What was it like, so many so close?

HF: I reckon you could say some people got short tempered sometimes, but a lot of times we pulled together. You know, we were all family, mainly. But other than that, it wasn't real bad.

MA: Her cousin who was flooded in Edgecombe County said that his house was just a little overstocked. Said he didn't mind the family and all being there, but it was just a little overstocked.

PA: My aunt and uncle took us in. And they were so accommodating. I know they saw our loss and saw how we were coping, but you know what? Even to this day you can't sit down at a meal and not bring up the flood. You can say, "Oh, well, guess what I found yesterday? I thought they had thrown them out." You know, there's something that's attached to the flood somehow. And then things like my wedding pictures, you know. Things like that that I lost, things that's not replaceable.

MA: Lots of things.

PA: And I had a lot of feelings in me. And I know the most important thing is that I didn't lose any of my family. I didn't lose any of my friends. We were very fortunate. It's just such a loss of personal things. And it's a lesson to be learned not to put so much value in personal things. My husband's always trying to preach that to me, about not getting attached to everything we own or whatever.

MA: When you are used to providing for yourself and all of a sudden you're away from home, then you don't have a home that you can go to. Can't go to the refrigerator. Can't go put on your favorite pair of blue jeans. You don't know where your favorite shirt's at. I mean, you're at somebody else's mercy. And finally they came to us in a few days after we figured out it was going to be more than a couple of changes of clothes. I mean me and Doug and Chad—we were about to wear our underwear out. And I think we had six pair between the three of us. You had to wear what you had to wear. We didn't have nothing. And then finally I guess it was the Salvation Army or somebody brought clothes down and put them in the barn over there. I don't know, it's hard to explain. But you know it finally dawns on you that you're helpless. You've got to go over there and try to find some clothes to wear until you can get back to your house.

PA: It was very hard when this lady handed me a bag of clothes and she says, "I brought these for you." And I said, "Well, you need to give those to somebody that needs it." That was my response. And then I had to back off and say, "Look, I am that person that needs it because I ain't got but two pair of shorts." Being a nurse, I've always been the giving person and I've never been on the receiving end that much. And I guess when people said, "Here. Here's some clothes for you," or "Here's some food for you." I'm like, "Hey, I've got plenty at my house. If I can ever get back to my home, I have plenty." It was very hard for me to swallow my pride and take a hand-out because I've never been used to that.

MA: And the other thing that was so bad about it—most people who have homes have got insurance to where if a tornado comes through and blows it away, they're covered. If they got fire, they're covered. We were in a situation where most of us had no insurance because nobody in a million years would have thought we'd have had water coming in like this. Nobody was prepared for it. I guess we're fortunate in one way because we lived in an old house that I was remodeling, and we didn't have a house payment. Now we're going to have a house payment because FEMA didn't help us. I think they helped a little bit but not enough to fix the house so we had to resort to a SBA loan. And I was thinking to myself how bad it would be to have a hundred and fifty thousand dollar mortgage and then have to turn around and get another loan on top of that.

HF: My house was paid for and I had insurance. Of course I didn't lose a lot of things in my house. I was one of the fortunate ones that didn't lose a lot of pictures and things like that. I mean there's things out there you just can't replace, you know.

PA: So if there's ever a storm, anything that's any value, you put it under your arm and take it with you.

MA: Wedding pictures and pictures of your family.

HF: Your great-great-grandmama, you know. She might have meant something to you and you can't retake that picture anymore.

PA: Well, you know you don't need all that stuff. When we took all that stuff out of our house, God, it looked like Mount Rushmore out there in our front yard. And it was stuff that we didn't need. I'm a pack rat. So we did some major spring cleaning. And I keep telling Mike, I say, "I'm not buying all that stuff like I bought before."

TB: And when I finally got back—I came back on the 25th of September and they had just gotten back to the house. And when I walked in there everything just looked like it had been through a tornado. Everything was upside down.

WM: Do you think it's made you a better person?

DE: I don't think it's made just one person a better person. I don't think it's just made me a better person. I just think it's made us ... well, excuse me, I think it made *part* of this community a better community. We saw that once the community gets in a bind we can pull together and we can come through.

PA: Well, some people—and this is not a put down. Do not get me wrong here. I mean no disrespect. But a lot of people now, they have come out better.

HF: Oh yeah, most definitely. The flood helped some people.

PA: Chad even said he likes the house he's got now better than the one he had before.

DB: That one was paid for. This one ain't.

PA: Well, and then you know Mike and I have lifted our house up off the ground—nine feet. We're going to be the oddball in the community. But our house was built in 1913 and some of our foundation had kind of settled. We were going to have to do a new foundation anyway. So Mike's motto here is: *It's going to be better than it ever was.*

MA: When I first started wanting to raise my house, somebody said, "Mike, there's no need to do that. If the Lord wants to flood you he's going to flood you." And I looked at him and I said, "Why that's like saying two people walking out in the rain, one carrying an umbrella and the other one not. And the one that's not carrying an umbrella says, "I'm not going to carry one because if the Lord wants me to get wet I'm going to get wet." You know, that's crazy. I mean you can still prepare under the circumstances. If it comes high enough to get us next time from a flood, everybody can just kiss their butt goodbye because it's going to get everybody.

PA: Well, people that didn't get flooded out, they say, "It's not going to flood again." That's almost like cuss words to me. Don't say that to me. You don't know. And this is such a concrete world, there's so much cement everywhere and asphalt and everything—there's nowhere for the water to go. And if the storms are going to get worse and worse and worse, you are going to see some flooding again. You may not see it of that magnitude.

MA: Well, I'm not perfect and I'm not a preacher but I look at everything from a Biblical aspect. And I know that the society in general is getting worse every year. Twenty years ago I went to sleep with my doors unlocked and didn't worry about anybody stealing anything out of my car. Now you lock everything up and just fear somebody's going to steal something. I'm not saying that all of society is worse, but society in general is getting worse. And historically speaking, if you look at the Bible, the worse a society gets, the worse the famines, the worse the economic situations. Those kinds of things start happening. The Bible says there'll be famine and earthquakes and all these different things in different places. I just think it's a sign of the times and I think you're going to see the weather getting worse. I think you're going to see things like that happen again.

But, you know, somebody said that a situation like this will do one of two things. It will either bring out the very best in people or it will bring out the very worst in people. One of our friends who came to get us on the boat, one of his neighbors had sat on the top of a house with a shotgun to keep the looters from coming in with boats and jet skis and all kinds of stuff. And I think that's very common, that somebody would come in and do something like that. That's the part of society that I'm talking about. But you know, they were trying to steal people's motors off their boats. And they were trying to go to the houses and steal stuff out of their houses. There was quite a lot of that going on. At the same time these good people were out trying to help one another, there was other people out trying to stab them in the back.

WM: Do y'all know of any examples of that kind of bad behavior that happened?

TB: Of people stealing stuff? Yeah, every one of us.

TB: You're told you can't salvage anything in your house. You're to throw it all away. But yet you've got people riding down the road and they're stealing what you're throwing out.

DB: Stealing everything you throw out.

PA: Out of your pile.

TB: You don't even get a chance to go back to see if anything is salvageable. But they're stealing it.

MA: When you get back to your home, you don't have anywhere that you could put anything. Everything is wet. You're trying to get everything out of the house to see what you can salvage. Or at least to air it out or dry it. We had clothes laying on the front porch drying so we could wash them when we could get somewhere where we *could* wash them. And there was people come by and stole some of our clothes. You see, when we first got to where we could go back to our homes, once we could get across the river, we worked for a living so we had to go back to work. We had to do our stuff in the evening after work. Well, Phyllis's mother is retired, so she would be over there trying to clean up her house or waiting for somebody to come and do something. And she would always be around during the day. And several times she would run out of the house and people would be out there taking stuff. She got the license plate of one car.

TB: The sheriff actually found the lady that stole Mike's coat—wearing it.

DB: They about cleaned our yard out.

TB: Doug's mom, she put her stove on her front porch. She thought maybe she could salvage it, you know, clean it up, see if it worked. And people went up there and took the burners right off. Stole the burners out of her stove.

WM: Did they think it was abandoned?

TB: From what Phyllis says, they were told that they could have what was in the yard that was considered trash.

DB: That was their excuse.

MA: You know, some people make comments like, "What did I do to deserve this?" or, "Why is God punishing me?"

PA: It took me a long time. I would say, "Why me? Why did I get flooded? Why didn't so-and-so over there? He lives on the same road I do, and his house is perfectly fine." You had two neighbors right beside you that didn't get flooded, you know. Why did it get everybody else but didn't get them?

MA: And if you want to go back to the Bible, the Bible says that rain falls on the just the same as it does on the unjust. I don't feel like it was punishment sent by God. I just feel like it was nature. It was just something that happened. And if it was a test, I don't think it was a test of punishment. I think it was a test of seeing how we were going to react and treat one another under the circumstances.

PA: Kind of like a wake-up call.

MA: Well, you get so busy tied up in this rat race of life chasing the American dollar—even though you owe it to somebody else you've got to chase it down so you can give it away. But most of the time you feel like you don't have time to stop to do anything. But something like this lets you know that you can stop if you have to. And, you know, sometimes you just have to let everything else go and then do what you can to help other people.

TB: My house got pulled off its foundation. Well, sitting on my dresser was my jewelry box. I had one that has the little drawer, and I kept all our rings—my high school ring, Doug's high school rings, my wedding bands, my cluster—everything that Doug give me that was valuable was in that drawer. Well, when I finally was able to get back to the house, we searched the house over and couldn't find it. Doug stopped by the store one day and [a woman] asked him, "What is your wife's name?" He said, "Tammy." She said, "Well, by chance was she a Mayo?" He said, "Yeah." She said, "Well there's this man looking for a Tammy Mayo. Will it be all right if I give him your work number?" So this man left a message for Doug to call. And he told Doug, he says, "I have your wife's jewelry." He says, " I found her jewelry box in my back yard on the cluster of picnic tables and porches and stuff. Can I meet you at my house? I want you to identify her jewelry." The man is located on Old River Road about two, two and a half, three miles down the road. So Doug went to the man's house, and he lives way back in the woods. Doug said it was just littered with all kinds of porches and stuff. And the man showed him, he said, "This is where her jewelry box landed." The drawer had got swollen and got stuck so it held all of my jewelry in that drawer. And he laid every bit of it out on the table. He said, "Is this hers?" Doug said, "Yeah. Here's my high school ring; there's my name in it. Here's her high school ring; that's her name in it. I had my name, Tammy Mayo, in mine. He had Douglas Bullock in his. So he was looking for Tammy Mayo. So that's how every bit of my jewelry got returned. He did not steal one piece. He gave every bit of it back to Doug. And Doug took it home and washed it up for me. When I got home he had it laying out on the table.

PA: Henry attends Lighthouse Church and their church was destroyed in the flood. And they had a highway patrol that came out of Randolph County that was riding around patrolling. They were sending law enforcement people from all over North Carolina to come in and relieve and help patrol and stuff. And that highway patrol was riding around and saw some people out at Lighthouse Church. And apparently God directed him to that church, because he called his minister who called people, and that church in Randleman restored, rebuilt, refurnished the one here.

HF: This was a small church that they had. And they completely done a job on our church. They done most of the work. They come down and volunteered. They donated the stuff, volunteered most of the work. I mean, their preacher was even down sanding, you know—their preacher.

WM: How do you think the flood has changed you?

DB: I don't know. It just shows you how quick things can be taken away from you. I mean how quick you can lose everything you got.

TB: You appreciate the day that you live. You can plan for tomorrow but you're not promised tomorrow. So you appreciate and you live that day and do all that you can for that day. I never felt like that this was the end of the world. Because God said He would never destroy this earth with water again. So I never felt like this was the end of the world even though I had no communication with my family. All I knew was that they were safe.

MA: I think it's made me more aware of other people that are in need. You know, when I'm watching TV and I'm flipping around the channels and I see one of these countries that has been flooded, and you see families and children starving and that kind of stuff. Before, I might look at it and feel sorry for them and just kind of flip the channel. But when I see it now it makes me stop and think that these are real people. They are really suffering and they really have need of help. And because I have gone through something like that, you know, I can relate to it. It's not just somebody on the TV and then change the channel. I mean it's a person that's got a situation and they need help. And it makes me more aware of that, more conscious of it.

WM: What about you, Doug?

DB: A lot of things changed. Because I've been on the Fire Department a long time and I've always helped other people, you know, all that time. And I didn't ever think I would need some help. I appreciate all the help I got. But you look at things a lot different. I've always helped people, you know, and didn't ever think about myself that much.

WM: When you say you look at things a lot different, how's that?

DB: I don't know. You just kind of slow down and take notice of things a lot better now.

PA: It's made me look at things differently. Like little things that used to really irritate me—now it's just a thing. You know, there's so many problems in the world, there's larger problems.

HF: I used to have a temper. Now I overlook everything. I mean, you know, nothing bothers me. I'm just thankful every day. It's just something there. I tote my fishing rod everywhere I go. I'm just, you know, thankful I'm living, I reckon. Used to, I probably wouldn't have cared. Now I'm glad I'm living and glad to be able to see it. Just thankful.

PA: I look at things different. Now I always ask myself, God had a plan for me here on earth and what is my plan? OK. Every time you turn around I'm on a committee. And it's always involving people in the community. I was on the Pitt County Hurricane Task Force, and now I'm on the Indigent Medical Care. I feel like it has mellowed me down. Not that I was way up in the sky, but it's brought me back down to earth. It's brought me back down to the real meaning of life. How easy you can have it and then the next day it's gone. And it's never promised. And you can put all the value into materials things, when that material thing is not really worth that much, and it's more important to have friends and family. But you know this flood, it wiped out our neighborhood. Like our road, I couldn't go help any of my neighbors because I didn't have anywhere to live either. If it had been a house here or a house there, I would have been there trying to help somebody. But I couldn't even help myself.

MA: Well I think pretty much from Greenville right on to Tarboro, Princeville, I don't know how far—anything that was close to the river pretty much got it, unless it happened to be sitting on high ground. I know Phyllis has an uncle that lives in Edgecombe County right close to Conetoe, and he's three miles from the river and he got eighteen inches of water in his house. So, you know, three miles from the river—that's a right good ways.

DB: And then, like they talk about hurricane season coming up again—I mean it makes you really think and you wonder what's going to happen, and just try to think of how you're going to handle it. Got to go on, you know, like she said, and just take it day by day and do what you can do.

WM: So, Chad, it's your turn. What are some of the things you look at differently now?

CB: Well, like Phyllis said, being the one that's always helping people and not really being able to let people help you, you know? What Phyllis was saying about swallowing your pride.

MA: It's a humbling experience.

PA: Yes. It brings you back down to earth.

DB: That's the truth.

PA: Well, you know what I felt? I felt sorry for Mike and I, but still classify us as being young even though we're in our forties. But I felt like Mike and I had another chance to start over. But my mother and my neighbors like Mr. and Mrs. Tucker, I really felt bad for them. I felt worse for them because they had worked so hard all their lives and now they're at this age and all that was taken away. And that's what my mom said when we moved her back in her home. She says, "But I have nothing now." And it was very hard on her, after working so hard so many years and retiring, to get back to her home and get her comfortable. And right now she will tell you it is not her home. It's not what she's familiar with and comfortable with. But it will take time and she'll become more comfortable. It's just different. I told her, I said, "Now you know they say that this year's hurricanes will be worse than last year." She said, "Well, if they start talking about a flood I'm going to go right out there and just fall right in it and let them just find me dead. Because I don't know if I can live through another one."

HF: My wife is petrified during hurricane season now.

WM: So are y'all making any preparations for the hurricanes now?

HF: Everybody's got insurance now.

DB: I got insurance but I wish my house was still higher than it is. Things still worry me.

PA: I'm going to rent a hotel in Greenville.

DB: I'm going to get a U-Haul truck.

PA: We will not be able to sleep again. We'll have to take shifts.

MA: I really think that if there was a hurricane and you flew over this road from Greenville to Tarboro and looked on everybody's front porch, you would see everybody's hand out there with a flashlight looking to see how high the water's going to get.

PA: With a boat out front.

MA: They won't go to sleep. I won't.

PA: I won't. Not again.

MA: We'll be watching the water.

BELVOIR IS A SMALL COMMUNITY

Eddie James

Belvoir is a small community with many churches. Although there are many churches, the community as a whole is very close. The community of Belvoir centers around the Fire Department, which is all volunteer. We had already been through one hurricane when the second hurricane started on us. We thought we were very fortunate to have survived two hurricanes. We never dreamed we would be flooded. Two days after the second storm, we were sitting in our house. There was no electricity so we were busy cooking all the food in the refrigerator and freezer on the grill. When the helicopter landed in our front yard, the Navy Seals grabbed the children first and escorted them to the helicopter. They told us they were leaving and we needed to join them. They stated that Rocky Mount was dumping ten feet of water a day on us and we would be underwater in a day. As we were in flight, our house and yard was the last land we saw. Everything was underwater and I was out of cigarettes. I was very ill.

IT APPEARED THE HURRICANE WAS OVER

Tammy Abeyounis-James

It appeared that the hurricane was over—the damage was done and basically my family and home were OK. Some of our neighbors were not so lucky and we had been down to their home and helped them move up to our house. Their home was already flooded. One friend had removed his family—son, daughter, wife, mom and dad—in a boat pulled by the tractor. When we got to our house, we felt safe. We were dry, had plenty of food and LP gas. In our minds, we were fine. The children were out playing in the paddleboat and riding it in our front yard. All of a sudden, a helicopter landed on the road and the Navy Seals started grabbing the children, telling them that they had to leave. I explained to them that we were fine, that we did not need to leave, and one of them stated, "Lady, they are dumping five feet of water on you twice a day. You are going to flood." I ran inside and grabbed the bags that were already packed. My husband was moving tax records upstairs and gathering all the cash that we had around the house. We all went to the helicopter and the Seals were gathering other people along the road and everyone was running around like crazy. The dogs were taken as well. The children were crying and afraid. So was I. Eddie's parents would not come, and the Seal came back and talked with Eddie. Eddie left and returned with his parents and that seemed to help the children. We never thought that we were going to flood.

While staying in a hotel in Tarboro, I met a very nice old lady. She was crazy about my dog and would often stop me so she could play with her. On the day that we were to leave, I asked her if she had had anything to eat and she responded no. I was angry at the way the elderly were treated; they were unable to walk across the road to the school where the food lines were.

ME AND MY BROTHERS
Mary James

Me and my brothers and sister and neighbor were playing in the front yard on the day of Floyd. We were playing in the water. My neighbor and his family had come to stay with us because their house had water in it already. We had no electricity and we played in the water just like nothing had happened, but we had a pool in our front yard. We were fixing dinner on the grill in the afternoon and then when we saw a helicopter land right on the road in front of the house, but not at the house, we got scared. My parents told me and my brothers and sister to pack our bags. So the kids got their bags and went to see what was going on while the parents were inside. The man on the helicopter just took us and put us on the helicopter and went to get my parents, neighbors and grandparents. My parents had my little dog. And my neighbors brought theirs. When the kids got on the helicopter it was really loaded. I didn't get to bring my two big dogs. There was no room. Then when everyone got on, the helicopter took us to Tarboro High School instead of Pitt County Schools. When we got there, there was no electricity.

IN THE FLOOD
Danielle Abeyounis

In the flood I had a lot of opportunities and disadvantages. The most surprising thing that happened was that I got taken out of my house and put on a helicopter. I was scared at first but after a while I got used to it. When we landed at Tarboro

High School, we just sat down and waited. It felt good that we could just sit down and not worry about anything. Until it came night. We were tired and cold and could not sleep there. So we went to the Comfort Inn. We finally fell asleep around 1:30 AM. The rest of my family and friends slept with the really nice man that we met. He let the dogs and people go to his house to stay. We managed to get to a Kmart to get some necessities. We used the pool water to wash our hair. At least we felt clean. The next few days were the same. We just hung around the hotel and ate, slept and played board games until the third day. On the third day someone managed to get to us and bring us home. Well, at least to Bethel. We stayed with my aunt for a week and then went home. It was an exciting adventure, but I am glad we are home. I don't think the "flood of the century" will ever be forgotten. At least not by me. The schools and all the communities really pitched in and helped a lot. Most everyone I know was affected by the flood. I don't think that there is a single person in Eastern North Carolina that wasn't.

❋ ❋ ❋

I LEARNED MORE ABOUT THE PEOPLE AROUND ME
Kristen Abeyounis

I learned more about the people around me during the flood than I ever have before. You don't realize how much you have in common with people you thought were so different until something like this happens to you. During this time I was volunteering down at the North Pitt High School at their shelter and I met some of the most amazing people. There were people there who had lost everything, people who didn't know their family was all safe or even alive because the waters had parted them, and they still were always smiling and ready to greet you. They were so grateful for everything that they did have they didn't worry about what they lost and that was just amazing to me. My biggest problem during the flood was, *Did I pack enough clothes?* And these people didn't even have any clothes except the ones they were wearing. I believe the person who amazed me the most and really sticks out in my head is a young lady who hadn't eaten for several days. She walked into the shelter and handed me her small baby. The only word in English she could say was "food," and she repeated it over and over. I felt so overwhelmed. Here is this lady I don't even know handing me her little baby and trusting that I will take care of her.

❋ ❋ ❋

WE WERE EVACUATED BY A HELICOPTER
William James

We were evacuated by a helicopter. We had to go to Tarboro High School. We tried to get to our house but the trucks could not make it to the high school. In a while the power came back on, so we went to a hotel to sleep there for the night. We didn't have any food to eat so we had to go to Kmart to get some. Of course, most of the stores were closed. Sometimes we went to the high school to eat lunch or dinner. We could not wash our hair and body because the shower would not run water. They had a pool so we got the pool water and took one in that water. We had a phone so we called some people.

WHEN I HEARD ABOUT MY FAMILY HERE IN NORTH CAROLINA
Benjamin James

When I heard my family here in North Carolina had a flood, I got kind of scared. I kept on thinking about what they were doing. One of my grandparents' house got totally destroyed. They had to stay at my aunt's house from when the flood happened to about two weeks ago. Now their house looks so much different. Luckily my other grandparents didn't have that much destroyed. My Pa-Pa said he would not ever fly on a plane, but when the helicopter came my cousins who lived next door made him get on. When we came down here for Christmas I felt bad when I saw all those houses damaged. I can remember my Pa-Pa telling me that there was a picture of him in the newspaper. I kept on wanting to go help my grandparents build their house. I can also remember my cousin's dog getting an infection and dying. He was a good dog. Now when I am living with my grandma, she is pointing to all the things that were really deep underwater.

Helicopter landing at Holly Hill Free Will Baptist Church parking lot, Belvoir.

Photo courtesy of Phyllis Adams.

You've got to go in and do things

Interviews with William Mansfield
William Mansfield with Charles Tucker, Gene Tucker,
Walter Allen, Ed Meeks, Robert Garrow and Ricky Gray

On June 5, 2000 William Mansfield met at the Belvoir Volunteer Fire Department with Charles Tucker, age 40, Chief of the Belvoir Volunteer Fire Department, his father, Gene Tucker, 72, Walter Allen, 63, and fellow Fire Department members Ed Meeks, 29, Robert Garrow, 31, and Ricky Gray, 42.

WILLIAM MANSFIELD: When you knew the hurricane was coming, did you make any special preparations for it?

CHARLES TUCKER: No, no more than I normally do for a hurricane. I also farm. So I had some farm damage that occurred from the winds. I made sure everything was tied up, put up the loose stuff so it wouldn't blow around. The hurricane went through on Wednesday and you could start seeing the water come up on Thursday. And we left on Friday. We were airlifted out by the Navy. When I left I didn't think I was going to get flooded. Now, my daddy lives right beside me. Water was in his house when we left. It wont in mine, but it was real close, and then apparently after we left, it came in. Our house is located six thousand feet from the Tar River. We saw the water coming up some on Thursday, but I didn't think it was going to go anywhere. And then even Friday morning I thought it was going to go so high and stop. But then, once it hit a certain stage, it sort of dawned on us to leave. The helicopters were flying on Thursday, getting some other areas. But this particular house I'm in—my grandparents was in it in the late thirties, and never had no trouble in the world. So that's why everybody sort of had confidence that it wasn't coming so high.

When I left, the water was level with the back stoop—the door steps. We could drive down the road a mile. But that was as far as we could go. We left on a farm tractor and a boat. The tractor was pulling the boat. My intentions were to play Noah. I had food and clothes and the family in the boat. Then when we got a little ways down the road, that's when the Navy landed and said it was a mandatory evacuation.

WM: Was the boat floating as you were going through the water or was it on a trailer?

CT: It was on a trailer. But when I was driving out of my house it was floating, the whole trailer and everything.

WM: Were you scared?

CT: It was a funny feeling. I don't know what kind of feeling it was. It was sort of like a defeated feeling. I like to be in control and you can't control that. I mean, like, if it's hot in this room I can go turn the air conditioner on or I can go outside. But in this situation I couldn't control the water. You knew the water was coming, there wont no stopping it.

WM: So, the helicopter saw you and landed?

CT: It landed in a certain area and sort of combed the whole area. I think it flew out with thirty-five or forty people, and nine dogs and all our luggage.

WM: So, you all went to the shelter in Tarboro. Did you stay at the shelter the whole time, or did you come back and pitch in with the Fire Department?

CT: We stayed at the shelter in Tarboro three days and then we could finally get back to Bethel. It took three hours to go from Tarboro to Bethel. We stayed in Bethel, how long, Ricky? About a week? Maybe two weeks. We came back and forth in the daytime but we spent the night there. Then we set up a camper out here, and stayed here.

WM: What was it like in the shelter?

CT: I wouldn't want to stay in there for long. When we got there it wont run by anybody, just the local community people. It was thirty-seven hundred people at one shelter with no electricity, no water, no food, and five port-a-johns. At that time the Red Cross or the National Guard hadn't got there.

WM: So it was just local people pitching in?

CT: They were doing the best they could. They were doing a good job. Some of that stuff—the sooner I can forget it, the better it's going to be.

WM: So, the National Guard didn't take over? Or the Red Cross didn't take over while you were in the shelter?

CT: No.

WM: Did you see many people that you knew at the shelter? Were they farmers like yourself?

CT: All walks of life. Our clan that flew up there sort of stayed together, you know, initially. Then somebody came out and picked up two groups of us, so we sort of went our separate ways that first night. Sixteen of us went to one house, and another family took the other sixteen in. So we really didn't stay in the shelter after 11 o'clock that night.

WM: And you went to different houses—just regular folks' houses?

CT: Yeah. After we left Tarboro we stayed with a relative of my uncle who lived in Bethel.

WM: What about the recovery efforts? How have they been?

CT: I personally would classify that as excellent. From the time we started on my house until the time we finished it, I probably had a hundred and fifty people to help me. Two churches in that community helped, Gum Swamp Free Will Baptist Church and Mount Pleasant Christian Church. And the West Side Christian Church out of Winston-Salem came down and helped tremendously. Plus just regular friends.

WM: Do you think that the flood brought the community together?

CT: Definitely. I think so. The day after the hurricane Bobby Joyner, who is the fire marshal for the county, called me and wanted me to come down here and open up the building for a shelter. They were going to start evacuating some people. And I laughed at him. I said, "Bobby, I can't get to the fire station." At the time the creek up here a little ways was blocking me. I couldn't get down here then. I was gone and I didn't get involved at all in the shelter.

WM: [to Gene Tucker] Have you ever seen anything like this before?

GENE TUCKER: The closest come here in 1919 about five feet lower than this was. And that's the only thing I've heard any of the older people say.

WM: Well, were you in the boat with the tractor pulling it?

GT: I was the first in the boat. I had a artificial hip put in my left hip. When I went in the boat, I couldn't control my feet fast enough to get in like I should, so I went in head first and then they had to straighten me up. But my wife and I was in it. Charles and his wife and two children was in it. We had the

112

dogs in it. We had sandwiches, drinks, ice, and dog food. We were going to make out for a week or so. We had previously hauled what tobacco Charles had out—loaded it on trucks and carried it to a higher hill. And the last thing Charles did, he went over to the fence and cut the wire to let out four cows. They were going to try to make it on their own.

WM: Did they?

GT: They went around the tobacco barns which was the tallest thing around and that's where they were when we left. And those four, they found the bodies in the woods. But the other herd of about twenty on the back field survived it. So he was fortunate to lose only four.

We left in the boat and went to the county commissioner's house— Eugene James. We were going to stay up there. Didn't have any water. We'd been there about thirty minutes when the helicopter landed in front of his house on the highway. They said, "The dam in Rocky Mount broke, and there's going to be eight foot of water here in thirty minutes. Let's go." Everybody went but Mr. James. And his son said, "Let me go back and talk to him. So he went back and told Mr. James that he had some grandchildren crying on the helicopter, and so Mr. James held his shoes in his hand and walked through water and got on the helicopter. For most of us it was the first time we went up on a helicopter. They took us up to Tarboro, which is Edgecombe County. Mr. James was chairman of the Board of Commissioners in Pitt County, and it upset him a tremendous amount that he was outside the county and couldn't help the county. He tried to get someone to come pick him up and they couldn't get up there. It was roughly a three-hour drive around south or a three-hour drive around north to make it there. And about 11:30 that night a couple—retired principal and the retired assistant superintendent of Edgecombe County—came by the high school and saw us sitting there with the dogs. They were going home to get the house ready and they would come back and pick us up, and the dogs, if we wanted to go. There was twelve people and eight dogs, I believe. And this couple took all of us to their house.

Some of us left the next day. Charles left about the third day. About a week later we went to my brother-in-law's house in Tarboro and stayed there for about a month. And then we started driving back and forth out here. We were helping clean it up. It's been a long job. We had about thirty churches in Virginia went together and adopted us, and came down here and spent seven hundred working hours on our house. And it's a four-and-a-half to five-hour drive one way from where they came from at Ashland, Virginia. We owe a lot to them. As my son said, they did things that you cannot expect nobody to do. But they did it. I think they really enjoyed coming down here and doing it.

WM: When you knew you were going to have to evacuate, was there anything you thought that you had to get out of the house?

GT: No, we just walked out and left it. My son and a couple of neighbors went back in and stacked some furniture up in his house. But in my house, when I saw it, it looked like someone had put a big eggbeater in every room and stirred it up. Furniture was all to pieces, paper, water, clothes. Everything was over the floor and around. And there was a group took everything out, probably ten to twenty people doing it. We didn't save nothing. We had two little chairs downstairs and we had two chairs that came out of the attic. Otherwise, we wouldn't have had but two chairs. We've replaced most of it now. We still have some work to do on the outside, but I think we're about over it now.

WM: Well, do you think you'll ever get over it?

GT: Well, I'll tell you one thing, I have flood insurance now. Hope I never need it.

WM: All right. Who wants to go next?

WALTER ALLEN: I'll go next. I live about five, six, seven hundred foot off NC 33. I got two houses back in the woods and my road runs about forty foot on the east side of Belvoir Free Will Baptist Church. When the storm came, I was standing watching and the trees was just falling all around my place. I lost about fifty trees right out in the woods and about thirty fell across my path. So the next day I was out trying to get the trees down. And the preacher and a couple of his boys and my boy and the Tony Bullock family came over with a back hoe. And James Brown. And they cut the trees in two and took the backhoe and pushed them back. It took about two hours to do that. If they hadn't come with the backhoe and done that I'd have been two weeks out there with a chain saw cutting them up. So while this was going on I didn't realize that the flood waters were coming like they were. I had a tree leant over on my old trailer and went out and winched it with cable to keep the pressure off of it. And the same thing with my garage. Then Saturday I heard these helicopters just continuously flying over—back and forth, back and forth. But I was busy so I wasn't paying them too much mind. Saturday night before I went to bed, I went down and checked the water in, they call it, Mayo Swamp. The headwaters start across the road and it comes over on my side and goes on out by James Brown's farm. And I checked the water before I went to bed Saturday night.

And then Sunday morning I looked out and the water was backing across the yard up on the other side. I looked out and I told the wife, I said, "We've got problems," because the water was backing up all the way from the river. It wont going out the Mayo Swamp side, you know. And so then I got out and looked, and between my two houses was a low place and the water was already about two and a half or three foot deep. So I walked through that and drove all the cars up on what we call "the hill" where my new house is, the highest peak up there.

I put me a mark up at the water level so I could tell how much it was rising. It didn't rise but about an inch and a half, two inches from ten o'clock that morning to about two o'clock that Sunday afternoon. And the helicopters were flying around and evacuated some people over there behind the church. Then they come over and hovered right around my house, one of these big Navy helicopters. So I told the wife, I said, "Look, it's time for us to go." I said, "They know something we don't know." Then our neighbors called and wanted to know were we coming out? We said, "We're going to try to get the tractor and come out." And they said, "Well, we'll come in and get you." The water had already filled down there at my old trailer. So they drove a four-wheel-drive Dodge in there, and I drove the tractor from my new house down to the old house and they took my wife and left. And I took the tractor and led them out down a path. And I left my tractor over at Belvoir Free Will Baptist Church. That was Sunday afternoon about 3:30. And as I went out I unplugged my deep freezers under my car shelter down there—had two upright deep freezers. I unplugged them and unplugged the refrigerator in the garage. Cut the power off. And the water didn't get but about eight inches under my old house, and got about a foot in my garage—we had a cement floor with 2 x 4 studs, so I didn't worry about that. And it got within fifty foot of my new house. So we were very lucky and we thank the Lord for it, too. It was only about three houses over in that area that didn't go down.

WM: Were you watching the news, listening to the radio, keeping up with events?

WA: I was out all day Saturday cutting up trees so I didn't really know what was going on except the helicopters were continuously flying over.

WM: Was your wife following it on the news?

WA: Well, she was laying in the bed reading. She loves to read. We went out Sunday afternoon and went over and stayed with the Tony Bullock family. And then along about Tuesday I guess it was they had set up out at Gum Swamp Church. So we went out and helped them on Tuesday and Wednesday, to disperse food and all. I wouldn't go back home until the waters peaked, and the river peaked at 2 AM on Wednesday morning. And I didn't go back to my house until late that afternoon, which was about twelve, fourteen hours later. And when I got there the water had already gone out. It was dry under my shelters. So I waited around until the next day and plugged my deep freezers up. They took right off. Refrigerator in the garage—plugged it up, it took right off. So I didn't lose any appliances.

WM: Did you lose stuff in the freezer?

WA: Yes, I did. As far as my garage, I just opened up the doors and let it dry out and I had no problem there. I had some tools that went under. I took all them all out and laid them out in the sun for about a week, didn't even try to mess with them, just sunned them each day. And both of them took right off when I fired them up.

WM: Did you know that your house had escaped before you went back?

WA: No, I did not. I kept watching how much the water was coming up though. By the time I went out on Sunday afternoon I figured it didn't come up no more than ten inches. We were very lucky. We didn't lose very much. And I found out I had some of the highest land in Belvoir. Because it was four foot of water right down near the interstate. And they did say it was seventeen foot deep on top of this bridge down here. They measured right straight down from a boat, and it was seventeen foot deep. But I've still got trees down. I've been cutting up trees all year.

WM: I guess you'll have all the firewood you need for some time. Now tell me what you did at the church.

WA: We'd go out and help unload food that was coming in on trucks and Army trucks and so forth. And eventually when they got where they could, they'd come in on transfer trucks. We'd unload them, and stack things back and people would come in with boxes and we would help them load it. Give out ice, give out water, whatever people wanted. And we'd just help them get it in their cars.

WM: So you were the supply and distribution place rather than a shelter?

WA: That's right. That was at Gum Swamp Free Will Baptist Church. When the Fire Department started flooding they moved the headquarters over there.

WM: Well, did anything about the community's response to the flood surprise you?

WA: Well, it's just like when we have a community gathering out here, like we have our big annual firemen's sale here, and everybody just comes together. And a lot of times we don't know where the help's going to come from. But on that date they just flock out here. And the same thing over there, we had plenty of help. We had to coordinate when those trucks come in. We had to make sure that we stacked food where people could get to it. And they started fixing boxes, you know, what they thought a person would need for a day's living, or two days. And when people come in, they'd look in it and say, "I'll take this one." It saved a lot of time too.

WM: Who took the lead? Was there somebody who kind of directed the relief efforts at the church?

WA: I think as far as taking control, it was the Forestry Service took over getting the food here and everything like that. But far as on the inside, if you went in and started doing a job they'd let you keep right on doing it. If they had any questions, the people of our church would answer their questions and help them along. But it just seemed to work real smooth. Anybody had any ideas, we'd see if it worked.

I think the community came together real good and if they had any differences, I didn't see them. They put them aside. And at a time like this I think they should. I think that's about it. I did keep a daily account of what happened, of what I did each day, where I could go each day, how far we could go and when the roads opened up, and such stuff as that. I figured that might be good for my grandyoung'uns some day to know that I lived and went through the Flood of '99.

WM: Anything you think you'd want to tell them that's special about that?

WA: Well, the thing to do is to use good common sense, because when floods and stuff like that comes, there ain't very much you can do. And the thing to do is just stay busy doing something.

WM: Tell me about your experience with the hurricane and the flood.

ED MEEKS: My name's Ed Meeks. I've been around here about six years now. I grew up in the Farmville community. Most of the family's around Falkland, Belvoir, that area. I lived in a singlewide at the time and we were up staying with my in-laws. They had gone to Missouri and were driving back home that Wednesday night because they were determined they could do something when they got here. I kept saying, "You just need to wait." You know, there was real high wind and stuff. About ten o'clock Wednesday night when all the wind was coming up, we had nine inches of water in the carport. And so I went to get my father-in-law's car out from under the carport and parked it at my house on the hill. We pretty much thought we had a little rainwater and it would be gone. And by I guess 3:30 or so Thursday afternoon all the rainwater was gone. I said, "We're out of the woods now." We didn't really realize what was going on. We didn't have power, but we had candlelight and I had my gas grill going so we had plenty to eat.

My in-laws got in about four o'clock that afternoon. They called me from Wilson that Thursday morning right in the heart of the storm and told me, "Look, it's got so bad we're going to stop right here in Wilson. Soon as it's over now, we'll be there." That was at 6:30. They pulled in our yard at 4:30 Thursday afternoon. Twice they got within a mile and a half of the house and they had to backtrack. They went to Rocky Mount, came back around Wilson, finally were able to fish around Greenville somehow and get back in here, about 4:30 in the afternoon. So that's when I started realizing, you know, that it was getting a little bad. If they had told me then that we'd have the water we got, I wouldn't have believed it.

So we basically just tied in for the night. No power, but we were fine. My wife was seven months pregnant, and I had a little girl that was about two and a half. We woke up Friday morning and nothing was out of the ordinary. I kept seeing some guys riding around with lights flashing, some of the sheriff's deputies. The road over in front of us, Stokes Road, had some low areas back there and they get a lot of water anyhow. I got out riding to check on friends over there. When I got there and saw my assistant chief's house, water was halfway to the windows of his house. He lives a quarter mile from where I live, so I said, "We got a problem."

We hadn't had a fire call the whole time, and about eight o'clock Friday morning they finally called us out. And the only way I could get to the department was to go back towards Greenville and come up 33. And I called my wife on the cell phone and said, "Look, you need to go ahead and start making some arrangements. Get with your parents. Pack some things. We might have to get out." That's when I started realizing it was more serious than I thought it was. I got back and we got the cars packed and I talked my in-laws into leaving. They didn't want to leave. But I talked them into leaving, and we came up to the Fire Department. And I was helping evacuate people, helping here that Friday. We had helicopters landing here picking up some elderly folks that had health conditions, carrying them to the hospital so they'd be close to the health care.

We had no idea it would get as bad as it got. And every time you looked it was getting a little worse. About three o'clock that afternoon, my father-in-law looked at me, and said, "Look, it ain't getting no worse than this, I'm going back home." So he and my mother-in-law took off, left their son with me and my wife. They headed out, went back home.

Well, we kept hanging out here. My main concern was with my wife and little girl. They were bringing in cots and stuff for us. And it so happened my cousin who's on the National Guard was on one of the trucks that kept bringing folks in and out. We'd been told all day Friday that there was no way to get across the river, that all the bridges in Greenville were closed. And he told me about six o'clock Friday night, "Look, the bridge at Hastings Ford is open. Don't know how long, but it is open." And I felt bad leaving because we'd all stuck together and I felt like I was letting them down, but at the same time I felt like it was the right thing to do to get my wife where she was OK with my parents in Farmville, and my little girl. I followed their truck out with my truck. And my wife had to call her mama on the cell phone and said, "Look, we're on our way to Farmville. Don't you want to come with us?" They wouldn't leave. And that was the hardest thing was leaving, knowing you were going to leave everybody else behind.

So we got round that way to my parents' house in Farmville. But my in-laws—my wife's sister and her family and my mother-in-law and father-in-law—were all flown to Tarboro. And a family there saw them at the shelter at Tarboro High School and took them in. And at first, we were kind of worried and then we found out that the man that took them in and my dad both retired from the telephone company. So you have a reassured feeling, you know—would love to meet these folks. And we went and got them that Monday and got them back to Farmville. And we had fifteen folks there in a two-bedroom house. It was kind of tight quarters. I hadn't lived at home in seven years. It was different. I was ready to get back home.

I had told everybody else I'd be back by morning and help out, but when I got back to Hastings Ford Saturday morning they wouldn't let us across. So I was pretty much stranded across the river for a good week and a half. We did come in that Wednesday. We snuck in. My brother-in-law come in from Missouri and me and my father-in-law and my brother-in-law snuck in through Rocky Mount, Enfield, into Oak City—the back way. Got to my preacher's house, who lives behind Belvoir School, and we got his johnboat and got to our house. I lived on some of the highest land in Belvoir and didn't realize it. We come in on a boat and my brother-in-law said, "What are you crying for?" I said, "There's grass in my yard."

This was on Wednesday. The water had just peaked. And everybody around me, all my neighbors, had a foot, two foot of water in the house. And the in-laws lived sixty yards in front of me and they had eighteen inches in their house. You were excited because you didn't have any in your house, but at the same time it was heart-breaking to see everybody you knew with water in their houses and all. I'm saying it was like the most helpless feeling; even though you didn't have any damage, it was helpless. Everybody, all your friends and family, had water in their houses. It was probably the following Saturday or Sunday before you could drive back in here. And even though you saw it, you didn't really believe it until you actually walked in your house. And even though we didn't have power and Lord knows all the food was spoiled, we were real blessed and fortunate, more so than you realized. It was a kind of heart-breaking and helpless feeling. I think it brought a lot of folks together. The Forest Service did a lot. They were stranded over here a week or so. All their families were across the river. And they were over here without their families—hadn't planned it that way, but that's the way it worked out.

WM: I know some people were actually getting angry.

EM: I never got mad. It was heartbreaking, wanting to help but at the same time there was nothing you could do. It was a helpless feeling.

WM: When was the baby born?

EM: It was born in November.

WM: What would you tell that kid about the flood?

EM: Well, believe it or not my little girl who's three now remembers a lot about it. Stuff that you didn't think she realized was going on, but she can tell you right now plain as day what happened, where the water was. Every time we go to her grandma's house, she says, "Memaw's house got flooded." That's the way it is. And, you know, my little boy he won't really know what happened. I'll just tell him he was here for the ride. I've got some pictures and stuff, but that still won't begin to explain it to him. Unless you actually saw it, you can't really visualize it. Guys I work with didn't have any damage, weren't in the flood. They were just without power for days or whatever. We get to talking sometimes, and they can't visualize some of the stuff I tell them about. They just can't imagine. They're like, "There's no way water got across that bridge." And I say, "Oh, it did."

WM: I've heard stories about young children and how when it starts raining they get scared.

EM: Now my nephew, it's bothered him. They flew out on a helicopter on Friday. And at first it was real fun, all he talked about was the helicopter ride. But after they got back in here and he saw what it had done to his house, it has really affected him a lot, even though he's not but four. You don't think they realize stuff, but they realize more than you think they're capable of.

ROBERT GARROW: I have three boys, and at the time their ages were four, seven and nine. And the four-year-old, still today when it rains for extended periods, he's constantly asking, "Is it going to flood? Is it going to flood, Mommy?" And you know it's on his mind. He's five now, but that's one of the first questions he asks. The other two children, they don't seem to be as affected by it as he was. I remember the day, Friday, we told them that we were leaving and that we were probably going to either take a helicopter ride or a boat ride. We gave them the option to get one toy and bring it with them. Well, my youngest one, he's an Elmo fanatic, and he went into the cabinet and got a plastic grocery bag, went in his room, picked up his Elmo—his Tickle-Me Elmo—and stuck it in the bag. And we asked him, "Why did you put Elmo in a bag?" "I don't want Elmo to get wet." That's the only thing he wanted. That was the only thing that he cared about. He was the same one that still asks the questions today, "Is it going to flood?"

I originally moved here from New York when I was seven. I live almost directly in front of Charles Tucker. I live across the field probably another two-, three-tenths of a mile away from the river. I ended up with twenty-seven inches of water in my house. I was just like him. I lost everything. Some people were actually washing toys for children with Clorox solution and things of that nature, but I threw it all away. I didn't want to take any risks. We were more concerned about contamination, illnesses to the children, so we didn't feel like anything was worth keeping. There was very little that we kept. Everything that was above the water line ended up in the water because furniture collapsed, entertainment centers collapsed. I had just bought my brand new home. I hadn't even lived in it a year, and it was wiped out completely.

WM: When did you first become aware that you were going to have to evacuate? Were you following the news?

RG: Well, I was one of those who expected the pager to go off if there was going to be a problem. And the pager never went off until the problem had grown to the point where there was nothing but last resorts. I got up Thursday morning, the morning the storm went by, and I received a call from my grandmother that a tree had fallen and brushed her house and her vehicle. She could not get out of her house at all and she didn't know who else to call. So I made an effort to go to her house in Scotland Neck to help her. I drove around probably six hours, but was unable to reach Scotland Neck at all. So I had to come back. I got here kind of late, and I was not able to drive my truck back across Thursday night to get home. Somebody over there had a large tractor and was helping pull cars out of the water. I parked my truck there and took a ride across the creek to my house. The water level comes up—you expect that after the rain. It comes up, it stays high for a little while and then it drops back down.

However, we woke up the next morning and it was six inches from going inside my house. We were awakened by the sounds of voices in the street. They were standing out there talking about us being in the house and the house was completely surrounded with water. I came out with my wife realizing that there was about two foot of water in my yard that was not there when I went to bed that night. There was no way to get out of the house without walking through it. At that point we realized something was wrong. The phone was still working. We called 911 to find out what was going on. The guy said that where we lived was already under a state of emergency and they were trying to evacuate everybody. About 10 minutes later at 8 o'clock, the pager goes off for the first time, which was very odd to me. You know, it's kind of late. By that time, there were already people down here though. The department was dispatched after people had already started helping. There were already some people in the department who had come down here by then and were trying to help.

About 11:30 the phone just went dead, and that was it. That's when you start getting to the point where you have lost everything now. You don't have any control, you don't know what's going on, there's no information coming in, there's no power. I didn't have a generator, but it would not have done me any good anyway because at 7:30 I had two foot of water in my yard. By 11:30 when the phones finally died it was up to about three foot. By the time the chopper finally arrived at about 1:30, the last thing we saw it was about three inches before going in the house.

This was Friday afternoon. Didn't know where we were going. We didn't know when the chopper was going to show up. We didn't know if it was going to show up. We didn't know if it was going to be at the point where nobody showed up until a boat comes along. You know, here we've got three children, the youngest being four, and just not knowing who, what or when was a helpless feeling. You knew something had to be done, but there was nothing you could do. Nothing. As far as preparations, as fast as the water was coming in, I didn't see any need to make preparations for the flood. Now we made a lot of preparations for the hurricane. And we were well prepared. We actually had water stored. We had tubs full of water. And by the time it was over, the entire house was full of water. It was just a big helpless feeling.

WM: Well, this is probably a silly question, but how do you stay calm? Because I know with your kids there you don't want to panic them.

RG: I knew I had to stay calm for my children. My wife was just as much aware of what was going on as I was. She knew there was nowhere we could drive in any direction to get out of there. She knew that the water was still rising. We could stand and see Hwy. 33 from our house, and there's a large upward slope hill between the two. And we could see the water coming across the field— the wrong way. When the water's traveling the wrong way, that's a reason for alarm. We tried to hide it from the kids the best we could. They knew it was coming, but I don't think they realized how bad it was until we went back for the first time and we wouldn't let them out of the truck. When they did go in, they were only there for a few moments. We never stayed more than a few minutes. They knew that it was bad at that point. We did a real good job of protecting them from what was going on.

My oldest son, I think he realized how bad it was when he was in the helicopter and he looked out and he said, "This looks like something you see on TV." And I said, "What do you mean?" And he said, " It looks like everything's covering up with water." And that's exactly what it looked like from the chopper. We were lifted about three miles west of here, and we were lifted across and went over towards Greenville, and then they diverted us over to one of the schools over here going towards Bethel. And we got a good view of how deep the water was Friday afternoon, you know, 1:30, 2 o'clock. You'd see tractors. All the tractors were on the hills. The farmers knew where the hills were and they had all their tractors sitting there. And you could see the water surrounding the tractors and it was coming in from all sides. You'd see water through the trees. You know basically like you'd expect to see on TV when they show weird movies that involve marsh or swamps. That's what it looked like from the air. It was something I'll never forget.

WM: The helicopter came and you all went out to it? Or did they hoist you up?

RG: There was still some area where they could land over there. There was plenty of dry land. There's a hill on both ends of the road across from my house. My house was not at the lowest part of the hill, but it was a lot lower than everybody else's. I received 27 inches; the house right across the street from me received a little less. My neighbor that lives right next door had some water damage on his floor; he had to redo everything under the house but as far as interior damage his wasn't extensive. His house is probably eighteen to twenty inches above mine, so he only received a few inches inside. And he was there fast, he started drying out and he managed to salvage a lot. And the water came in and dropped and then stayed for such a long time. The initial drop that came in greatly helped him. Didn't do anything for me, but it helped him a lot.

WM: Well, when you knew you were going to have to evacuate, was there anything it felt like you needed to save out of the house? Anything important?

RG: No, we're the type of family that likes outdoors events—camping, hiking, things of that nature—and we always have basic necessities at hand. We knew where we needed to go to get certain things. We grabbed the necessities and we told the children to get a toy, and that was all we worried about, you know—just get out.

WM: You didn't think about papers or photographs?

RG: No. In all honesty, I had heard the water was supposed to reach halfway to my window, and I believed it at that point. And it actually reached probably six or eight inches below the windows. Everything in the house could be replaced. That was my opinion. I did have flood insurance, so I wasn't all that concerned about personal effects. I knew there was going to be a lot that I would lose that I could not replace, but I didn't want to delay the inevitable.

WM: Can you tell me a little bit about your experience at the shelter?

RG: The shelter I went to wasn't pleasant at all. The people who were volunteering there—not all of them, don't get me wrong—but one bad apple can spoil the bunch and there were a few people there that acted as if they were doing you favors. They finally decided that they were going to feed everybody. It was in a school, so what they were going to do was to take the school supplies and feed the people who were there. One woman in front of me had a little boy and she said, "My son can't eat that, he's allergic to it." And the response was, "What do you think this is—Burger King? This is Emergency Services." And I said, "Lady, you don't need to act like this. If you don't want to do this, leave." And she looked at me with this look of surprise, you know, like either she didn't realize what she had said or she couldn't believe that somebody would say something like that to her.

There was an announcement that the county or city, I don't remember which, was under a state of emergency, so at seven o'clock they decided they were going to lock the doors. If you were in the building and you left, you would be cited. There was deputies there. You would be cited for leaving the building. If you were outside the building and they locked it, you weren't coming in, regardless. Which I thought was very wrong. I mean you have four hundred plus people in this gymnasium, locked in. Well, you know, that's asking for trouble in my opinion. That was asking for trouble. Luckily, I finally reached somebody and I was out of there about five minutes till seven. And the deputy told me on the way out the door, he said, "Get out as fast as you can because they've got me doing some stuff I don't understand." He said, "If you're not out of here by the time I lock these doors and you go out," he said, "I'm going to have to cite you." It didn't make sense to me.

WM: Where was this?

RG: It was the school just across from what used to be Burroughs Wellcome, Wellcome Middle I think it is. Some of my neighbors flew over in the same chopper that we did, and they were treated the same way.

WM: Who was administering it? Was that the Red Cross?

RG: Red Cross.

WM: One of the stories I heard said the local people were doing things and helping folks but the Red Cross had rules that they were supposed to follow that conflicted with what the local folks were doing.

RG: When they were going to lock it down, they didn't even have anything in there for people to sleep on. It was basically three hundred fifty, four hundred people in this gymnasium. It was warm. It wasn't extremely hot, but it was warm. It was good and toasty in there. And people were saying, "Well, can't we leave the doors open to get a breeze through here?" "No, we got to lock it up." The people who were outside with their dogs, they couldn't come inside because they weren't allowed to leave their dogs unattended, yet they weren't allowed to bring their dogs inside with them, regardless of the size of the animal. And they were going to be locked out and they were—from what I understood, I don't know if it ever occurred—they were supposed to be cited for being outside after 7. I'm saying 7, it might have been 8. But there was actually a curfew in effect and we were within the boundaries of that curfew. And the Red Cross hadn't brought anything in yet, but they did have one person there from the Red Cross that I guess was pretty much overseeing it and making sure everything was running fine. There was also some other Emergency Service people, there was supposedly a doctor or a nurse coming to see to anybody's needs. And there was supposed to be a social worker coming for people who needed to talk. You know, it was just that I was very stunned at the way we were treated there. Everybody there was there for a reason. They didn't choose to go there. I didn't know a single person there who chose to go. This shelter was opened as a last effort because the others that were opened originally were overloaded, so they needed extra places to put these people. Wellcome was the secondary one.

I finally got in touch with my step-dad and he actually drove through some pretty deep water to get to us. And we went and stayed over there for a few days. It was Tuesday before I could get back over to Belvoir.

My truck was parked here, and I got my truck. I drove it down to the corner and I drove it through water that came up to the door handle on the truck. I drive a Dodge Dakota. And from that point on, that truck was used, because I had just filled it up with gas prior to the storm. That's one of our preparations. I went over to Gum Swamp. I helped them transport food to Wellcome. I helped them move some food from the chopper to here, from here to there. I didn't do a whole lot of that. I helped out at Gum Swamp a little bit as far as helping people carry their groceries to their vehicles, various deeds around there. Where I did most of my help was actually in Edgecombe County. I knew a lot of people over there and a lot of them didn't have vehicles. A lot of people, you know, were still without power. And I went to different shelters over there, collected supplies and took them to them. That was how we dealt with it. You know, we could not sit still. When I say we, I'm referring to me and my wife. We could not sit still and just think about it. We had to keep busy, we had to keep doing something.

The help that everybody talks about that was right here—I saw it as far out as Speed, and from Speed all the way up through here. Everybody was helping everybody. I saw a great big helping hand. I remember seeing things on TV, you know, you see there's floods over here and you see people driving through in their trucks. I remember thinking to myself, "What are these fools doing? Why don't they get out of the truck, get a boat, you know, get somebody to help them?" And then I caught myself doing the exact same thing trying to help other people. You always hear, "Don't criticize somebody else till you've walked a mile in their shoes." Well this really put a lot of things into perspective. I was driving through water where somebody would come from the other way, and if I didn't have my window rolled up, the wake from their vehicle would roll over into my truck door. And I was surprised I didn't destroy my truck. The only thing that happened was I got some water in the transmission and I had to clean it out. I was lucky. They told me I needed to get a gray stripe and put the water line on the truck. Because it was door handle deep and the breather for the truck is at that very same level. You know, another inch or two and I probably would have filled it full of water.

WM: Now it's your turn. What's your story?

RICKY GRAY: My story? I didn't really lose anything personally. I lost financially because of work at Ready Mixed Concrete on Greene Street. We actually received nine feet of water there. And I'm responsible for all of that equipment—well, the whole facility. And one of my main concerns was that Thursday morning when we got up, I was blocked in. I couldn't go but maybe half a mile each way. Got a call from the church, Gum Swamp Church, saying that a tree had fell in the fellowship building. So I couldn't get there. And I couldn't go anywhere, not at that time. My first concern then was that I couldn't go toward the church, couldn't get to Greenville and try to see what I could do about work.

Friday morning, they had cleared out a way where I could get to Greenville. Well, police were blocking everything off. They had no consideration or understanding whatsoever, you know. I've got two million dollars worth of rolling equipment down there. If I can get in, I can move it. I can put it up to higher land. It might help. You know, none of this stuff is insured. We're all self-insured. But no, they don't believe in that whatsoever.

So what I did was parked a mile and a half away and walked down the railroad track to it. And called a couple of people to come down and help me start moving trucks. They walked from the other end on the railroad track, from the town end. I know the police are trying to protect lives, but then there is situations where you've got to go in and do things and so that's what we did.

We went in and where the trucks were setting, it was about up to the headlights. We couldn't get out in the street because it was deeper there, so we moved them up on the high side of our property. Put them on bricks. Actually parked some of them on the railroad track because water had never come over the railroad track before. So we put them there.

I went in the office and took the computers and put them up overhead. I took all the important papers and I put them up on top of the refrigerator in the break room, and put stuff up as high as I could. Put up everybody's telephone, trying to save every little thing I could. Which didn't do any good. The water got nine feet so it didn't actually do any good there. But then it was really the same situation when you could get back in.

Now, looking back, it seems the people that were able to get in quick—I mean just as soon as you were able if you had to put on boots to walk through the water and start doing things—were the ones that were able to get their stuff back in line quick. I mean they were able to get work done, get permits. If you waited any amount of time until everything hit the city of Greenville, you couldn't get anything done because everybody was flocking there for this permit and that permit. They didn't have it figured out yet. They didn't know what to do. So you had to be one of the early ones to get the permit. And that's what we did. We got permits. We got moved back in quickly where other businesses are not back in yet, you know, some of them. But we received a lot of damage. We had twenty-six pieces of equipment there. We lost ten of them, but we would have lost all of them if we hadn't gone in and moved stuff.

We actually had a tractor-trailer that was floating out. The fence was the only thing that kept it in. It was a tanker, so it was like a boat, just about. But it would float the tractor right on with it and it floated that out to the fence. I mean, I don't know where we would have found it. Really, it was that strong coming through there.

Like I said, Friday I was able to get there and then when I come back out somebody had cleared a way where we could get to the church, so I come down to the church and looked at the damage there. And I actually didn't come down to the Fire Department. They hadn't set pagers off yet. I really didn't realize, I guess, how bad it was on this side over here. And Saturday afternoon I come back down towards Belvoir this way, and that was when it was coming up around the Fire Department and it was time to move. So that's what we did and went to Gum Swamp Church.

And somehow we became a distribution center. Maybe it started out with bottled water, but then there were some calls made. People were actually hungry around here. They had no way of getting out, and what supplies they did bring out with them were becoming depleted. So somewhere around Tuesday or Wednesday we started getting supplies in, and we kept getting them in and getting them in, and I stayed there about eight days, you know, working well from sun up to sun down, I guess.

WM: Were you doing the same things that eight days or did you change your job daily?

RGRAY: No, I was basically doing the same thing. I was more or less in charge of outside, telling them, when a truck come up, where we were going to put this. What they needed inside, we'd keep it stocked. We had so much stuff we couldn't actually put it all on the inside, we had to start stacking stuff on the outside.

The way we worked it was we'd form a line outside and let them go in. We'd actually fix them a box of groceries. If we had children, we'd put that kind of items in. We didn't let people go in and grab what they wanted and come back out. We'd try to fix them a box. Had everything from peanut butter to toothpaste to diapers or whatever. You'd ask how many people were in their family and what their ages were, and you would just more or less put that stuff in there. Most of the time, try not to ask people, like, "You want Peter Pan peanut butter or Skippy?" You'd give them peanut butter.

WM: Did you have to deal with folks for whom English is a second language?

RGRAY: Yeah, and with no problem. They were just thankful to get something, you know. Anything that you would give them, they were thankful for, they really were. They more or less just followed the leader, you know. They'd follow the line of people going in and they'd get a box and they'd come back out.

WM: Was there any problem communicating?

RGRAY: No, not really, no. We had tried to have a sign-in sheet where each person would sign in, and that person might have had a little bit of trouble trying to get their names, but that was really about the only thing.

WM: Well, you said you worked from sun up to sun down?

RGRAY: It was a tiring job. I mean it was a whole lot harder than you'd normally work. It really was. I mean that would be Saturday and Sunday, right on through, you know. You were back each day. And you'd see the same people each day, you know, the same people would come back and get supplies. They would need to, you know, because of having to live each day. And then we started seeing an influx of people that you'd never seen before, that you knew weren't even from this area. The roads had opened up and they found out, I think, that Belvoir had supplies. Like I say, they were hitting every spot and the car would be full of groceries.

WM: Tell me a little bit about the good you saw.

RGRAY: Well, people actually helping one another. People coming up that were getting supplies would pitch in, help unload a truck, carry stuff out for people. And then others that would come up acted like, you know, this is a grocery store and you're going to take it out for me. You're going to carry it out to my car. That's not my brand of cereal. They would actually complain about some things. And you'd take it out to the car for them and the car was so full at that time you couldn't hardly get it in there for them. They'd been around to every center there was. You know, that kind of deal. Got me a little disgusted with it at the end. In the beginning it was good for four or five days, and then the last four or five days it was being taken advantage of. It really was.

WM: Some people were milking it for all it was worth? Those were the folks that wanted stuff rather than folks that needed stuff?

RGRAY: Yes, they really were. There was a lot of them that were.

RG: I saw that in other counties too.

RGRAY: And that put a bad taste in my mouth. I know we did a good thing out at Gum Swamp Church and I'm glad we did it and we'd do it again. It's just some things like that leave me with memories about the flood that I don't really like to remember. We had stuff actually taken from here in the Fire Department, you know. It was not a lot of it, but it was going on and you couldn't stop it. You couldn't turn people away. Just things like that.

But other than that, the community itself, it did pull the community together, and it still is together. We really kind of dreaded our farm sale this year. We have a farm sale each year that supports our Fire Department. It's the only way we actually make money. It's an auction. It's where people can bring equipment in here to the Fire Department, and we hire auctioneers and we auction it off. It's a big fundraiser for us. I mean we can clear anywhere from ten to twenty thousand dollars, you know, for that one day. We get a commission. We really thought that it might be a small turnout because of the flood, that people were burnt out from helping, you know, and they wouldn't come down and help this year. But it was probably one of the better sales we've ever had.

WM: Well, did you end up suffering from burnout?

RGRAY: No, not really. I mean I was glad when it was over with. I was ready for it to be shut down, I really was. And we just made a decision that such and such a date we were going to shut it down. I can't even remember what day it was now. We kept it open a good ten days, I believe.

WM: When you say you made the decision, was that the Forest Service or the church people?

RGRAY: Church people. I saw a lot of people that did a lot of good. And we had no problems with everybody working there. I mean everybody did a good job. And I might be a little negative about things, sometimes, but I saw it bring out a lot of good in people. But I saw it bring out a lot of bad in people too.

It was hard

Interviews with William Mansfield
William Mansfield with Sheila King and Mary King

Sheila King and her ten-year-old daughter, Mary, live on Floyd Harris Road in Belvoir.

WILLIAM MANSFIELD: Can you tell me about your experience with the flood and the aftermath? When the storm was coming, what kind of preparations did you make?

SHEILA KING: Well, we were listening to the radio, and they said that the hurricane was coming. And as I was living in a doublewide, and mobile homes just don't seem that safe. I packed my kids' clothes, me and my husband's, grandkid's clothes, and stuff. Things that I thought we could just get by with for at least a few nights. I had no idea that it was going to last like it did. The night the water rose, I had some dogs out in the back yard in a pen and they were just barking and carrying on, and we went out there. It was dark, and I had my van in the back yard where my dog pen was, and the horn was blowing and the lights was on. We couldn't figure out what was going on because it was dark and we couldn't see. So I went back in the house and I got my husband. He went to step off the porch, and he stepped off in water.

WM: That must have been something, stepping off the porch and finding out you're knee deep in water.

SK: We were actually scared to cut on the lights on the back porch, but we cut them on and it was really shocking to see that much water in my back yard. I was just scared it would short circuit because I'm scared to death of electricity. By that time the water had gotten up into my van. It wasn't drivable because we had to take the battery cables off to shut the horns and the lights off and everything.

WM: The water rising made the lights come on and the horns start flashing?

SK: Yes, sir. That's the only thing we could give an account for it because it was all the way up to the dashboard of my van. We pushed the minivan out so it wouldn't keep rising in there. And that was a job, trying to push that van through that water and it was already full of water. We pushed it out into the front where it wasn't so much water. Well, we got through the early morning and my husband left to see if he could find any type of drinks or anything because we knew with all this much water coming around that probably the lights were going to go out. And while he was out, I think Doug, the assistant fire chief, he got David and asked him would he help get people out of their houses. I think they were on River Road, where it hit the deepest, and up towards the Tarboro area.

He called home and I asked him what should we do? I had my two kids and my grandbaby there at the house, and two expecting women there. And he told us to get a place out there in the back yard and look to see if the water was rising. When the water got rising to a certain place, I called the Fire Department and let him know. So he come and he got us out. And so we come down here and stayed down here at the Fire Department. I didn't know where my kids were going to eat. And I think a lot of people was facing that, too. My grandbaby at the time wasn't but nine months old or so. And my two girls, they were little. And it's a hard thing to face when you don't know when or where you're going to feed your kids or when they're going to get the next meal. Or where they're going to stay.

WM: That must have been pretty scary?

SK: It was very hard. After we stayed here at the firehouse we went to the shelter at the schools. Well, I'm a heart patient and I have high blood pressure too. And the National Guard told me with my situation and with the children that I would be better off to go to one of the schools. That way if anything happened to me, they could get a helicopter in to carry me to the hospital if I needed to go. So we went to North Pitt first, and the water got to rising over there, and then they said that they were going to have to cut the water off because they didn't know if it was contaminated. And so we went from North Pitt to Bethel Elementary School. And that was a trip. Because we all had to get back on the truck and go over there and had a certain time over there that you had to be in, and a certain time that you could go outside. And you had to sign in and sign out. I guess it was just to make sure that the ones that signed in was being looked after and everything.

WM: Well, how when you got there, did you pitch in to help or were your hands full looking after your kids?

SK: Well, we really didn't have to do much over there at the schools because by the time we got there Red Cross was there and they pretty much had everything under control. But if they needed volunteers, I volunteered and my husband volunteered. My sons, they helped unload helicopters and big trucks and we just done whatever we could help to do.

WM: How long were you in the shelter before you went back home?

MARY KING: [*Sheila's daughter*] It was a long time.

WM: A long time. I bet so.

MK: Boring.

WM: What was it like staying in the shelter for that length of time?

SK: Well, you never get used to it because you have a certain time that you have to eat, and you have your breakfast, then you have your lunch, and you have your supper. Sometimes the little kids, they would get snacks and sometimes wouldn't. It all depended on what they had because there was a lot of people in them shelters. The day that we got to North Pitt, I think there was something like 500 people already there. And later on that evening they told us that 200 more was going to come. And everybody was wondering where they were going to put them, because we already had the hall floors covered. They weren't opening up the school classrooms. It was something that I don't ever want to experience again.

   If you had a family and you could get one corner, you stayed pretty much to your corner. You kept your corner cleaned. At first they were letting people bring their food back to wherever they were staying. And then people didn't want to clean up behind themselves and drinks were getting poured all over the floor. So they just decided to have us eat in the dining area.

WM: Seems like it would be a huge campout for three weeks with no real privacy.

SK: Well, there wasn't any privacy at all. When you took a shower, you took cold showers. And that was really cold. That water was like ice.

MK: And it was really, really cold.

SK: It seemed like there was no air conditioning at all. I guess it was because there was a lot of people there. And you had to have some means of taking a bath and stuff, so you just went in and gritted your teeth and took it as fast as you could.

WM: The people in the shelter, were any of them your neighbors or folks that you knew or were they all strangers?

SK: A lot of them were. We had a lot of people that we knew, not just from the Belvoir area but from all around that had got flooded out. It made it a little bit easier because you had someone to talk to. And you made new friends there. A lot of people too was there that wasn't flooded but they had to leave their homes because they didn't know if they were going to flood and they didn't want to take that chance.

WM: Well, was there some way you worked to get along with the people? Did you find yourself, you know, biting your tongue?

SK: At times you did because some people had kids and they didn't want to look after their kids and they were just running all over. And there was a lot of elderly people there that had a lot of handicaps, and the kids would just run into them and about knock them down. And you're not supposed to say anything to somebody else's kid, and it's just hard, you know, to see how kids act, and later on the grown people too.

WM: Could you describe a typical day?

SK: They would call over the intercom, what little bit of intercom that they had, and they would tell you that breakfast was being served from six o'clock to eight o'clock and that you had to be there in between that time to get breakfast. And it was really hard on some of the kids because there was a lot of little kids there. And from six to eight a lot of kids sleep in, and you had to wake your kids up to make sure that they got breakfast and everything. And then they would call about 12, 12:30 for lunch. They had spaghetti and chicken and pizza and they pretty much looked out for the little kids with what I would call finger foods—pop tarts and things like that kids would eat. And we had a hot meal each day, at least one hot meal. And if we had the hot meal for lunch and if it wasn't all eaten at that time, we would have it that night for supper with something else to go with it.

They had what they called a clothes house. And you could go down there and help sort out clothes. And if you knew anybody that needed anything who wasn't able to come to the clothes house to get things, then we could look for their size and get them clothes. Because a lot of people that was handicapped couldn't get to the clothes house. Some of us volunteered to clean up and to pick up the trash that was in the hallways and sweep up a little bit what we could. Because you didn't want to go in somebody's little area and move their stuff, so we just swept around it. And we tried to keep it as sanitary as we could with that many people.

About nine o'clock was lights out. It wasn't really dark, but they asked you to keep your kids to your section unless they were accompanied by an adult. Just trying to keep a lot of the hostility down. At times it was a little bit hostile in there because when you got that many people rooming together, this one's getting on this one's nerves, and this one's getting on that one's nerves. Your nerves was all upset and you didn't know what to expect. And you just didn't know what to do. And of course probably some of us let off steam at others that we shouldn't have. And there was a lot of little babies there that were crying. They provided a lot of baby foods and milk for little ones, but sometimes it wasn't the milk that they were used to and it took a toll on the little ones.

WM: I'm interested in how you managed to hold on.

SK: It was hard to hold on. Sometimes we would break down. We just had to make the best out of a bad situation. And Red Cross, they were doing everything that they could to try to help the people, and the medical teams tried to help a lot of people that didn't have their medications with them or they ran out while they were in the shelters.

WM: Well, did they keep a special eye on you?

SK: Yes. While I was there, my blood pressure went sky high. It was about 300. And they told me that if I didn't get my blood pressure down I could have a heart attack or a stroke, and it's really hard to try to stay calm in a situation like that.

WM: What did you do to try to stay calm?

SK: Well, we went outside with the kids and we played with the kids. And we volunteered to do different things. If they needed help, we tried to help with that. And we just tried to stay as busy as we could so we wouldn't have to sit there and just think about it.

WM: Do you think it made it easier pitching in to help?

SK: Yeah, because it took your mind off of it, some. Because you just weren't sitting there thinking about, "Well, am I going to even have a house to go back to?" So it helped to stay busy.

WM: Well, you were pretty glad when it was time to go home.

SK: Yes, sir, I was, because I told my husband, I said, "Well," I said, "if I can find a loaf of bread or a pack of sandwich meat," I said, "I'm carrying my kids home." I said, "They can survive off of that and a bag of ice for a while." We came home and we didn't have any lights, and we used candles and we made the best of a bad situation. It was nice to come home and sleep in your bed and not on a hard floor, because the only thing you had was a little thin blanket and a hard floor. And it was really hard to lay on that floor.

WM: How do you think this has changed you?

SK: Where we would take little things for granted, I don't take them for granted no more. I guess you have all these fancy things—fancy furniture, fancy clothes, and things like that. You don't need them, just the necessities.

I keep pretty much to myself, but I think I'm a little bit more open than before. I talk to strangers more now. I guess it's just the way that I was brought up. My parents told me you never talk to strangers and that's what I always did. Now I'll say, "Hey," to people I don't even know.

My house was standing and it had been flooded but we had survived. We stayed there until we could get us another place to move to. And around the Belvoir area, people was really scared about buying land and stuff because just about everywhere in Belvoir had been flooded. When we finally found us a piece of land, everybody was asking us, "Well, why are you going to stay in Belvoir?" I said, "Well, because my kids go to Belvoir School."

134

I'm thankful for the people that volunteered to help out when other people wouldn't. The community fed my kids and they made sure that we were looked after. I knew there was a lot of people that wasn't flooded that could have helped, that didn't help. And a lot of people that was flooded that didn't have anything, helped out as much as they could. I met a lot of good people down here that I didn't know was in Belvoir.

WM: Well, how long do you think it will be before you get over it?

SK: I don't know because I have not got over it. Sometimes I think about it and I break down and I go to crying. A lot of my close friends, they have lost everything and they're having to start over and it's really hard because you don't have a lot of money and you can't help out. After the flood went away my kids would see water in the ditches and they would ask me, "Mama, are we going to get flooded again?" And it's really hard to explain to them because we didn't lose everything that we had. And my oldest little girl, she really took it hard. When it would rain outside, she'd be petrified. She's beginning to get over it. Or we could go across the river bridge, and we would just hold onto each other. There was more water than we have ever experienced.

I took it personally

Bruce and Wendy Brady, who live on Porter Road in Belvoir, "one hill away from the flood," are originally from Tarboro. Phyllis Adams also attended this session with William Mansfield at the Belvoir Volunteer Fire Department.

BRUCE BRADY: It happened so fast. By the time we realized it was going on, it was just about too late. You wake up after the storm and the water was everywhere, and then it was gone the next day, and then you look back out your window and you see water coming back up again.

WILLIAM MANSFIELD: Were you listening to the news about the storm coming on the radio or TV?

BB: Well, the hurricane, yeah, but we stayed at her mother's Wednesday night, the night of the hurricane. We stay in a doublewide and they was talking about how bad it was going to be, and her mother's old house was pretty old so we figured it had stood some storms before.

WENDY BRADY: The next morning we went to check our house and make sure everything was intact.

BB: Water was pretty much everywhere then, not like it was when the water backed up, but just in isolated areas the roads were flooded and stuff. But I think it was the next day it started backing right back up, or the day after.

WB: To my knowledge, there wasn't any forewarning of the water. I'd had a phone call from my brother in Tarboro who said it was headed our way. He said that it was bad in Tarboro but I didn't realize it. I thought it was exaggeration. We went and helped a friend of ours get her horses and her dogs and cats out, and that was bad. I mean, it was up about to my waist walking through the water, and I thought that was horrible. But as far as seeing water at the rooftops and stuff like that, I would never have imagined anything like that.

BB: Later that week the water started backing across my driveway and up beside the house. It was the last night the river was supposed to crest. That was the night we were really concerned because they kept saying it was going to crest that Monday and it didn't. It went on another week before it did crest. I had a tractor at my house and a big trailer, so if anything really got desperate, I was going to load the wife and the kids up and leave on the tractor and the peanut truck. And if it got too deep on that, I'd have turned around and come back and got the bossman's combine.

WM: So you had a plan to get out of here?

BB: I had a plan to get out. As long as it didn't get fifteen, twenty foot deep on the highway, I was going somewhere.

WM: What brought you down to the firehouse?

BB: Well, I just know everybody, just something we took on our own. We had somewhere to lay our heads, but a lot of folks didn't. The first two or three days we were down here, everybody was going out and rescuing. We just hung around helping out the folks that came in and stuff like that. And the military was getting some folks out, and we were making sure everybody got loaded up on trucks. And then everybody had to move out of here to Gum Swamp Church because the water was coming on up and we still didn't know how high it was going to rise.

WM: What were some of the things that you did?

BB: One night I cooked down here on the grill for a lot of them, for most of the Sheriff's Department that was going out on the boats and stuff.

WB: Bruce told me that there was a lot of rescuers still working and nobody had had any dinner. And I knew that there was still a lot of pork chops here and stuff, so I came back that Friday night and we cooked on the grill to feed them.

BB: There was a bunch of stuff that Billy had across the street that was going to go to the bad, so we went ahead and put it on the grill and cooked it before it all spoiled. Anybody that wanted to eat, just eat. And then the next day we wound up having to move everything up to Gum Swamp. And then by that time I think they started bringing in some food because there wasn't no more cooking going on. We moved everything up there but we didn't cook anything up there at the church.

WB: When they went to the church, I more or less just tagged along with them and just stuck it out. And then when we come back here, I stuck it out until they got ready to close up.

WM: What role did you play down at Gum Swamp Church?

BB: We unloaded trucks and unloaded the boxes. I just more or less brought it in off the trucks and then stacked it in different places, you know, same variety of everything would be set up like a grocery store. And then when people came in, they'd give it out. And then toting their stuff to the car. Stuff like that.

WB: I come down here every morning about seven thirty, I guess, and left about seven thirty at night. I did more or less whatever anybody needed. If somebody come in and just wanted to talk, I listened. We packed up supplies and handed out supplies and tried to give out whatever we had to give out, tried to do it so somebody could get what they needed. Of course, there was a lot of greed involved, but you couldn't control that.

WM: Tell me a little bit more about that, if you don't mind. I'm just curious to know, because you saw it and I didn't.

WB: But that's just a few bad people out of a bunch of good, you know. You had people that would come back and felt that they needed this and they needed so much of that. And a lot of times you knew that that person was sitting over there in a dry place, but at the same time maybe they *do* need it, you know, and it's just in a different form.

WM: What surprised you the most about the flood—how things were done? How people reacted? Did they disappoint you? Did they meet your expectations?

BB: Well, a lot of folks disappointed me, but I'm not calling names, and a lot of folks done more than they should have. You had a lot of folks that didn't get flooded, and all they was doing was worrying about whether they could cut the grass the next day and stuff. And there was a lot of folks that could have got out and helped some, that didn't do it. I don't reckon they felt like they were obligated, but they would have wanted the help if they were in the situation that all the other people were in. I mean I didn't have to do nothing I done, I just done it because I wanted to do it.

WB: Most of the people that was doing all the volunteer work were flooded themselves. And he felt like they were the ones that needed assistance and they needed some relief. They wanted to see what was going on at their houses. But they were busy trying to rescue other people and worrying about where other people were going to stay, and they didn't have anywhere to stay themselves. About the whole Volunteer Fire Department was flooded. And they were worried about the other person. I think that's more or less what he's trying to express, is that he has a problem with the fact that a lot of people that weren't flooded, more of them didn't come out and volunteer their time and service. And it wasn't like you had to do it, but it's what he thought anybody *would* have done, you know, that it's just human kindness. You would do it regardless. And would hope that if you were in that situation somebody would help you. Is that what you're trying to say, honey?

BB: Yeah, pretty close.

WM: Tell me about the best thing that you saw, an instance of someone being really good and decent.

WB: It was the group from Hillsborough, or Cedar Grove, North Carolina. That group come in and they set up the kitchen, and to me they took control. Phyllis and Doug and all of them had control of the situation during the flood when the waters were rising. They knew what to do as far as go in and help get people out and help get animals out—it didn't matter what, you know. Phyllis went several times to a gentleman's house that did not want to leave, but she tried her best to get him to come, but of course he didn't come. But to me when Cedar Grove pulled in and they set up their kitchen out back, right away they just more or less took control as far as fixing the food and then people knew they were going to be fed, you know, there was going to be meals there. At that time the Salvation Army or the Red Cross hadn't come in yet. Belvoir was almost forgotten for a while. I think Phyllis was important too in getting the news out that Belvoir needed some help, for some of the people that needed medicine or needed medical supplies. Phyllis worked day and night—and she was flooded, terribly flooded—but yet she worked day and night to make sure that she could help everybody that she could. And at the same time her mom was flooded, her brother was flooded, you know, just everybody. But they didn't stop, they just stayed here.

WM: Can you tell me a little bit about the bad stuff? I don't want to get up any dirt on anybody, but you know we need to get the whole story.

WB: The way I saw things—I don't know that this is all fact, either, and this is later on—was that a lot of people that got help or was the fastest to receive help, were people that didn't justifiably need it. That's the way I saw it. Yes, they were affected by the flood because all of us were. I was, and I didn't get flooded. But at the same I saw a lot of greed. A lot of greed in our own community, in other communities, and everywhere you went—there was just this tremendous amount of greed from people. I don't know if it's because they experienced a week when they didn't know whether they were going to have food to eat or they couldn't get to a grocery store if supplies were running low. I don't know what made them act that way or respond the way they did.

We had people come in that did not need supplies who would stand in line and wait their turn to get their supplies. And if you were on the low end, and if you made a comment about it, they thought they were justified to get the same amount as everyone else. And in all reality, I guess they were. But I myself could not see me standing here in line trying to get something when I could make do with what I had at home because I had a home.

There was people that received a lot of stuff that they shouldn't have received during the process. And I was probably responsible for some of it, because I was right in the middle of it the whole time. But there was a fine line there, I guess, to determine who did need and who didn't need and for what reason they needed and for what reason they didn't need. The way I saw it, if you lost everything in your home, you needed anything that was offered out there. If you did not lose your home, then you should have took your time to help the people that did lose their home or stay out of it. I mean, that's the way I saw it. So, as far as the way that FEMA or anything like that worked, I don't know.

WM: Folks here last week said that this thing brought out the best in people and it also brought out the worst in people.

WB: And it did. It did. And it showed me—as far as in this community—it showed me the people that if I was in trouble, who I would want on my side. And it's sad to say that most of the people that before this happened I would have wanted on my side, I wouldn't want now on my side. The ones I least expected it from are the ones that helped. I took it personally and should not have. I mean I saw the bad side of people I did not want to see. And hope I never have to see it again.

WM: Well, do you feel like you saw more bad, or more good, or about an even mix of the two?

WB: I wouldn't say there was more bad. I saw so much good in so many people, but it was the same people. I mean, it wasn't like every day there was this new goodness coming in. I saw it differently than the ones that were flooded, of course. I don't know how to explain it except that I found out a lot about people I would not have wanted to know and was very disappointed in a lot of people. And that's the way it affected me. I don't regret what I done. I'd do it again tomorrow. I mean, as far as that, I don't regret any of that. And I'd do it for the ones that disappointed me, too. Because it might be me next time. Pray there's not a next time, but it could be me.

WM: Do you feel like this event has changed you?

WB: I was probably known as a snob or something. I didn't get out in the community, and I wasn't very friendly with a lot of people. I stayed home, I took care of my kids, my house. And that was it, you know, more or less. This brought me out in the community more. Now I put my nose into everything. But no, I don't think it changed me a whole lot, not as far as the person that I was. It brought me out in the community more. It made me faster to voice my opinion. Now I'll tell you more or less what I think, if I know you and you ask me, I'll go ahead and tell you up front. But other than that, I don't think so, no. But that's enough.

WM: Do you think you're a better person after this?

WB: I think I'm the same person I was before. I wouldn't say I was a better person because I feel like I was a good person anyway. And I don't feel like I done anything special for anybody. I don't think anything I done was anything that I need praise for. I don't see that any of it was special. I think it should have been expected.

PHYLLIS ADAMS: Excuse me. I have to interrupt here, please. She is being very modest here. I guess that's the way we do ourselves when we're talking about ourselves. But, you know, you keep talking about the flood and things that kind of happened around the flood. She's not telling you what she did after the flood for months and months. So she needs to elaborate a little bit more because she was a special person in our community.

WM: What did you do after the flood?

WB: Well, when Cedar Grove come in they set up a wish book, more or less, under the tent. We called it the "Feed Tent." And they set up a wish book and everybody that went back to get a meal had the opportunity to write down on this list what they needed or what they thought they were going to need and so forth. And when they went back to Cedar Grove they raised a lot of funds for just this community, not to go outside this community. And they kept coming back and doing volunteer work, helping on some homes and stuff like that. And they didn't know how to distribute the funds. And I sure didn't know. But we come up with helping get some supplies. So they opened an account at Lowe's in Greenville and each family that they felt needed it, they gave them four hundred dollars for supplies the first time. And I helped out on some of that. After that money was more or less liquidated, then they come back and done some gift certificates. And there weren't a whole lot of those gift certificates but the ones that had children got a Wal-Mart gift certificate. And that was through Cedar Grove. I distributed those out. And then the ones that didn't have young children, if they needed Lowe's or Wal-Mart, we gave them another small gift certificate. That was all money raised from Cedar Grove. I just helped to pass the certificates out.

WM: Does that mean you just sort of took the applications, or did you help make some decision about where the funds went?

WB: I helped make a lot of decisions about where they went. Most of them I'm happy with. Some of them I'm not. I went through the list that they had kept in the tent, the wish list. A lot of the people you could see were flooded and really did need something. It had to be in the community and we wanted it to be people that was literally flooded. And I went down this list and put some people on the top, you know, and came on down until the funds run out. I'll be honest with you, the people that went on top were the people I saw directly. I mean it wasn't friends or family, or anything like that, it was people I saw that was working here in this flood, that was helping the other people that were flooded. They were the ones that went on the top of the list when I made it. I mean they were the ones that had the least on the wish list, and some of them didn't even fill out the wish list. They had lost everything. I mean, no clothes, no home to go to, just everything. Phyllis didn't even have a brush, didn't have a hair dryer.

PA: And no makeup!

WB: Yes, and no makeup. So because I was directly around those, they were the ones that went on first. There wasn't any application to fill out. We'd had a couple of, like, committee meetings, and I guess you were more fortunate if you had came to the meeting and if you were one of the first ones to get on the list. I mean, until it run out. I think though there was probably fifty families that was helped one way or the other—at least fifty, probably greater than that—that was helped one way or the other through the gift certificates or the purchase of supplies at Lowe's. I done a lot of riding to see the houses for myself, but there was a lot of people on that list I did not know, had never laid eyes on before the flood. Not that I didn't trust any of them, but, you know, I did a lot of riding. Bruce was with me on several occasions. We'd go to the house and speak to them and see what was going on, and just generally look to see whether they looked like they were getting a lot of help or not. And so, that's more or less how it was determined. It might not have been the right way, but that's the way it was done. So, that was probably the biggest part I done after the flood.

PA: And the furniture and the shoes and clothes.

WB: Well, that was other stuff that had been donated, and Hillsborough helped bring a lot of that in. And also a group out of Pulaski, Virginia, had brought in a lot of appliances and furniture, and sheets, towels, linens. And we went probably through a month or two months with that group, and they would just keep sending. The Fire Department was kind enough to let me store a lot of it right here. Then we stored right much of it over there in the tire shop, and then when I got time we'd just go through it and try to see that whoever still needed the stuff, got it.

WM: So you helped distribute the relief supplies and because you knew the community, you were more aware of who needed what.

WB: It wasn't really because I knew the community. I didn't know my own community even though I'd lived here about eleven years. I didn't know it that much until the flood came. That gave me the opportunity. I knew there was good people here and I'd talk to them, but as far as really knowing the community itself, I didn't know it until the flood come. I guess that's why I was so disappointed too, in the way some of the other people were in the community.

WM: How do you feel about your knowledge of the community now?

WB: I love everybody here and would be glad to help them in any way I can. But I have a better perspective on who I can depend on, if I get in a bad situation. So, it taught me a lot.

WM: When you said that you have some regrets about some of the decisions you made, what kind of regrets?

WB: I think as far as giving people enough, no, they didn't get enough. But I think most of them fairly got what I had to give them or what was offered to give them that I had control over. There was probably a few that I think got unfairly, which I gave to them. It wasn't all my decision. Cedar Grove knew who got what. They made quite a bit of the decisions that I was unhappy with, and I actually distributed out. But everybody had their own story and their own reason, and everybody had their own effects, you know, from the flood, and they felt they deserved their share. And rightfully, they probably did. But there was just a few that I was uncomfortable with. But then again, like I said, that was just my personal opinion.

I do want to say one more thing if I could. I know that Phyllis Adams has thanked them, but the North Carolina Forestry Service was not mentioned tonight and I just want to make sure that they are. Because without them I don't know what any of us would have done. And Tom Harris and all of them were wonderful. We would have all been lost without them and the Belvoir Volunteer Fire Department.

These people have very interesting stories to tell

Allen Smith
Belvoir Writing Workshops

THESE PEOPLE HERE HAVE VERY INTERESTING STORIES TO TELL. THEIR FIRST-HAND accounts of what happened are really emotional and touching, I almost feel like my experience is inferior to anything they went through. I was truly fortunate. We all were in many respects. I didn't realize how bad it got over here. It must have been a sight. I became emotional myself tonight when I started talking about my granddaddy. It was a very trying time, but like the others said it brought us closer together as a community. Maybe that is what we all needed. I have always thought that God has a plan for everything that takes place. Maybe He knew that the community would pull together because of this tragedy.

The most emotional experience for me was to see the train that I once played on toppled over on its side. It really made me think about how bad it really got. However, there is always a peace after the storm, so to speak. I am more at peace with myself now than I have ever been. My granny complains a lot, but it really didn't bother me that much those two weeks. I thought it was funny how she complained about losing her car. It wasn't funny that she lost her car, it was funny because all she used her car for was to get the paper out of the mailbox. I have so much to say, it is all beginning to come together. I thought it was funny how my mom over-reacted. She called us every day panicking about everything. She really panicked when me and my granddaddy tried to get out. We didn't get very far. We got stopped right at 264. We saw an Army truck flood out.

I still keep thinking about that caboose. It really made a lasting impression on me. I just remember how I used to play on that thing all the time. Everybody thought you were so cool if you could climb to the top. It was just so sad to see it toppled over. I went by there a few weeks ago, and it wasn't there. It is extremely sad to think that children in the future will not be able to enjoy that little red train like I did. That was the main feature of the Elm Street Park in Greenville. I always thought about bringing my children to play there. I would probably be like my mom too. "You are getting too high up there!" "Stop throwing rocks!" "You are going to fall and break your neck." "Do you want a spanking?" "Stop hitting your brother." "Allen, what did I tell you?" It seems like that was yesterday.

Elm Street Park Caboose #1.

Photo courtesy of City of Greenville.

I loved Belvoir the moment I saw it

Sharon Abuarab (now Sharon O'Neill)
Belvoir Writing Workshops

MY FAMILY LIVES ON HWY. 222 NEAR BELVOIR CROSSROADS, ALMOST TWO MILES from the Tar River, and we've lived there since 1995. We spent two weeks following the flood at my mother's house in Greenville. She had left a key for me to check on her house while she was in Massachusetts for a week and we decided to go to her house to get hot showers, hot food, and to check the news. After we had been there for a few hours, the electricity in town went out also and the roads back to our house had already been closed, so we were stranded. Unfortunately, she left no perishable food in the fridge and very little in her freezer or pantry. We drove around town, looking for Red Cross distribution stations, which, it seemed, were constantly moving. We applied for emergency food stamps and FEMA relief because, in the end, we didn't know what, if anything, would be left of our house.

The thing I remember most was the tension and the anger of people around me. Not the people I lived with because for the most part we had to be there, together. The people I remember most were the ones in lines, the endless lines that snaked everywhere, the crowds that would grow and press together whenever something was offered for free. Some people were deliberately overfriendly with each other, not in a false way but a more nervous, "I'm-so-glad-to-be-alive-and-if-I-don't-laugh-I'll-cry" kind of way. Their desperate, hollow, too-loud voices could turn to shouts easily if the line stopped moving—and it always did.

Waiting in line for emergency food stamps seemed endless. We started early and it got hot early. The closeness of the others was oppressive, breathtakingly so. I could feel the heat of the people around me as the crowd swelled, standing in the bright sun, waiting like cattle to be prodded, moved along, only to be told, in the end, to just go home, come back tomorrow. Not exactly a slaughter, but an emotional dagger each time. Come back tomorrow, do it again and again. A week spent trying to get food? How are we supposed to live like this? I was running out of gas, couldn't get any money and by the time we got through that line and they sent us home, everything, even the Red Cross, was closed. My kids.

Just tell me you understand that we are angry? Does anyone understand? Yes, I'm thankful, grateful for the help, but dammit, I was angry and I'm not even sure why. And what could I do about it but swallow it, swallow my pride over and over, asking for help when I wouldn't normally dream of it. Embarrassed for accepting free water. WATER? Yes, I was embarrassed that the people handing it out would pity me. It's hard putting aside your pride.

I hate putting people out. I hated being in my mom's one-bedroom duplex with three adults and two kids with nothing to do but watch the same clips on TV and try to keep my mom and Mohamed from fighting. I guess a lot of the anger I felt then is still in me, but it's not so intense. Maybe it rubbed off onto me while I was standing in line, waiting for food stamps, waiting for tetanus shots, waiting for toilet paper, waiting for my life to get back to normal—like I was a receptacle of all this surrounding undercurrent of rage.

I used to be patient but I don't wait well now. I feel so anxious for everything now. Now. I want to get back to myself now. And I want to stop being angry now.

I really hated those lines, can ya tell? I hated standing all day only to be turned away empty handed, tears stinging my eyes, my face afire with shame. After being away from home for two weeks, I found my stuff ended up being OK and I was left with boxes of guilt in the form of canned beans, cocktail wieners and stale white bread that I couldn't bring myself to eat. I turned around and gave most of it away, and I would give everything I have away, every thing, not to have had to go through this, for my community not to have had to go through this.

My community. I had never really been a part of a community before. Well, growing up, I had "the neighborhood" but when we were still in Massachusetts

Highway 33 under water.

Photo courtesy of Phyllis Adams.

when the kids were born, we lived in a city with no sense of community. It was cold, impersonal, big. I wanted so much to belong to a community when I moved here.

I loved Belvoir the moment I saw it. I felt a sense of something I had been missing. We came in '95 and I found I had a home to make and a community to join, but I never quite felt welcome. Not sure why, I just didn't. Maybe it's because I don't go to church, that really does determine your community. Five years and I am still alone out here. The flood could have changed that but when we left to go to my mother's I was cut off from the community even more. I could not help, I could not reach out, I was not a part of them. I didn't even know what was happening to my home. I was totally cut off from the community I longed to fit into, but probably never will, just as they were totally cut off from the outside world.

For a while we were together

Pat James
Belvoir Writing Workshops

Pat James is married to Eugene James, Pitt County Commissioner for Belvoir.

MONDAY NIGHT. I WAS REALLY TIRED. I HAD BEEN AT THE GUM SWAMP
fellowship hall over twenty-four hours. Most of the firemen and sheriffs were
talking quietly or had gone to sleep. Gene and I took a Sunday School room to
sleep in. I had gotten to bed on the floor and after a bit I had just about fallen
asleep. I heard a loud noise, men talking, laughing. It seemed they were having
a really good time. I understood how men tell stories when they are together
and I was glad if they could have fun. But then I detected what I thought was a
woman's voice. Could there be women there? Why were they there? Had the men
brought in women? I finally decided since I represented the Gum Swamp Church
I should investigate.

When I went in I found several drenched men and women. I failed to mention
it had been raining very hard.

The newcomers were a group of people called Animal Rescue. They were cold,
wet, and hungry. I quickly got the coffee making and we still had food on the table
that had been brought earlier. They were so appreciative. After they were fed, we
began looking for some dry clothes for them. We had some bags of clothes that
had been left for flood victims. Luckily most of the clothes were a big size. Men
and women got dry clothes and changed. Men looked funny in women's pants
and shirts. Women had clothes on mismatched and too big. But they were dry. As
they drank coffee and warmed up, I found they were from several places in the US.
One lady was from California, a man from West Virginia, a lady from Black Jack
in Pitt County, a man from Chapel Hill, a man from Morehead City, a man who
lived on my road four houses away but whom I had never seen until then. I don't
remember where the others came from.

They had been out that night rescuing animals when the rain had caused them
to abandon the mission. They had left their boats and were under the corn house
shelter when our firemen had found them and brought them to the fellowship
hall. They were so thankful to find food, shelter and warmth.

The people of the Belvoir community have always been pretty much divided
by what church they attended. Blacks were isolated from whites, and each group
was then divided by what church they attended. Then all those people who attend
Belvoir School or Wellcome or North Pitt are in a group. Then there are those
who attend private school. This causes another division in the community.

All these groups were united in the Fire Department. Except there are no blacks in the Fire Department at the present time even though there have been some. They moved away. When the flood came to their homes, people moved to the Fire Department. When the water came into the Fire Department, they moved to Gum Swamp Church fellowship hall. Everyone that was keeping check on the community, on homes that had been left empty, was staying at Gum Swamp.

For a while we were together, the flood victims. As more neighbors began to hear of the food and supplies, they came to get some. Then they started coming back to offer help. Some people came and worked all day. There was a very cooperative spirit as men, women, and children worked together.

After the bridges and roads were opened, the distribution center closed. The majority of the Belvoir area people had so much to do with the clean-up that there was little time to help others. Again the community reverted back to the church groups helping others in their church to recover from the flood.

Section III: SOMEONE TO TELL THE STORY

Flooded mobile home park.

Photo courtesy of Ana Cowó.

As long as there's no one to tell the story it never happened: The Hispanic community and the Floyd flood

Ana Cowó
Assistant Editor and AFTUR Committee

WHEN HURRICANE FLOYD HIT NORTH CAROLINA I WAS STARTING MY SECOND YEAR of graduate work at East Carolina University in Greenville. I am originally from Belize, Central America, so the threat of hurricanes was no news to me; however, I had never actually experienced one. When the warnings were announced, Shau-Ann, my roommate at that time, and I didn't panic. We did what we were advised to do—filled containers with water, bought non-perishable food, and then went over to a friend's house. Our experience of hurricane Floyd was so much different than what we saw on television later on. Our "time off" from school and teaching was spent doing useless activities. We heard a couple of stories and even contributed a dollar or two to help the victims. True, the images on television gave us an idea of the horror of the flood, but we did not realize the true extent of the damage until much later.

Right after the flood, we saw images of people affected. We saw Princeville destroyed and the African American community displaced, but we saw and heard very little of the Hispanic community in the Eastern Carolina area. Back then, I didn't care. Now, two years later, my feelings are different.

As I got involved with the Hispanic community through church, my job with the Migrant Education Program with Pitt County Schools, and through my work with other non-profit organizations, I got exposed to the reality of hurricane Floyd and the struggles of the Hispanic community before, during and after. Since my involvement with the Hispanic community, I've realized the obvious—that as long as there's no one to tell the story, especially in English, it never happened.

When Julie [*Fay*] asked me to participate in this project, I accepted gladly. This was an excellent opportunity to recount the *historias* of some Hispanic families that suffered during the time of the flood—stories that would otherwise go unheard.

Antonio Ponce, who at the time of the flood was the manager of a Mexican restaurant in Greenville, made appointments to meet with the three families whose stories are included in this section. Antonio made it clear that he would not be a part of the actual interviews, but inevitably his name came up in all three interviews as someone who had volunteered during the time of need, so we have to thank him. We met at Tienda Acapulco on Dickinson Avenue one evening and drove to Farmville to interview Norma and her mother Victoria. When we got there, people were gathered for a birthday celebration. Many of them I knew from St. Gabriel's Church.

Norma and Victoria told their stories, which were moving, although some details were unclear after the years. We were in the living room, with a party outside, and everything seemed normal. However, we were listening to the stories of a family that suffered a lot during Floyd. It was almost unbelievable to notice that everything had gone back to being normal. After the interviews, Antonio and I were asked to stay and socialize for some time, a true mark of Hispanic hospitality, and as Hispanics we knew we had to say yes. I could see the unity among the families and it was wonderful—just minutes before we had discussed a tragedy and its consequences, and now we were once again eating and laughing.

Our second stop was at the home of Arturo, Pilar and Wilber. When we arrived, Don Arturo was sitting outside waiting for us. He had a cooler full of cold drinks and a grill full of meat cooking—wonderful. We sat around and talked for a short time until Pilar and Wilber arrived, then we moved inside to start the interview. The family was very sincere when telling their story about the flood. They told me about their experiences of having to stand in line to get food and help. It was interesting to listen to a family who ordinarily did not need help, did not ask for it or accept it, tell stories of when they had to stand in line for hours or when many of them had to sleep in a one-bedroom apartment and had to be out of their house for months, only to have to start all over again after losing everything they had worked so hard to get. It was amazing to see them sitting together, remembering those difficult times with laughs. Once again I could see the unity in the family. By the time the interviews were over, the food was set on the table—grilled pork and chicken, hot corn tortillas and tomato salsa. We had our second dinner for the evening, not daring to refuse the hospitality and the appetizing food.

Our last stop of the day was back at Tienda Acapulco where I interviewed Jorge. Jorge's story came from a different perspective. He was not affected by the flood as much as the others, but his experience working with Hispanics during that time made an interesting story. Jorge was able to volunteer with the Red Cross because of his bilingual skills. That's how he met a lot of people and was able to tell them of help and resources available to the victims.

All three families were in some way touched by hurricane Floyd. There was general agreement on how great the Red Cross was in helping the victims, including the Hispanics. At the time of hurricane Floyd and afterwards, there were several complaints about FEMA and the distribution of help. Norma and Victoria did get help from FEMA. However, Arturo's family did not receive any help from FEMA. This was true for many other Hispanics as well either because they never got the information or because they were undocumented.

These are the stories of three Hispanic families. In no way do they do justice to the struggles of many, many other families, but at least some voices will be heard and there will be many more to be heard, in some way or another. This is only the beginning.

Si no hay nadie que relate la historia es como si nunca sucedió: La Comunidad Hispana y la inundación

Ana Cowó
Asistente del editor y miembro del comité AFTUR

CUANDO EL HURACÁN FLOYD LLEGÓ A CAROLINA DEL NORTE, YO COMENZABA EL segundo año de estudios graduados en East Carolina University en Greenville. Soy de belice en centro america (peninsula de yucatán), donde siempre hay amenazas de huracán, pero en realidad nunca había tenido la experiencia de estar en uno. Cuando comenzaron los avisos yo y mi amiga Shau-Ann no nos preocupamos, simplemente llenamos cubetas con agua, compramos comida y nos fuimos a la casa de un amigo. Nuestra experiencia del huracán floyd fue muy diferente a lo que vimos por televisión. El tiempo que pasamos fuera de la universidad lo empleamos haciendo cosas inútiles. Escuchamos una que otra historia y hasta donamos uno o dos dólares para ayudar a las víctimas. Es cierto que las imagenes en el televisor nos dieron una idea sobre el horror de lo sucedido, pero la verdad es que no comprendimos el grado del desastre hasta mucho después.

Después de la inundación, vimos imagines de la gente afectada. Habían imagines del daño ocurido, pero no había nada sobre la comunidad hispana de área de carolina del norte. En ese tiempo no me importaba mucho lo sucedido porque en realidad no estaba expuesta a la diversidad en la sociedad. Ahora dos años después, pienso diferente. Mientras más me involucré en la comunidad hispana por medio de la iglesia San Gabriel, mi trabajo con las escuelas del condado de Pitt en el programa de educación migrante y otras organizaciones, aprendí sobre la realidad de huracán floyd y los esfuerzos de la comunidad hispana antes, durante y después del huracán. Desde entonces me he dado cuenta de lo obvio, que si no hay nadie que relate la historia (especialmente en inglés) es como si nunca sucedió. Cuando Julie me propuso trabajar con este proyecto, estuve muy contenta en aceptar. Pensé que esta sería una gran oportunidad de contar historias de algunas familias hispanas que sufrieron durante el tiempo de la inundación … historias que de otro modo no se sabrían.

Antonio, quien durante el tiempo de la inundación era gerente del restaurante mexicano en la calle diez en Greenville, hizo cita con las tres familias cuya historias son incluyidas en esta sección. Antonio fue muy claro al decir que él no estaba interesado en ser parte de las entrevistas, pero sin querer su nombre fue mencionado en las tres entrevistas como alguien que brindó ayuda a esas familias durante el tiempo de necesidad. Es justo darle las gracias.

Me encontré con Antonio en la Tienda Acapulco en Dickenson Avenue en Greenville. Esa tarde fuimos a Farmville a hablar con Norma y su mama Victoria. Cuando llegamos a la casa, había gente celebrando un cumpleaños. Yo ya conocía a la mayoría por que son miembros de a la iglesia San Gabriel. Norma y Victoria relataron sus historias y aunque ya pasaron algunos años y los detalles no estaban tan claros, las historias fueron muy conmovedoras. Estabamos sentados en la sala, había una fiesta afuera y todo era muy normal, sin embargo estabamos escuchando las experiencias y historias de una familia que sufrió mucho durante floyd. Era increíble creer que todo había regresado a ser normal. Después de las entrevistas, nos pidieron que quedaramos un ratito, muy típico de familias hispanas, y como "mero" hispanos nos quedamos. Era muy obvio la unidad entre las familias presentes. Solo minutos antes habíamos hablado de la tragedia, y ya estabamos comiendo y sonriendo.

La segunda parada fue en la casa de la familia de Arturo, Pilar y Wilber. Cuando llegamos, Don Arturo estaba afuera esperándonos. Tenía una hielera con refrescos y estaba cocinando carne a la parilla. Nos sentamos a conversar mientras esperabamos a la señora y a su hijo Wilber. Cuando llegaron, entramos en la casa para comenzar la entrevista. La familia fue muy franca en relatar sus aventuras durante el tiempo de la inundación. Sin pena me contaron como tenían que hacer fila para conseguir ayuda y comida. Fue muy interesante escuchar a una familia que típicamente no necesitaba, no pedía, ni aceptaba ayuda ajena, relatar historias de cuando tenían que pararse en líneas por horas, cuando tenían que dormir muchos en un apartamento y andar fuera de casa por tanto tiempo solo para tener que empezar de nuevo después de perder todo lo que habían conseguido con mucho esfuerzo. Fue sorprendente verlos sentados juntos, recordando con risas esos tiempos muy difíciles que pasaron. Una vez más era obvio la unidad de familia. De acá que terminaron las entrevistas ya estaba listo la comida—carne asada, tortillas de maiz calientitas y salsa de tomate. Así fue como comimos nuestra segunda cena de la noche.

La última parada de la tarde fue en la Tienda Acapulco donde hablé con Jorge. La historia de Jorge fue de otra perspectiva ya que la familia de él no fue afectada por la inundación tanto como las otras familias. La historia de sus experiencias ayudando a otras familias hispanas durante ese tiempo fue muy interesante. Jorge, porque habla ingles y español, pudo ofrecer su tiempo como voluntario en la Cruz Roja. Así fue como él conocio a mucha gente y pudo informarles de algunos recursos disponibles a las víctimas. Todas las familias fueron afectadas por el huracán floyd de una manera u otra. Todos parecieron estar muy satisfechos con la ayuda brindada a los hispanos por la Cruz Roja. En el tiempo de la inundación y después, algunos tuvieron quejas sobre FEMA y la ayuda. Norma y Victoria consiguieron ayuda de FEMA. La familia de Arturo no consiguieron ayuda de FEMA esta fue la situación de muchas otras familias Hispanias que no consiguieron ayuda porque no supieron porque no calificaron por falta de documentos. Estas son las historias de tres familias. Hay muchas otras familias que fueron afectadas, pero al menos algunas voces serán escuchadas y ya habrán muchas mas. Este es el cominezo.

Flooded trailer park.

Photo courtesy of Ana Cowó.

Interview

Ana Cowó with Norma and Victoria

Norma and her mother Victoria live in Farmville, NC. At the time of the flood they were living in a mobile home park in Greenville. Norma is a single parent. She and her daughter live with her mother, father, sisters and brothers. Victoria has a disabled child who cannot walk or talk.

ANA COWÓ: Where were you living at the time of the flood?

NORMA: At the time of the flood we were living in Greenville.

AC: What part of Greenville?

N: By Hwy. 33.

AC: Where were you working?

N: In the tobacco plant.

AC: Did this change after the flood?

N: No. We continued working there.

AC: Did you have to leave your home?

N: Yes, we had to get out of there.

AC: When did you decide to go and where did you go?

N: We left when the flooding started. We went to the school and from the school we rented a house and then from that house we came to this one.

AC: So it was right after the flood that you moved?

N: I think it was more like, I'm just remembering. I was pregnant during that time. I was in my last month of pregnancy. Back then I wasn't working. The hurricane came and we waited that day in the house and after the hurricane we saw that the water kept rising and it came to the point when they told us that we had to evacuate the place. The firemen came and told us we had to move, to get out of there so we left. Fortunately, we went to Antonio's house. He had a separate place where we stayed. We were there and even then we had to leave from there because the water kept rising up to a certain height. We left and that's when we went to the shelter, which was Wellcome Middle School.

AC: How did you get out of the house? Did you have to rent a vehicle or did you leave in your own cars?

N: In our own cars.

AC: So you packed up everything that you had in there?

N: The little bit that we could, we packed and like I told you, I was pregnant so I couldn't move a lot. My little brother is sick and she [*Victoria*] had to struggle with all the children and all that. It was very difficult. Most of the furniture and everything stayed behind.

VICTORIA: This child [*pointing to son sitting on the floor*], since he's big, it wasn't possible to carry him around and take everything out. We either carried the child around or we carried the things. We left the things in order to carry the children—there were many small children.

AC: So, when you left the house, you went straight to Antonio's house?

N: Yes.

AC: And after that?

N: After that we all had to leave and go to Wellcome [Middle School].

AC: How long did you stay there?

N: I think we stayed there for almost two weeks.

AC: And after that, where did you go?

V: To another school.

N: After that we came to this side, here in the school in Farmville.

AC: Which school?

N: Farmville Middle School.

AC: OK.

N: And from there we left. We left because my father rented a house here in Farmville. We stayed there and that's when I had my daughter. Two months later we bought this house and we moved here.

AC: Did you have trouble communicating with or getting help from relief workers?

N: No, I don't think so. I think that a lot of help was given through volunteers and all the programs and everyone.

V: The Red Cross.

N: We had a lot of help, including free public telephones to call relatives. They had the phones outside.

V: They didn't charge anything. We even called Mexico and they didn't charge us.

AC: Did you find that the community agencies were helpful? FEMA?

V: Yes, FEMA helped us. They helped us a lot. What FEMA gave us, we used for the down payment on this trailer.

AC: Do you still remember details about the flood? Days, dates, names of people you met?

V: Well, there were a lot of people but I don't remember names. When we see each other on the street we say hello and we remember that we lived there in the school, but names I don't remember. Only by sight.

AC: Do you still see some of the people?

V: Yes, we see a lot of people that were there with us in the school.

AC: Do you still talk with friends and loved ones about the flood?

V: We do, yes.

N: Yes, yes, always.

V: We'll never forget that day.

N: Never, never.

V: It was really sad.

AC: Are you in a better or worse situation than you were before the flood? How does that make you feel?

N: Better. We are better but at the same time, what you lost, you lost, and you will never get it back. Maybe it wasn't much, and maybe it was less than what we have now, but its something that you had and you suddenly lost and you will never get back, no matter how much they replace it with something new, you lost it. It is more emotional. It's more the emotional than the . . .

---

v: Material.

AC: Are there still places you won't go or things you won't do since the flood?

v: For us, yes, it's still the same. The only difference is the distance to town, but then again, it's close by. Where we used to go a lot, Wal-Mart, we still go. The mall also. It didn't change much.

AC: Does anything "trigger" intense emotions for you about the flood?

N: For example, when the news that a flooding that occurred recently in some state here, when they showed those scenes I remember that we have been in that situation. Or, for example when they say that you could donate something for certain things, today with more enthusiasm we give because we say that we have been in their place. They gave us a lot of help … so we start thinking that we have been there, why shouldn't we help someone else?

AC: Did you have trouble in your personal life after the flood? Sleeping? Health troubles?

N: Maybe I did. I was pregnant so I was always nervous about what was going to happen or where we would end up. We didn't have a home; we didn't have anything so I wondered where I would be when my daughter would come. I worried about my mom mainly, and the children.

v: And our child got sick also. There were too many people.

AC: When you were staying in the school?

v: Yes. They took him out in a helicopter. The doctor said that my son had gotten an infection; and that's why they put us in a classroom with only one family, which is my *comadre* [*godmother*] Olga and *compadre* [*godfather*] Jorge. They left our family and the godparents there alone.

N: He is very vulnerable to anything. If the children are outside and they come in and bring soil/dirt from outside or microbes, that's bad for him. One has to be very careful with him.

AC: Did they offer you any help?

v: Right there, from the school they called the hospital and they sent a helicopter. They took care of him immediately.

AC: How has your perspective changed? On life, family, community . . .

v: Before, I never believed that any of the agencies would help. With this that happened to us, well, we believe that yes, they help people when there's a disaster. It's like my daughter says, now when we hear something and they ask for help or donations we also help. But yes, it changed a lot because we would say, "Oh, what are they going to give you? They don't give anything. Those are lies. They keep the money," and "No, no, no, don't give them anything." And … because now we had our turn and we know that yes, they do help, and more the Red Cross. FEMA also helped us. Now if they ask for a donation, we give it—food, money, we get together and amongst ourselves, "How much are you going to give?" "No, well I'll give $10. No, well, I'll give $5, and I'll give this . . ." And we get together and do it like that.

v: In the stores where they have the little balloons where you write how much you donate and all that, my children immediately ask us to donate money, "Look, Papi, this and that for the hungry children from I don't know where." They know. They know more than I do because they are in front of the television more. Yes it changed a lot.

AC: Do you think that you were treated in any way different than others?

v: No.

NR: Nothing.

v: It was the same for all the races.

N: The same requirements. I can say that because I went to the Red Cross so that they could help us with furniture because they were giving vouchers to go to the furniture stores or to the clothes shops to get clothes, and I saw that there was no distinction for being Hispanic or not Hispanic or white or any other race. There was help. What I did see was a lot of abuse by many people—the people abusing the agencies. A lot of people that did not lose anything were there. They were probably there before the people that were affected. There were Hispanics who were very afraid to ask for help because they were illegal. I would tell them, "Go, go. That doesn't matter." One has to go and has to say, "It happened to me."

AC: How was your community changed? Have things returned to "normal"?

N: Well, the Hispanic community is growing a lot. There are a lot of people now who weren't here during that time. Now, I see more unity. We still need more, truly, more unity with the Hispanics, but there is some.

AC: So, after the flood, do you think that people united to help each other?

N: Yes, of course.

AC: For you, has everything been back to normal?

v: For us, yes. We are more calm. For us everything is back to normal.

AC: Is there anything else you want to add?

v: No, only that everything is fine. We got a lot of help. FEMA helped us, and the Red Cross also.

Entrevista

Ana Cowó y Norma y Victoria

Norma (hija) y Victoria (mamá), viven en Farmville, North Carolina. En el tiempo de la inundación, vivían en una vecindad en Greenville. Norma vive con su Mama, Papa, hermanitos y hermanitas. La señora Victoria tiene un hijo que no camina ni habla.

ANA COWÓ: ¿Dónde vivían durante el tiempo de la inundación?

NORMA: Vivíamos en Greenville.

AC: ¿En qué parte de Greenville?

N: Por la carretera 33.

AC: ¿Dónde trabajaban?

N: En la planta de tabaco.

AC: ¿Cambió esto después de la inundación?

N: No. Seguimos trabajando allí.

AC: ¿Tuvieron que salirse de la casa?

N: Sí, tuvimos que salir de allí.

AC: ¿Cuándo decidieron irse y a dónde se fueron?

N: Nos fuimos cuando comenzó la inundación. Fuimos a la escuela y de allí rentamos una casa y de allí vinimos a éste uno.

AC: ¿Entonces se movieron después del huracán?

N: Creo que más bien, me estoy acordando. Yo estaba embarazada durante ese tiempo. Ya estaba en el último mes de embarazo. Entonces yo no estaba trabajando. El huracán vino y esperamos ese día en la casa y después del huracán vimos que el agua seguía subiendo y llegó al punto que nos dijeron que teniamos que evacuar. Llegaron los bomberos y nos dijeron que teníamos que salirnos de allí, así es que nos fuimos. Afortunádamente fuimos a la casa de Antonio. El tenía un lugar aparte donde nos quedamos. Estuvimos allí y después nos tuvimos que ir porque el agua seguía subiendo. Nos salimos y allí fue cuando nos fuimos al refugio que fue la escuela de Wellcome.

AC: ¿Cómo se fueron? ¿Tuvieron que alquilar carro o se fueron en sus propios carros?

N: En nuestros propios carros.

AC: ¿Entonces, empacaron todo lo que tenían?

N: Empacamos lo que pudimos y como te dije, estaba embarazada así es que no podía moverme mucho. Mi hermanito está enfermo y mi Mamá tuvo que batallar con todos los niños y eso. Fue muy difícil. La mayoría de los muebles se tuvieron que quedar.

VICTORIA: Este niño [*señalando al niño que estaba sentado en el piso*] ya que es grande, pues para andarlo cargando y sacando cosas, no se podía. O cargábamos al niño o cargábamos cosas. Dejamos cosas por agarar a los niños porque estaban chiquitos.

AC: ¿Entonces, cuando se fueron de la casa de ustedes, se fueron a la casa de Antonio?

N: Sí

AC: ¿Y después?

N: Después tuvimos que salir y fuimos a Wellcome.

AC: ¿Cuanto tiempo hicieron allí?

N: Creo que estuvimos allí por casi dos semanas.

AC: ¿Y después, dónde fueron?

V: A otra escuela

N: Después nos vinimos a este lado, aquí en Farmville

AC: ¿Cual escuela?

N: Farmville Middle School

N: Y de allí nos salimos porque mi Papá rentó una casa. Encontramos una casa aquí en Farmville, lo rentó y allí estuvimos y allí fue cuando yo me alivié. Tuve a mi hija. A los dos meses compramos esta casa y nos vinimos aquí.

AC: ¿Tuvo usted dificultad en comunicarse con alguién, o en conseguir ayuda?

N: La verdad no creo que fue. Sí hubo bastante ayuda por parte de voluntarios y de todos los programas y de todos.

V: La Cruz Roja

N: Hubo mucha ayuda. Había incluso teléfonos públicos gratuitos para llamar a familiares verdad, que uno quisiera avisar, llamar allí en la escuela. Afuera los pusieron.

V: No cobraban nada. Hablamos para Mexico también y no nos cobraban.

AC: ¿Cree usted que las agencias de servicios para la comunidad fueron servicial?

V: Sí, FEMA nos ayudó, mucho nos ayudó. Con lo que FEMA nos dió fue con lo que dimos el "down" [pago inicial] de esta traile.

AC: ¿Se acuerda usted de detalles de la inundación? ¿Días, fechas, nombres de gente que usted conoció? ¿Qué recuerda?

v: Pues de gente, había mucha pero los nombres no me acuerdo. Cuando los vemos en la calle sí nos saludamos y nos acordamos de lo que estabamos viviendo allí y todos nos ponemos a recordar lo que pasamons allí pero pues nombres, no me acuerdo. No más de vista.

AC: ¿Entonces siempre ven a algunas de las personas?

v: Sí. Vemos mucha gente que estuvimos todos en la escuela.

AC: ¿Siempre habla usted de la inundación con sus amigos y seres queridos, o prefiere evitar hablar de ello?

v: Nosotros sí.

N: Sí, sí. La verdad sí siempre.

v: Nunca se nos olvida ese día.

N: Jamás, jamás.

v: Fue muy triste.

AC: Está usted en una situación major o peor después de la inundación?

N: Mejor. Mejor pero a la vez lo que perdiste lo perdiste y jamás lo vas a volver a recuperar. Tal vez no fue mucho y tal vez es menos de lo que ahora tenemos o x, pero es algo que tenías, que de repente lo perdiste y ya nunca, por más que te le reemplazen con algo nuevo, lo perdiste. Es más lo emocional que lo . . .

v: Material

AC: ¿Hay algunos sitios que usted ya no frecuenta o cosas que ya no hace desde la inundación?

v: Para nosotros sí, sigue igual. Pues, no más la diferencia es del pueblo (Greenville) pero pues está cerquita. Y donde ibamos mucho pues a Wal-Mart, siempre vamos. El mall pues también. No cambió mucho.

AC: ¿Hay algunas cosas que le traen emociones intensas de la inundación?

N: Por ejemplo cuando las noticias por ejemplo, que una inundación que fue hace poco en algún estado de aquí, cuando pasan estas escenas, me acuerdo que hemos estado en esa situación o por ejemplo cuando dicen que verdad, si uno quiere donar algo para ciertas cosas o sea hoy con más ganas uno dice, uno estuvo en ese lugar y nos ayudaron y nos dieron mucha ayuda entonces uno se pone a pensar yo ya pase por allí ¿porqué no voy a ayudar a otra persona?

AC: ¿Tuvo alguna dificultad en su vida personal después de la inundación? ¿Problemas en dormir? ¿Problemas de salud?

N: Tal vez yo sí. Yo porque como estaba embarazada eran los nervios constante de qué va a pasar o dónde vamos a ir a dar. No tenemos hogar, no tenemos nada y embarazada, a dónde va a llegar mi hija. Por mi Mamá principalmente por los niños, preocuparse de todo eso.

v: Y se nos enfermó el niño también.

AC: ¿Cuando estaban allí quedando en la escuela?

v: Lo sacaron en helicóptero porque tanta gente, dijo el doctor, que era que el niño había agarado infección y por eso nos pusieron en un salón de clase nada más con una familia, que es la comadre Olga y el compadre Jorge. La familia y la comadre allí solos nos dejaron.

N: El es muy propenso a cualquier … si los niños estan afuera y entran y traen tierra de afuera o microbios, para él es mal. O sea uno tiene que tener mucho cuidado con él.

AC: ¿Le ofrecieron ayuda?

v: Allí mismo en la escuela le hablaron pa' el hospital y mandaron un helicoptero. Lo atendieron luego luego.

AC: ¿Cómo cambió su perspectiva? (sobre la vida, la comunidad, agencias del gobierno, de los esfuerzos de recuperación?)

v: Yo antes no creía nada en la ayuda de todo eso. Con esto que nos pasó pues sí. Creemos que sí, sí ayudan a la gente cuando hay un desastre. Pues es que como dice mi hija ahora nosotros cuando oyimos algo y piden ayuda o donación también ayudamos. Pero sí, cambió mucho porque nosotros decíamos no, «Hay no te van a dar, si no les dan nada» y «son mentiras, se quedan con el dinero» y que no se que, no, no, no, no des nada. Y ahora no porque ahora nos tocó a nosotros y sabes que sí, y más la Cruz Roja y FEMA también nos ayudó mucho. Ahora si piden una donación sí la damos. Que comida, que dinero, nos juntamos entre todos y «¿cuanto vas a dar?» «No pues que yo diez, no pues que yo cinco, que yo esto» y juntamos entre nosotros y así lo hacemos. En las tiendas que hay los globitos asi que ponen cuanto donan y todo , los niños míos luego luego. Los niños también, «mira papi que esto que el otro para los niños que estan sin comer en no se que partes.» Ellos saben. Ellos saben más que yo porque en la tele no mas mirando. Y sí, cambió mucho.

AC: ¿Usted cree que hubo diferencias en la manera en que trataron a los hispanos, de la ayuda que consiguieron?

v: Nada

N: Para nada

v: Fue igual para todas las razas

N: Los mismos requisitos. Yo puedo decir eso porque fui a la Cruz Roja que nos ayudaran con los muebles y eso porque estaban dando "vouchers" [cupón] para ir a las mueblerías o a las tiendas de ropa a conseguir ropa. Y yo ví o sea no había ninguna distincción por algunas personas por ser hispanas o no hispanas o blancas o cualquiér raza. Hubo ayuda. Lo que sí ví fue mucho abuso por parte de mucha gente. La gente abusando de las agencias porque mucha gente que no perdieron nada estuvieron allí . Estuvieron creo que antes que las personas que sí. Hubo personas hispanas que tenían miedo, por ser ilegales, de ir a pedir la ayuda. Yo les decía, vayan, vayan, eso no imoprta. Uno tiene que ir y tiene que decir. Yo fuí o sea a mi me pasó.

AC: ¿Como ha cambiado su comunidad? Han regresado las cosas a ser normal?

N: La comunidad hispana de hecho pues está creciendo bastante o sea mucha gente que en ese tiempo no estuvo aquí, pero hoy hay mucha gente aquí que veo un poco mas de unidad. Falta más, verdad unidad de uno hispano pero la hay.

AC: ¿Entonces después de la inundación usted cree que se unió un poco más la gente para ayudarse?

N: Sí, claro

AC: ¿Cree que ha regresado todo a ser normal?

V: Yo creo que sí.

AC: ¿Para ustedes ya regresó todo a ser normal?

V: Nosotros si ya , ya estamos mas tranquilos. Ya todo está para nosotros ya todo está igual.

AC: ¿Alguna otra cosa mas que quieren añadir?

V: No, no más que todo está bien, nos ayudaron bastante. Mas FEMA, FEMA fue el que nos ayudó mas. Mucho y la Cruz Roja también.

Ana Cowó with Pilar, Arturo and Wilber

Arturo and his wife Pilar participated in this interview, along with their older son Wilber. Arturo and Pilar have three other children—two daughters and a son. At the time of the flood, they were living in the same mobile home park. Wilber and his wife were living with his parents at the time of the flood. Since then, they have moved out but live in the same mobile home park.

ANA COWÓ: Where were you living at the time of the flood?

PILAR: At the time of the flood, we were living in this same mobile home park.

AC: Where were you working?

P: He was working at a plant.

AC: And you?

WILBER: In the same place.

AC: And you?

P: I wasn't working.

AC: Did that change after the flood?

P: Yes. Well, we got disoriented because at the time of the flooding my husband didn't want to leave. They told us to leave and he said no because after all it was nothing serious and it wouldn't affect us. I have another daughter who is fourteen and she insisted that we leave, and seeing that the girl was telling us to leave and was crying, I told him that we should leave at least to satisfy her. Well, when he saw that I was agreeing to leave, he said that we should all leave. My son was also saying that he would stay in the house and I told him that no, that we all either stayed or we all left. That was when we all decided to leave and we went to Wilson. We went to Wilson and we spent that night there but we didn't think that it had been anything major because we heard the wind and the rain.

It was the night of the hurricane. We didn't feel too much wind. We were at my daughter's mother-in-law's house and it's a house so we didn't experience much. The following day we got up at around 7 in the morning, and the men went out to look around. When they came back and they said that some parts were really bad.

There were parts of Wilson that were flooded really bad. We were uneasy because we wanted to come back to Greenville, so around 9 in the morning we tried to leave. We hadn't even left Wilson when we had to come back because there were no exits to Greenville. My son really wanted to return and he said that we would look for other roads. That day we were out until 5 in the evening looking for roads that would bring us all the way here and everything would be blocked and we would go to another one. It was getting dark and he was still saying that he wanted to come back and I was telling him, "No, son, let's go to Wilson. Let's go back to Wilson because it's getting dark. We don't know how bad the roads are." Then he decided to go back to Wilson and we got up early on the second day and around 7 in the morning we started back to Greenville.

We got to Greenville around 2 in the afternoon and we tried to get on to Hwy. 11 towards the airport by where we lived, and we couldn't because the bridge by the airport was blocked. We kept on looking and we went all the way to Greenville Boulevard by Hwy. 264 and we got through there and we came. There was one section by Hwy. 33 where the water was high. It was rising too much but my husband took the risk. We wanted to get back to where we lived so he took the risk and we traveled, like, two miles, or maybe three and we started to drive back because there was no pass.

w: I did manage to get to the house.

AC: So you were traveling separately?

w: Yes, I was ahead of them. They stayed behind but I managed to get through. Right here by the little store and gas station, there was two feet of water and there was a line of about ten cars. Nobody wanted to cross so I crossed with my truck, and when I crossed everyone came behind me. When I got to the mobile home park, there was only a slope so I managed to get up to the slope. I couldn't get to our trailer because there was a canal in the middle of the mobile home park. I turned around and on my way back I met them. That's when they told me that they couldn't pass so I told them that, yes, they could pass, to follow me, and that's how we came back.

We wanted to take some things out because the water was still underneath the trailer, it hadn't risen, but we knew there were some electric cables and we thought they were underneath so we didn't want to risk it. We returned and went to a friend's house for the day. Later, we couldn't get over to the other side because even the bridge on Hwy. 264 was underwater.

AC: The one going towards Washington?

w: Yes.

P: It was on that same day. The bridge got flooded the same day.

w: The case is that we were on the other side for about a week, on the Greenville side, since you know that it's divided—Greenville is on the high side and the river is low. We stayed on the Greenville side for about one week right?

AC: Where did your friend live?

w: He lived behind Hastings Ford on Tenth Street. I was there for about a week and we weren't working for about four or five days. Work was on the other side. We had to go around to Little Washington to get to our house. I went around with some friends. We took about two hours to get across a little part that is about five miles. When we got there I tried to go to the house and get clothes. The water had risen more and my two cousins and I got in and tried to get to the house but when we were crossing, the water started covering us so we turned around and then we borrowed a canoe from someone.

AC: The man who lent you the canoe, did you know him?

w: No, we were going to my cousin's house and we saw a man pass by with a canoe on his truck so we followed him until he got to his house and asked him if we could rent the canoe because we wanted to get some things out. He told us that he would not rent it to us, that he would lend it to us. It was the first time we had seen the man. During that time it seems we all became sentimental. The material things didn't matter much. If we saw anything, we helped. We didn't care at that time. That day on the canoe we passed a trailer where the water was close to the door. We could hear dogs inside and little puppies, so we tried to get them out but it was a pit bull and the mother wouldn't let us. The only thing we did was tell people from the Army, then someone came with pens and took them out.

When we were rowing, we could touch the cars underneath. When we got to the house we couldn't open the door because the current was too strong. When we finally opened the door we got in and the water was already inside the house. It reached up to my chest inside the house. We took out a few things that we could, clothes and all that.

P: He took out the things that were on top, what hadn't gotten wet.

w: That's what I managed to get out and we got back to the canoe because we couldn't go anywhere else because of the current. We went to the other side where the water was lower and we came out and came back to my cousin's house and we were there for about a week. We used to live together and during that time we got separated because they stayed at some friend's house. They were staying at a friend's house. When I crossed the bridge to the other side where we used to live, I had to stay at my cousin's house.

P: During those eight days they had to go with a cousin to stay and we stayed— my husband and I and this other child—stayed with some friends. My other daughter went to her mother-in-law's in Wilson and my younger daughter, the fourteen-year-old, also went with her sister because there were about twenty of us living in the house. Yes, like twenty. And another friend who had an apartment, there were also … about how many?

ARTURO: About thirty.

P: Ah, in one small one-bedroom apartment. Everyone was sleeping beside each other.

We stayed only with what we were wearing. I didn't get anything out. It was sudden and we didn't have anything. I used to say, "What does it matter that everything was lost? The main thing is that we were all OK." And it made me feel good that we were all fine and the material things, we could replace them little by little. But yes, we still feel a little sad. On the second day after the hurricane, the husbands said that there were no supplies, food, nothing, so they went out to Ayden. Someone told us that in Ayden there was a store that was open so they went to Ayden to get milk, water and things like that for the children.

A: Only a gallon of milk they would allow you to buy per family. There was none. Everything was closed here in Greenville. You couldn't get anything. We went all the way to Ayden only for a gallon of milk and some gallons of water.

P: And you took a long time right?

A: Yes, there were a lot of people.

P: And then, you couldn't go straight on the road. You had to go around. It took like half a day to get to Ayden. Here in Greenville all the stores were closed. It wasn't until maybe the third day that things started to get back to normal and the gas stations opened and the stores started giving away water and help started to come.

W: For the first couple of days after the flood, we didn't really care. But when the food and water started to run out and we saw that none were available and there was no movement and everything was quiet, then we started to get worried about what was going to happen and that's when we felt it more.

P: And then the house where we were living had no lights, no water, no telephone, nothing. So they brought a grill for us from Wilson. We would cook outside. Yes, we would cook outside and we would feed the children first and then we would eat. After about three days we started to get more help from the churches and other places.

AC: So what did you do about water and electricity?

P: Well, we didn't have any.

AC: How long did you live like that?

W: Like three days, and then we went to Target to buy clothes.

AC: So Target was open at that time?

P: For a little time.

---

w: It was dark. I think that they only had a generator because they would do the totals …

p: By hand.

w: With pencil or pen because the computers weren't working. I think that people would take things from there because all of a sudden you would see people dressed differently.

AC: How did you find out about the help that was available?

w: We went out looking for help. Wherever we saw people lining up we would ask them what they were giving away. And we would stand in line for water.

p: Nobody cared—we were all in the same situation.

w: We were doing it out of necessity, not because we liked it.

AC: What type of help did you get?

p: With the Red Cross? During that time, we were disoriented and we didn't know anything. We saw that there were a lot of people standing in line.

AC: Where?

p: At the Red Cross. We got help from the Red Cross. When we saw that a lot of people were standing in line, we went to see what was going on and what type of help they were giving. When we got there they told us that it was the Red Cross and that if we had been affected, that we could stand in line so that we could get a number for an interview, and well, we had to wait a long time for the interview.

AC: Did you have the interview on that same day?

p: No, about two days later. There were some people who did not realize that help was available so it took them longer to get help because they were staying in the shelters and they didn't know about it because they couldn't leave the shelter since they had no cars.

AC: So no one informed them?

p: No, no one told them

AC: Where were they?

p: I think they were in one of the schools. It took longer for them to get help, and they needed urgent help also. I told them about the Red Cross and told them to get in line and to wait until they got called and not to leave. I told them they would get help—they just had to stay there for a while. We got a lot of help from the Red Cross, so now when they are asking for help, we help them. We will give a little bit of what they gave us.

A: They treated us well, all of us. They never humiliated us, or anything.

AC: During that time when you had to move around, did you meet a lot of people?

A: Yes, we met Antonio, we met Jorge. Antonio helped us. He lent us a little trailer for us to live in and didn't charge us anything. Later we got a trailer and everything.

AC: How long did you stay at friends' houses?

P: Like, three months.

AC: And after that you moved to your own place?

P: No, actually we stayed, like, a month in my friend's house. After that, they told us that Antonio had a little trailer and that possibly he could lend it to us. I wanted to be alone with my children so we went to ask him if he would rent it or lend it to us, and he lent it to us.

AC: Do you still talk with friends and loved ones about the flood?

P: Yes, and now we believe. Before we used to say, "No, no, nothing's going to happen to us." And my husband never wanted to leave and he would say that nothing will happen, but now we do think that it can happen again.

AC: How long did you have to wait before going to work?

W: One week.

W: There are many contracting companies in the plant so two people from each company had to stay there on the night of the hurricane in case any windows were broken or any pipes were damaged. They told me that I had to go but at the last minute I went to Wilson. It was my turn to go to the plant and to make sure everything was taken care of.

AC: All day and all night?

W: Yes, during the night and during the day just in case any windows broke or anything, that's what they needed us for.

AC: So you would have had to fix anything right there?

W: Yes.

A: Our boss helped us out a lot.

AC: What type of help?

A: Well, he helped us with money.

AC: Was this after you went back to work?

A: Yes, when we got back. When we came back from Wilson we told him what had happened to us. He even offered us his house, that my family could come to his house, and he gave me money.

P: He gave us groceries.

A: He gave us groceries and told me that if we had to stay in a hotel, that he would pay.

W: Yes. There were about … about how many people working so, you think?

A: It is a huge plant, maybe like a thousand.

W: No, maybe like three thousand employees and from those three thousand, only like thirty of us were there. We were walking around cleaning up and picking up things that were broken. When things started to get back to normal, they called us, the ones that were there, and they thanked us.

W: We had reported to work and they asked us to help clean. It was, like, thirty of us, and, like, fifteen Mexicans.

AC: Are you in a better or worse situation than you were before the flood?

P: Better.

AC: Why?

P: Well, we don't lack work, thank God, and we feel content.

A: And we live in the same mobile home park, so we're not afraid. We were affected but it's a mobile home park where we live content.

P: Yes, and we wanted to move somewhere and it's a struggle to find a lot and all that, so I told my husband to come back to the same one since we were living well and peacefully and if it happens again, well we would just get it a second time.

A: It would be our turn to lose again, but this time we have insurance and we even insured inside. When we were in the other trailer we didn't have insurance so we lost everything. We were left out in the street. We were left with nothing. They paid the trailer but that was it.

P: What happened is that the insurance paid what we owed on the trailer and as soon as they gave us the check, we paid the trailer but we were left with nothing. The only thing is that we had a clean record, but we had to start all over again.

AC: Are there still places you won't go or things you won't do since the flood?

W: Yes, I don't have anywhere to cut my hair. There was a barbershop by the river and before the flood I would go there, but after the hurricane it got flooded and who knows where they moved to.

AC: Are there things that you avoid talking about the flood?

P: No, we are fine talking about it.

A: Well, it was an experience that we didn't believe in. That was one of the things that I didn't believe in. I would think, "That won't happen," or "No, I'll wait for it sleeping." My daughter Cristina, when she was leaving she would cry a lot and wanted to drag me out, but I would insist that I would stay.

AC: How old was she at that time?

P: She was 14.

A: She would not leave me alone. She is a very nervous person. She was not happy and I was one of those people that would insist on staying. No, but now I believe.

AC: Does anything "trigger" intense emotions for you about the flood?

P: Well, we get sad when we remember we had to struggle.

A: It is very sad to have to be out of your house. Like now … we have everything and by tomorrow, nothing—to have to go to other houses. Even if they are family or good friends, you still don't feel content like you do in your house. My children suffered.

P: They tried to make us feel at home where we were staying, and we did feel good but we were sad because the family was separated. Some were here, some were there, and we didn't know how the ones in Wilson were doing and they didn't know how we were doing here.

AC: You didn't have a way to get in contact with them?

P: No, there were no telephones or anything, and the only way we could communicate and find out about our friends was through the radio, through the radio station.

AC: In Spanish?

P: Yes. That's how we knew that they were at a certain location and that they were fine and they knew we were here.

AC: You would send messages?

P: Yes.

AC: Did you have trouble in your personal life after the flood? Sleeping? Health troubles?

P: During that time I was suffering from asthma. I got sick with asthma and I was feeling sick.

A: Depression.

P: A lot of depression. I was very depressed and then apart from the depression I was sick with asthma.

AC: Did they offer you any help?

P: I didn't ask.

AC: How has your perspective changed? On life, on community agencies …

W: Well, you lose pride. When nothing goes wrong, you have a lot of pride, and when the things happened, we had to stand in line asking for water or asking for food. When we are doing fine people would say, "They are giving away food over there," but we would feel ashamed.

A: What will you do there? You don't need it.

W: You lose your pride during that time, and you don't care about doing anything that is necessary.

A: Burger King was giving away hamburgers and we stood in line.

P: Before, we were the kind of people who didn't like to go asking for help because we would say that there are people who need it more than we do so they should have the opportunity to get it instead of us. But when that happened and there were lines of people asking for help we would stand in line and I wasn't ashamed because I was in need of help. Before that happened to us, we would say, "No, how are we going to take something if there are people that need it more than we do?" But at that time, we also needed help.

W: And we felt as if we were in Mexico because we were riding bicycles downtown and we were riding at the back of trucks and we were walking around only in shorts because we had to get in the water. We felt as if we were in Mexico—Mexican style.

AC: Has your community changed?

W: Yes, all the neighbors that lived around here, the African Americans, we never saw them again. The area where we were living was on the other side of the mobile home park, and during that time nobody knew where everyone went.

P: We all got along very well and when everything was over, we didn't know where they were.

AC: Do you think that everything is back to normal like it was before? In your life, in the community?

P: Yes.

A: Yes, I think so.

P: Only the fear. We get scared when we hear that there's a hurricane, but we're more alert. Now we're saying that we will get out.

AC: Is there anything else that you want to add?

A: The story of a dog named Chicano. Well, we left him here when we had to go in the night, and as the water started to rise he moved to the edge. My younger son really liked him, so when the water went down and they started rescuing the dogs and all that, we started going to the dog pounds to look for him because he wanted to find his dog. They would ask him, "What does the Chicano look like?"

w:	[*quoting his little brother*] "Well, he is a black dog, and he wags his tail."

AC:	And did you find him?

A:	Yes, Wilber found him.

w:	I found him here in the mobile home park when I returned to look around. I think the dog recognized the noise, and when he heard the truck he ran towards it and that's when I put him in the truck and I took him with me. I took the dog to where I was living, then they took him to Antonio's house and he corrupted Antonio's dog Mailo. He turned him into a partying dog.

AC:	Would you like to add anything?

A:	We hope it never happens again.

w:	Thanks to the Red Cross.

P:	And the Salvation Army also.

AC:	Do you think that people got together in unity during that time?

P:	Yes, yes.

AC:	I think this is all, thank you very much.

Pilar (mamá); Arturo (papá), Wilber (hijo mayor). El Sr. y Sra. tienen tres otros hijos-dos hijas y un hijo. En el tiempo de la inundación, todos vivían en misma vecindad. Wilber y su esposa vivían con los padres de él en el tiempo de la inundación. Desde entonces, se han cambiado de domicilio pero siempre viven en la misma vecindad.

ANA COWÓ: ¿Dónde vivían en el tiempo de la inundación?

PILAR: Cuando pasó la inundación estabamos vivieno en, la dirección es 1689 … en este mismo parqueadero.

AC: ¿Dónde trabajaban?

P: El trabajaba en una planta (*señalando al esposo*)

AC: ¿Y usted, Wilber?

WILBER: En la misma parte

P: Yo no trabajaba

AC: ¿Cambió esto después de la inundación?

P: Sí

AC: ¿Cómo?

P: Pues nos desorientamos mucho porque el día de la inundación, mi esposo no quería salirse. O sea nos avisaron que nos saliéramos y él decía que no que al cabo era algo asi sencillo que iba a pasar y que no nos iba a afectar. Tengo otra hija, una hija de catorce años que ella decía que sí, que nos saliéramos. Ella lloraba porque quería que nos saliéramos. Entonces yo le dije a él que nos saliéramos no más por complacerla a ella. Pues el al ver que yo sí ya aceptaba salirnos dijo pues nos vamos a salir pero ya nos vamos a salir todos. Mi hijo también decía que él se quedaba en la casa y le decía yo pues no o nos quedamos todos o nos salimos todos. Entonces fue cuando ya pensamos irnos todos y nos fuimos a Wilson. Nos fuimos a Wilson y después ya o sea que esa noche en Wilson no pensamos que había sido así gran cosa porque sentimos la lluvia y el aire.

Y pues pensabamos que no había sido mucho porque no sentimos mucho el viento y es que nosotros fuimos a la casa de la suegra de mi hija y allí es casa, entonces como que allí no sentimos tanto. Y al otro día en la mañana cuando nos levantamos como a las 7 de la mañana ellos se salieron allí afuerita a dar la vuelta e ver qué se veía y ya cuando ellos regresaron no, decian que habían partes muy feas.

Habian partes inundadas, o sea que estaba feo. Y nosotros estabamos desesperados por querernos venir. Entonces como a las 9 de la mañana comenzamos a venir. No salimos de Wilson pa' cuando nos tuvimos que devolver porque no había pase para acá para Greenville y mi hijo quería llegar a fuerza y él dijo que no, que vamos a buscar caminos. Y ese día anduvimos buscando camino y caminos que nos trajeran hasta aquí y no, no, no todo se cerraba y nos devolvíamos por otro y así ya se nos estaba oscureciendo y él todavía decía que él se quería venir. Yo le decía no mi hijo no, vamos para Wilson. Vamos a regresarnos a Wilson porque ya se está oscureciendo. No sabemos como esten de mal los caminos. Entonces él ya aceptó regresarse y al Segundo día, temprano nos levantamos como a las 7 y otra vez como a la siete de la mañana a regresar pa' aca pa' Greenville. Pues de siete de la mañana hasta como a las 2 de la tarde llegamos aquí a Greenville a donde andábamos buscando caminos donde hubiera pase y que nos daban o sea que había gente que guiaba para que les siguieramos y así o sea o sea que como quien dice desde las 7 la mañana hasta las 2 de la tarde llegamos aquí en Greenville y todavía llegamos aquí en Greenville y nosotros tratamos por el 11 [carretera 11]. De 11 quisimos agarar para aca para el aeropuerto que es por donde nosotros vivíamos y no pudimos pasar porque el puente del aeropuerto estaba … no había pase. Y todavía nosotros buscándole, nos fuimos hasta allá que es el boulevard Greenville. Por allá agarra uno otra vez el 264 [carretera 264] y allí sí hayamos pasada y ya nos venimos. Y por el 33 [carretera 33] hubo una partecita donde estaba el agua muy alta. Estaba subiendo mucho y no, es que mi esposo se arriesgó a pasar. Nosotros lo que queríamos era llegar aquí donde nosotros vivíamos y él se arriesgó y pasó pero fuimos, que sera, como unas dos millas? Tres? Y ya nos devolvimos porque ya no había pasada pa' aca.

w: Yo sí llegué. Yo alcanzé llegar.

AC: ¿Entonces usted venía por separado?

w: Sí, yo me venía adelante porque ellos se quedaron atrás. Yo alcanzé a pasar. Aquí en la tiendita de aquí de la gasolinera, la carretera tenía yo creo que como unos 2 pies de agua y estaba una fila de como unos 10 carros. Nadie quería cruzar pero yo cruzé. Todos se vinieron atras de mí. Cuando llegué al parqueadero no más había como una loma y nada más alcanzé subir hasta la loma y para la traila de nosotros ya no se podía porque había como unos 5 pies de agua porque corre un canal por medio del parqueadero. Ya me devolví y cuando me devolví fue cuando me los tope. Y allí fue cuando me dijeron ellos que no había pasada y les dije yo que sí, que si había pasada, que me siguieran y eso fue cuando fuimos a llegar y cuando llegamos queriamos ir a sacar cosas porque o sea que todo el agua estaba abajo y no quisimos porque como corrian electricidad pensamos que corrian por debajo y no quisimos arriesgar sino que nos devolvimos y nos fuimos pa, la casa de un amigo hasta pasar un día ya no pudimos cruzar para este lado porque el le puente de aca del 264 también se inundó.

AC: ¿El que está en camino a Washington?

W: Sí

P: Ese mismo día. El Puente se tapó ese mismo día.

W: El caso es que duramos como una semana de aquel lado de Greenville, ya ve que se divide. Greenville queda alto y el rio queda abajo. Quedamos como una semana de aquel lado verdad?

AC: ¿Donde vivía su amigo?

W: El vivía en la calle 10 por donde está la Hastings Ford, atrás. Allí duramos como por una semana. Duramos como unos 4 o 5 dias sin trabajar. El trabajo de nosotros nos quedó de ese lado. Tuvimos que ir a rodear hasta Washington. Yo fui a rodear. Yo y unos amigos anduvimos como dos horas. En un pedacito que se hace 5 millas tuvimos que ir a rodear como 2 horas. Ya cuando llegamos quise volver a venir a sacar ropa pero ya el agua estaba más alta y nos metimos yo y dos primos más a querer llegar a la casa. Cuando veníamos cruzando para llegar a la casa el agua nos fue tapando. Mejor nos arrandamos y fuimos y prestamos una chalupa.

AC: ¿El señor que les prestó la chalupa, lo conocían?

W: No, ya nos íbamos a la casa de mi primo y en eso vimos a un señor pasar con una chalupa en la troca y lo seguimos. Lo seguimos hasta que llegó a su casa y allí cuando llegamos a su casa nosotros le dijimos que si nos rentaba su chalupa porque queriamos sacar cosas y se nos había inundado y nos dijo que no, que no nos la rentaba, que nos la prestaba y ya fuimos. Sí, era la primera vez que lo veíamos. En esa temporada como que uno se hizo de sentimientos o sea que ya las cosas materiales, como que ya no le importaban a uno. O sea que si uno miraba cualquier cosa uno daba ayuda. Ese día que nos metimos nosotros en la chalupa en una traila estaba alta el agua y llegaba como hasta la puerta. En esa traila se oyian perros dentro y perros chiquitos. Nosotros quisimos sacar los perros con la chalupa. Cuando quisimos tocar a los perros, era una perra, una pit bull que tenía perritos, no pudimos porque era muy brava y nosotros lo único que hicimos fue avisar a la gente del army. Ya despues vinieron especialistas yo creo porque trajeron como pinsas para los perros y luego los sacaron.

Cuando veníamos remando con la chalupa, los carros estaban abajo. Cuando llegamos a la casa no podíamos abrir la puerta porque la corriente del agua estaba muy fuerte. Ya cuando abrimos la puerta nos metimos y el agua estaba dentro de la casa. A mí me daba aquí en el pecho. Sacamos cositas que podíamos sacar como ropa y todo eso.

P: O sea lo que había quedado mero arriba. Lo que no se mojó.

W: Eso fue lo que saqué. Nos aventamos pues, en la chalupa porque no podiamos andar pa' allá por la corriente de agua. Fuimos a salir a otra orilla donde estaba más baja el agua y fue donde nos salimos y regresamos pa' la casa y duramos como una semana. Vivíamos juntos pero en esa temporada nos tuvimos que separar porque ellos se quedaron en casa de unos amigos. Cuando yo cruzé para este lado, yo me vine para la casa de un primo mío.

P: O sea que en esos 8 dias ellos se tuvieron que ir con primo de él a vivir y nosotros nos quedamos. Yo y mi esposo y este otro niño nos quedamos con otros amigos. La otra hija mía se fue con su suegra a Wilson y la otra hija más chiquita de 14 años también se fue con su hermana porque allí en la casa de los amigos que nos dejaron vivir, habíamos como, eramos como 20 viviendo en la misma casa. Si, como 20 y otros amigos que tenían un apartamento por allí mismo, habían como … como cuantos?

ARTURO: Como unos 30.

P: Ahá, en un apartamento chiquito de una recámara, y pues durmiendo en hilerita todos. Nos quedamos nada mas con lo que llevabamos puesto o sea nosotros no sacamos nada. Fue tan derepente y no tenía uno nada. Yo decía «¿qué hace que todo se haya perdido? Lo principal es que todos estabamos bien.» Me sentía yo bien de que todos estabamos bien y las cosas materials, pues poco a poco se recuperan. Pero sí, como quiera se sentía uno triste. El Segundo día despúes del huracán los esposos pensaron que no hay mandado, no hay nada y se fueron a Ayden. Les dijeron que en Ayden estaba una tienda abierta y se fueron a Ayden a traer leche, agua y cosas para los niños.

A: Un galón de leche nada más dejaban comprar por familia. No había. Aquí en Greenville estaba todo cerrado. Aquí no conseguía usted nada. Nosotros nos fuimos hasta Ayden no mas por un galón de leche y galones de agua.

P: ¿Y tardaron mucho verdad?

A: había bastante gente.

P: Y luego el camino también que no se podia ir directo. Tenían que ir rodeando. Tardaron como medio día para llegar hasta Ayden. Y aquí en Greenville pues todas las tiendas estaban cerradas. Hasta como al tercer dia empezaron a normalizarse las cosas y ya las gasolineras se abrieron, las tiendas empezaron a regalar agua y asi empezó a llegar ayuda.

W: Los primeros días como que no le importaba a uno, pero cuando empezó a apretar la comida, el agua y que miraron pues que no había ningún

---

movimiento, todo estaba muy aplacado, pues nos empezamos a preocupar de lo que iba a pasar. Nos sentíamos asi como mas apretados.

P: Y luego la casa donde vivíamos no tenía luz, ni agua, ni telefono, ni nada. Lo que hicimos es que de Wilson nos trajeron una cosa para afuera y cocinabamos allá afuera. Cocinabamos afuera y le dabamos de comer a los niños primero y después nosotros. Después de como tres días empezamos a conseguir más ayuda de las iglesias y otros lugares.

AC: ¿Entonces como le hacían sin agua y electricidad?

P: No pues, no había.

AC: ¿Por cuanto tiempo estuvieron viviendo así?

P: Como tres dias y después fuimos a Target a comprar ropa.

AC: Estaba abierto Target durante ese tiempo?

P: Un ratito

W: ¿Estaba oscuro. Como que tenian no más un generados porque hacían las cuentas. ...

P: A mano

W: Con lápiz y pluma porque las computadoras no funcionaban. Yo creo que la gente se llevaban cosas de allí porque de repente miraba uno a la gente vestida diferente.

AC: ¿Cómo supieron de servicios que estaban disponibles, de la ayuda?

W: Andábamos en el centro buscando. A donde mirábamos que hacían fila, pues les preguntábamos que había y nos informaban y nos formabamos a agarrar agua.

P: A nadie le importaba porque andábamos todos igual.

W: Lo haciamos por necesidad, no por gusto

AC: ¿Qué tipo de ayuda consiguieron?

P: Con la Cruz Roja. En esos momentos como que uno andaba muy desorientado y no sabía uno. Vimos que había mucha gente allí que estaban haciendo fila.

AC: ¿Donde?

P: Allí en la Cruz Roja. Recibimos ayuda de la Cruz Roja. Cuando vimos que había mucha gente que estaba haciendo fila, llegamos a ver qué clase de ayuda estaban dando y pues nos dijeron que era la Cruz Roja y que si nosotros habíamos sido afectados que hicieramos fila para que nos dieran un número para la entrevista, y pues tardamos mucho pero tuvimos la entrevista.

AC: ¿Tuvieron la entrevista ese mismo día?

P: No. Duramos como dos días. Hubo personas que no se daban cuenta de la ayuda. Para ellas les tardó mas en conseguir ayuda porque ellas estaban en un albergue y allá no salían porque no tenían como.

AC: ¿Y nadie les informó?

P: No, no les informaban.

AC: ¿Donde era? Cual albergue?

P: Creo que estaban en una escuela. Les tomó más tiempo y pues sí, ellos también necesitaban urgentemente la ayuda y pues yo les dije pues que aquí es la Cruz Roja, que se formen y esperen que les hablen y no se vayan. Les dije que sí iban a recibir ayuda, no más que tenían que tardar allí. La Cruz Roja nos ayudó mucho y ahora nosotros ayudamos. Cuando están pidiendo ayudas, damos un poquito de lo mucho que ellos nos dieron.

A: Nos trataron muy bien. Nunca nos humillaron ni nada.

AC: ¿Durante ese tiempo cuando se tuvieron que mover de un lado a otro, conocieron gente?

A: Sí, conocimos a Antonio y a Jorge. Antonio nos prestó ayuda. Nos presto una trailita para vivr allí sin cobrar nada. Después conseguimos una traila y todo.

AC: ¿Cuanto tiempo hicieron en la casa de sus amigos?

P: Como tres meses

AC: ¿Y de allí se fueron en su propia traila?

P: No, en la casa de amigos anduvimos como un mes. Ya después nos dijeron que Antonio tenía una trailita y que posiblemente nos la podia prestar y pues yo ya quería estar sola no más con mis hijos y fuimos a preguntarle si nos la rentaba o prestaba y nos la prestó.

AC: ¿Siempre habla usted de la inundación con sus amigos y seres queridos?

P: Sí, y ahora creemos. Antes deciamos no, que no iba apasar nada y él nunca quería salirse. Ahora sí pensamos que nos puede volver a suceder.

AC: ¿Cuanto tiempo estuvieron sin trabajar?

w: Una semana. Somos varias compañías de contratistas en la planta y de cada compañía dos personas se tenían que quedar en caso que se quebraran ventanas o pipas. A mí me dijeron que tenía que ir pero a la mera hora mejor me fui para Wilson. A mí me iba a tocar quedarme en la planta y andar cuidando.

AC: ¿Todo el día y toda la noche?

w: Era el transcurso de la noche y el transcurso del día porque si se quebraban ventanas o cualquier cosa, para eso nos querían.

AC: Entonces tenían que componerlo allí enseguida?

w: Sí

A: El partrón nos ayudó también

AC: ¿Qué clase de ayuda?

A: Pues, nos ayudó en lo económico

AC: ¿Esto fué después, cuando regresaron a trabajar?

A: Sí, cuando ya regresamos de Wilson, le platicamos lo que nos había pasado. Incluso hasta ofreció su casa para que yo me fuera con mi familia pues, y me dió dinero.

P: y mandado

A: Dió mandado y me dijo que si me quedaba en hotel que guardara los recibos del hotel y el me lo pagaba.

w: Si, habiamos como … como cuantos empleados tendrá ésta?

A: La planta es enorme. Como mil …

w: No, como unos tres mil empleados y de esos andábamos como 30 y anduvimos limpiando y recogiendo cosas quebradas. Cuando todo se empezó a normalizar nos hablaron a todos los que estuvimos allí y nos dieron las gracias. Nosotros reportamos al trabajo y allí fue cuando nos pusieron a hacer eso. De los 30, como 15 eramos Mexicanos.

AC: ¿Está usted en una situación mejor o peor después de la inundación?

P: Mejor

AC: ¿Porqué?

P: Pues, no nos hace falta trabajo gracias a Dios y nos sentimos a gusto.

A: … Y vivimos en el mismo parqueadero, no tenemos miedo … (risa) Sí nos afectó pero es un parqueadero donde vivimos muy a gusto.

P: Sí, y nosotros lo que queríamos era una parte donde vivir, y se batalla para hallar un lote y todo eso y pues yo le dije a mi esposo que regresemos al mismo pues al cabo allí viviamos muy a gusto y tranquilos y si vuelve a suceder pues ya nos tocaría otra vez.

A: Nos tocaría perder otra vez. Ahora sí lo tenemos asegurado por fuera y por dentro. Cuando estábamos en la otra traila no teníamos aseguranza, o sea que lo perdimos todo. Nos quedamos pues en la calle. Nos quedamos sin nada. Nos pagaron la traila pero no, más eso.

P: Lo que pasó fue que la aseguranza pagó lo que se debía de la traila y nosostros, así como la aseguranza nos dió el cheque, pagamos la traila pero nosotros nos quedamos sin nada. Lo único fué que se quedó el "record" [reporte de crédito] limpio pero nosotros tuvimos que empezar de nuevo.

AC: ¿Hay algunos sitios que usted ya no frecuenta o cosas que ya no hace desde la inundación?

W: Ya no hay donde cortarme el pelo. Allí junto al río estaba un local donde cortaban el pelo y antes de la inundación yo siempre iba allí. Cuando sucedió lo del huracán y se inundó, no supe a donde quedaron.

AC: ¿Hay algunas cosas que ustedes evitan hablar sobre la inundación?

P: No, nos sentimos bien hablando.

A: Pues fue una experiencia que no creíamos. Eso era una de las cosas que yo no creía. Yo pensaba «Qué va a pasar esto» … o «No, déjenlo. Aquí lo espero dormido». Mi hija Cristina cuando se iba a ir, lloraba mucho y quería sacarme. Yo insistía en quedarme.

A: No me dejaba en paz. Es muy nerviosa. No estaba contenta y yo era de las personas que insitía en quedarme. No, y ahora sí creo.

AC: ¿Hay algunas cosas que le traen emociones intensas de la inundación?

P: Pues, nos ponemos tristes cuando recordamos que anduvimos batallando.

A: Está muy triste andar fuera de su casa. Como ahorita tenemos todo y que para mañana no tengamos nada … tener que ir a otras casas. Por familiares que sean o muy amigos pero no se siente muy a gusto como en su casa. Mis hijos sufrieron.

P: Allí donde estabamos viviendo, nos dieron mucha confianza para que nos sintiéramos a gusto y por ese lado nos sentíamos a gusto pero se sentía uno triste porque toda la familia desparamada, o sea que unos allá, otros acá. No sabíamos como estaban ellos en Wilson y ellos no sabían como estabamos nosotros aquí.

AC: ¿No tenian como comunicarse?

P: No, no había teléfonos ni nada. La forma en que nosotros nos comunicabamos y supimos de amigos, era por medio del radio, por medio de la estación.

AC: ¿En español?

P: Sí. Fue así que supimos que estaban en tal parte y que estaban bien y ellos sabían que nosotros estabamos aquí.

AC: ¿Ustedes mandaban mensajes?

P: Sí

AC: ¿Tuvo alguna dificultad en su vida personal después de la inundación? ¿Problemas en dormir? Problemas de salud?

P: Durante ese tiempo tuve mucha asma.

A: Depresión

P: Mucha depresión. Me sentía muy deprimida y estaba enferma con asma.

AC: ¿Le ofrecieron ayuda?

P: no la busqué

AC: ¿Cómo cambió su perspectiva sobre la vida, la comunidad. Agencias del gobierno?

W: Pues, no más que pierde uno el orgullo. Cuando no le pasan a uno las cosas se siente uno con mucho orgullo. Y cuando pasaron las cosas, teníamos que estar haciendo fila, pidiendo agua o pidiendo comida. Cuando está uno bien, dicen «allí están dando comida» pero como que uno se averguenza.

A: Qué va a andar uno allá. Ni que tuviera tanta necesidad.

W: Pierde uno el orgullo y no le importa a uno cualquiera cosa que tenga uno que hacer.

A: Burger King regalaba hamburguesas y hicimos fila.

P: Antes éramos de las personas que no nos gustaba pedir ayuda porque decíamos que hay personas que la necesitan más y hay que darles la oportunidad que la reciban mejor ellas. Cuando nos pasó eso, habían filas para pedir ayuda y nos poníamos a hacer fila y yo decía que no me da verguenza porque sí estaba necesitando la ayuda. En ese momento también la necesitabamos.

W: Y se sentía uno como si anduviera en Mexico porque andaba uno en bicicleta en el centro y andaba en la caja de las trocas. Andaba uno encuerado, en puro shorts porque se metía uno en una parte donde había agua. Se sentía uno como si andaba en Mexico, al estilo Mexicano.

AC: ¿Como ha cambiado su comunidad?

W: Los vecinos que teníamos alrededor de raza morena, nunca los volvimos a ver y no supimos donde quedaron. El area donde vivíamos era por la otra orilla del parqueadero y en esos momentos nadie supo donde quedó ni un vecino.

P: Todos allí nos llevabamos bien y ya cuando pasó todo eso ya no supimos donde quedaron.

AC: ¿Cree que ya llegaron las cosas a ser normal como eran antes? ¿En su vida? En la comunidad?

P: Sí

A: Yo creo que si.

P: No más con el temor. Se asusta uno cuando va a haber un huracán pero ahora estamos mas pendientes. Ahora decimos que sí vamos a salir.

AC: ¿Alguna otra cosa que quieren añadir?

A: La historia de un perro que se llamaba Chicano. Lo dejamos cuando salimos en la noche y conforme iba subiendo el agua, él se iba orillando y luego como mi chavalo lo quería mucho, cuando bajó el agua y empezaron a rescatar a los perros, íbamos a los albergues de los perros a buscarlo porque él quería hallar a su perro. «¿Como es el Chicano?» le preguntaban.

W: «Pues es un perro negro, y menea la cola» (risa)

AC: ¿Y lo encontraron?

A: Sí. Wilber lo encontró.

W: Lo encontré aquí en el parqueadero cuando vine a dar una vuelta. El perro como que conocía el zumbido de la troca y cuando oyó el zumbido, corrió a la troca y fue cuando me lo eché adentro y me lo llevé. Lo llevé donde estaba viviendo y después se lo llevaron para la casa de Antonio y echó a perder al perro de Antonio, Mailo. Lo hizo parrandero.

AC: ¿Alguna otra cosa?

A: Ojalá que no vuelva a pasar.

W: Y darle gracias a la Cruz Roja

P: Y al Salvation Army

AC: Usted cree que se unió la gente durante ese tiempo?

P: Sí, sí.

AC: Eso es todo, muchas gracias.

Flooded backyard.

Photo courtesy of Ana Cowó.

Interview

Ana Cowó with Jorge

Jorge currently lives in a mobile home park in the Belvoir area. At the time of the flood, he was living in the same mobile home park with his wife Olga, her mother and sister.

JORGE: During that time we were getting ready to open the store so we were working here in the store.

ANA COWÓ: Did this change after the flood? Did you have to move from where you were living?

J: I wasn't affected too much. My trailer wasn't affected.

AC: So you didn't have to move from your house or anything?

J: No, we did leave when we were watching on the television that the hurricane was coming. My other sister-in-law called that they were going to a hotel and we could go with her.

AC: Here in Greenville?

J: Here in Greenville. My parents also called me from Wilson and told us to go to Wilson. Finally we left to go to the hotel. I left my car and we all went in the truck. We went to the hotel and we were all sleeping in rows. We all slept there and we got up the following day at about 7 in the morning, and seeing as how my truck was four-wheel drive, we went to look around and we saw branches and trees on the ground and there was water everywhere. We went by Hwy. 264 and I went towards the mobile home park and the water was high in some parts but I went ahead and went to the house. The water was covering a little bit of the street but I went ahead and when I got to the house the water was higher. I went in the mobile home park with my truck and then I left and went back to the hotel.

AC: You didn't get anything out?

J: No, we didn't take anything out, except clothes to take to the hotel so that we could take baths and other little things that my wife took out like her jewelry, and her earrings and rings—all that that was valuable. We got it out and came back. That evening they blocked the streets and no one could cross the bridge. You couldn't cross to the other side. We stayed in the hotel for another night. When we wanted to return on the following day, almost everything was blocked so we couldn't get there. They wouldn't let you get to [the mobile home park]. I still went in because my truck has four-wheel drive. We then went to Antonio's house. We stayed with Antonio.

AC: How many days did you stay there?

J: We stayed like, one day with Antonio, maybe two. We stayed two days with him and then we had to leave that area because he lives behind the airport and they took us out of there. During those days I still kept an eye on my trailer. I would go in the mornings or in the evenings. I went often but then the water rose and it would reach to the middle of the door of the truck, but since it was a four-wheel drive I would still go way inside and would leave with no problem. So they told us we had to leave Antonio's house and we went to Wellcome Middle School. We were there for about two days and then I called my mom. There was no way to communicate except with cell phones. I called my mom in Wilson and she told me to go there, and we tried to leave but there were no exits. Finally we did leave but we spent the entire day getting to Wilson. I had to go through Rocky Mount and go up by Hwy. 95. I stayed there with my mom for about two days also and then we came back through Hwy. 264. There were exits to get here and we came back.

AC: And you went back to your house?

J: Ah, hhm, how was it? I think that we came back to Antonio's because the water was still high. We were out for about a week. I think that yes, yes, we came back to Antonio's and then we went home.

AC: Did any water get inside your house?

J: No, it got to the skirting underneath the trailer by the door and the porch, but it didn't get inside. What did happen was that they stole from us. On one of those days that we were out, someone broke into the back doors of many trailers. They stole little things from me like two pairs of boots, two hats and two belts. They stole my wife's wristwatch and my sister-in-law's CDs, little things that they could take. They stole $500 from my neighbor. He left for one night. I helped him get out. There were many small cars that would stay behind and I would pull them out. He came back the following day and that's when we all noticed that the trailers were vandalized.

AC: Did you ever find out who did it?

J: Well, we did the report with the Sheriff's office and they came to take fingerprints but we never heard anything. I had insurance so they paid for what was lost in the robbery and they paid for the damages to the trailer. The cars would pass and the waves would hit the skirting and it bent. They paid for that and they paid for the air conditioning head unit that was outside. The insurance paid for that but nothing was damaged inside.

AC: You mentioned that you had some difficulties getting in contact with people.

J: There were no telephones. I think there was a telephone at El Ranchito Restaurant and I came with Antonio. We came here to the restaurant and got some food. But, the truth is that I don't really remember. I think that I called my mom with the cell phone only.

AC: So, did you try to get in contact with anyone for help?

J: Well, I speak English and Spanish so I didn't have any difficulties. However, I went to help at the Red Cross as a volunteer and interpreter. Some Hispanics would come. I didn't need the help. Thank God, I did not have to ask for anything, only what they stole from me and that was material, things that could be replaced. I didn't have any problems for anything. The Red Cross and Salvation Army would give out ice at the Piggly Wiggly. They had a trailer and were distributing bags of ice. I think that they were giving out two bags so we went for that; but apart from that, no. We did have problems at a gas station by Wellcome Middle School. They were charging three times the amount for things. I went to get some gas and my wife bought two sodas and he wanted to charge her a lot of money so she told me and I went back to check. He realized that I could talk English really well so he gave us the change and apologized. There were a lot of people there so he was trying to take advantage.

AC:	From what you observed, do you think that the Social Service agencies or agencies that give service to the community and FEMA, do you think that they did a good job helping the Hispanic people?

J:	Yes, I think they did a good job. When I was a volunteer, what I noticed was that many African Americans came back more than once. This one time we caught someone who had been there in the morning and then came back in the evening and since there were security guards and sheriffs, they asked the person to leave. When we were filling out the application forms, they would ask the people for Social Security numbers and many were disappointed. Some of them didn't speak English. They were people who really needed the help. The Hispanic community was the one that suffered the most, I think. They didn't receive help from FEMA like the Americans did, the ones that live here. For instance, they got trailers by Hwy. 33. It was mostly whites and African Americans, and our people if they didn't have insurance, like Don Arturo, well they only got their trailer paid and nothing else. They didn't get any money for the damages inside. FEMA did a good job for those that had Social Security cards, documents, but those who didn't have any suffered a lot. There were people who didn't know that they could get help and the truth is that most were discouraged because they were asked for Social Security numbers or other documents and they wouldn't get help if they didn't have them. The Red Cross, while I was there, would give help to everyone that came. They would get little things like bottles of water, diapers for the babies, all that. It was great help for the people.

AC:	Do you remember any other details about the flood? Days? Dates? Did you meet anyone that you keep in contact with until now?

J:	Well, the only family is Don Arturo's family. I knew them only by sight and we would say hello.

AC:	From where?

J:	From the dances, or maybe we would see them at the mall or Wal-Mart.

AC:	This was before the flood?

J:	Yes, before. We became friends and started visiting each other during that time when they were living with Antonio. I was with Antonio, so occasionally I would go there so we got to know each other better. Now we grill together and we get together. They were the only ones I got to know. When we were in Wellcome [Middle School], we also saw a lot of people, Latinos that we knew by sight maybe from church or around.

AC:	Do you still talk about the flood with your friends and relatives?

J:	Not too often, more with Antonio. I don't get together with people too often. I leave the store and go straight home. I do talk about it with Antonio. Sometimes we remember when were driving around and pulled out many cars with my truck.

AC: For people you knew?

J: No, people whose cars got stuck there or who were driving around and the motor would get wet so the cars would stop. Antonio and I would pull them out. I only talk to him and to my sister sometimes but not too frequently.

AC: Do you think you are in a better or worse situation after the flood? How about those people you know?

J: The same, I think. Everything is back to normal.

AC: Does anything trigger intense emotions for you about the flood?

J: No, there isn't much. Thank God, my family didn't suffer.

AC: How has your perspective changed? About life, family, community, etc.?

J: Well, now when they say that hurricane season is here, I have my First Aid kit, my flashlight, my little radio, everything. I have everything prepared and since I'm in the Reserves, I have a box of MREs, those things that you eat. I have a box of those. Yes, we take it more seriously because we know it has happened and we lived it. Many people died in that tragedy so I give thanks to God that everything went and nothing happened to my family and we take it more seriously. When they say another hurricane is coming, we know we are prepared and that sometimes we have to leave. The next time I will go to Wilson. I also make sure that I have good insurance for the house and everything.

AC: How has your community changed after the flood?

J: I think that people are just like me, they have lived it so they take everything more seriously now and they believe that it can happen again. Likewise, with their trailers or homes, they have flood insurance so they are better prepared. Many Mexicans and Hispanics have their trailers and they don't have insurance—the trailers that they get cheaper, like two or three thousand dollars and they pay in cash. I have talked to some others and told them to go to All State or wherever they have their car insurance and get insurance for their trailers. A few of them have done it.

AC: So you think everything is back to normal in the community?

J: Yes. A few mobile home parks, for example where Don Arturo lives, were filled before the flood but now there are only a few trailers. Pinecrest also. It got affected and it hasn't opened again. A lot of people were living there, and a lot of Hispanics. The businesses—yes, they're back to normal, but the mobile home parks that were beside the river, those have not gotten back to normal.

AC: From your point of view, since you volunteered with the Red Cross during that time, do you think that everyone was treated in the same way?

J: I never went to FEMA, but for the two or three days that I spent at the Red Cross, I noticed that people were treated in the same way. I saw Hispanics, whites and African Americans and they seemed to be treated equally. I don't know what happened inside with whoever they got because you had to take a cart and the volunteer would take you to the lines and they would give you a little bit of everything. They would tell you to choose. I noticed that for some of them, the volunteers would put the things in, but the majority of the people took the stuff and put it in their carts. They were treated equally.

AC: Is there anything else that you observed from the people you helped, or anything that you want to add? Antonio mentioned that there was a man who lived behind his house . . .

J: Oh yes, Bill. It was during the time when we were there with Antonio. He is an older man. The people from the Fire Department passed and told us that we had to evacuate the area. The people that they would meet on the streets, they would tell them they had to leave. After a while a sheriff passed by, and everyone started to leave. I remember asking Antonio about his neighbor and he didn't know. We were leaving already so Antonio told me to go check to see if he was still there and, yes, he was. I told him, "Bill, we gotta go." And he told me that he would stay. I told him that the Fire Department said that we had to go, but no, he didn't want to leave. So finally I convinced him. He wanted to stay in his house because he said that it was the only thing he had.

AC: He didn't have any relatives?

J: He has a brother, but his brother lived by Bethel. I think he has two sisters but he was living alone. I finally convinced him so he asked me what he should take and I told him to take some clothes for a couple of days and some blankets. He is a really nice person. So I got him out and I took his clothes because the water was rising. The water was rising by Antonio's house. We got out and I took him and took his clothes and he had two flashlights so we took those and locked his doors and turned everything off. We left, so I helped him up to the truck and we went to Wellcome Middle School. And wherever I went, I would take him with me. He didn't want to leave. I got really close to him. I got to appreciate my grandparents even more because I noticed that he got close to me. He didn't have anyone so he would stick by me. When we were at Wellcome Middle School, he would stay with me in a corner. He was very humble and calm, a little shy but we talked. He told me his life story, about his wife and about himself. I got very attached to him and then we went to Wilson with my parents and took him also. I didn't want to leave him there. I told him, "Bill, we're going to Wilson with my parents, do you want to come?" And he said yes because he didn't know anyone and he didn't want to stay alone so he would go with me. So I told him that I had taken him out [of his house] and I would be the one to take him back to his house. We went to Wilson for about two days and my mom lent him the washing machine and he washed his clothes during those two days that we were there. When we came back here the water was still high and he wanted to go back to his house and I told him, no.

AC: Did his trailer get flooded?

J: It's a house. No, no it didn't get flooded. Antonio's didn't get flooded either. It only got to the last step but it didn't get all the way inside. We went to his house [Bill's] to check on it because he has cats. The cats had stayed on his porch and we left food for them. We came back and they didn't have any food left so we gave them some more. He wanted to stay but I told him to wait until they told us we could return. So we went back to the school.

AC: This was after Wilson?

J: Yes, we went to Wellcome. So we were there for two days more and then we came back home and I took him back to his house also. The water was still high but it had gone down a little. I would go there often to check on him because he's diabetic and has high blood pressure, and when he was going around with me he would have his pills and would take them. I do remember him … he didn't want to leave.

AC: Does he still live there?

J: He does. Lately, it's been like three months since I've been around there. I think he's still there. He's really nice, really nice.

AC: Anything else that you want to add about your experiences or what you observed from other people?

J: Well, only that I think that the Hispanic community suffered the most. The Red Cross helped. Like I told you, there were some people that didn't speak English.

AC: Were there any other bilingual volunteers apart from you?

J: I was there, my niece and my sister-in-law were also there. When the water went down I started working here in the store and got busy here. There were more people apart from us.

Rescuing belongings from the flood waters.

Photo courtesy of Ana Cowó.

Entrevista

Ana Cowó y Jorge

Jorge vive en mobile home park en el area de Belvoir. En el tiempo del huracán, él vivía en el mismo sitio. Jorge vive con su esposa Olga, su suegra y cuñada.

AC: ¿Dónde estaba viviendo durante el tiempo de la inundación?

J: Estaba yo en mobile home park.

AC: ¿Usted y su esposa?

J: Mi esposa, mi suegra y mi cuñada.

AC: ¿Dónde trabajaba?

J: Yo en ese tiempo no trabajaba, estábamos abriendo la tienda. Estábamos trabajando aquí en la tienda.

AC: ¿Cambió esto después de la inundación? Se tuvo que mover de donde vivía?

J: A mí casi no me afectó. A mi traila no le afectó.

AC: ¿Entonces no se tuvieron que mover de la casa ni nada?

J: Sí nos salimos. Estabamos mirando la television y en eso me llamó mi otra cuñada , que ella iba a ir a un hotel y que nos fueramos con ella.

AC: ¿Aquí en Greenville?

J: Aquí en Greenville. Y también mis papás me llamaron de Wilson que nos fuéramos con ellos en Wilson. De último nos fuimos al hotel.

Todos nos fuimos, hasta mi suegra, y entonces dejé mi carrito y el de mi esposa y todos nos fuimos al hotel en la troca. Pues allí estuvimos en surquitos, todos allí dormidos hechos bola. Nos levantamos el próximo día como a las 7 de la mañana y como la troca mía es alta, 4-wheel drive, pues nos fuimos a dar una vuelta. Había ramas tumbadas, árboles, había agua en partes y en eso nos fuimos por la 264 [carretera 264] y agarré para el [mobile home park]1 y ya salimos y el agua estaba alto en lugares. Me metí y el agua estaba tapando la calle un poquito y entonces cuando llegué a la casa ya estaba más alta el agua y entonces me salí y me fui para el hotel.

AC: ¿No sacaron nada?

J: No sacamos nada. Lo único que llevamos fue ropa para bañarnos y cosillas así que mi esposa sacó, como sus joyas y anillos. Sacamos todo lo que era valuable y entonces nos fuimos atrás. En la tarde ya estaban cerradas la calles y el Puente, ya no se podía cruzar para el otro lado, y entonces nos quedamos en el hotel otra noche. Al siguiente día cuando quisimos regresar ya casi estaba todo cerrado, ya no dejaban entrar para el [mobile home park]. Yo sí entraba por lo mismo de la troca pero no había salida para allá. De último nos fuimos para la casa de Antonio.

AC: ¿Como cuantos dias se quedaron?

J: Con Antonio nos quedamos como dos dias y luego de allí nos sacaron porque él vive atras del aeropuerto. Nos salimos de allí. En esos dias yo le echaba vuelta a mi traila. Iba en las mañanas o en las tardes. Iba seguido y ya esos dias el agua llegaba a la mitad de la puerta de la troca, pero como era 4-wheel drive, pues yo me metía hasta adentro y me salía sin ningún problema. Entonces de allí nos sacaron y nos fuimos a Wellcome School. Allí estuvimos como 2 dias y luego me comuniqué con mi mama en Wilson y me dijo que me fuera para allá, pero no había salida. A última hora sí salimos pero tardamos todo el día para llegar hasta Wilson. Tuve que ir por Rocky Mount y subir hasta arriba por la 95 [carretera 95]. Allí me quedé con mi mamá como por dos dias también y ya después nos regresamos por la 264. Ya había salida para acá.

AC: ¿Regresaron a la casa de ustedes?

J: Ahmm, como está? Creo que regresamos con Antonio porque estaba alta el agua y sí, porque tardamos como una semana afuera yo creo y este, pero sí, sí, llegamos con Antonio creo y después nos fuimos para la casa.

AC: ¿Pero no les entró agua ni nada dentro de la casa?

J: No, a mi me llegó hasta la traila, donde está la puerta, el porch y todo eso pero no se me metió pa'adentro. Lo malo que sí pasó es que nos robaron. Esos dias que nos salimos … en todo el parqueadero allí, a varias trailas les quebraron la puerta de atras y se metieron y a mi me robaron como cosillas así. Tenía botas, dos sombreros, dos cintos. A mi esposa le robaron un reloj, a mi cuñada le robaron CDs, cosillas así que podían llevarse. A mi vecino le robaron como $500 que tenía guardado. El se salió no más una noche. Yo lo saqué porque habían carritos que se quedaban y yo los jalaba. A él yo lo saqué. El regresó al siguiente dia y allí fue cuando se dió cuenta de lo que le pasó al lor trailes.

AC: ¿Y supieron quién fue?

J: No pues, hicimos el reporte con el Sheriff's Office y fueron y sacaron «finger prints» [huella digital] pero no, hasta ahorita no supimos nada. Como tenía aseguranza me pagaron lo del «robbery» [robo]. Me pagaron los daños de la traila como el agua … pasaban los carros y aventaban las olas. Y el "skirting" [la orilla] que tenía allá abajo me lo dobló. Me pagaron eso y me pagaron el sistema de aire acondicionado que estaba afuera. Se hechó a perder y la aseguranza me lo pagó. Adentro no le pasó nada de daños.

AC: Entonces mencionó que tuvieron un poco de dificultad en comunicarse con gente.

J: No había telefono. Yo creo que había un teléfono en El Ranchito y yo vine con Antonio. Vinimos aquí al restaurante a sacar comida, pero la verdad casi no me acuerdo. Creo que llamé a mi mama por «cell phone» [celular] nada mas.

AC: ¿Ustedes trataron de comunicarse para pedir ayuda?

J: La verdad, como yo hablo ingles y español, no tuve ninguna dificultad. En cambio, me fuí a trabajar con el Red Cross de «volunteer» [voluntario], pues de interprete allí, y llegaban mucha gente … La verdad, gracias a Dios yo no perdí nada, solo lo que me robaron, pero eso eran cosas materiales que se pueden comprar. No tuve problema para nada. El Red Cross, el Salvation Army por ejemplo, se pusieron a dar «ice» [hielo] aquí en la Piggly Wiggly. Hubo un traile allí donde estaban dando bolsas de hielo, te daban dos. Eso sí. . . ibamos por hielo nada mas. Donde sí tuvimos problema fue en la gasolinera de allí por Wellcome Middle School. Estaban cobrando a lo triple por las cosas. Yo fuí a echar gasolina y mi esposa compró como dos sodas y quién sabe cuanto le querían cobrar. Entonces ella me dijo y yo me regresé y le dije que le estaban cobrando de más a mi esposa. Ya vió que yo hablaba ingles bien y regresó el cambio. Se quiso pasar como había mucha gente.

AC: ¿De lo que usted observó, cree que las agencias de servicios a la comunidad y FEMA hicieron un buen trabajo en ayudar a la gente hispana y todo?

J: Sí, si hicieron un buen trabajo. Cuando estaba allí de «volunteer» [voluntario], lo que sí miraba que llegaban los mismos morenos, más que una vez. Me tocó una vez incluso, que estaba allí, agarrar a una persona que había ido en la mañana y regresó en la tarde. Como había Sheriffs y todo eso, le dijeron que mejor se fuera. Cuando llenábamos las aplicaciones, pedian seguro y mucha gente se desanimaba. Luego como unos no hablaban inglés: Era gente que necesitaba la ayuda. La comunidad Hispana fue la que sufrió más yo creo. Ellos no recibieron ayuda de FEMA como los americanos, los que viven aquí. Por ejemplo, les daban traila allá por la 33 [carretera 33] pero puro Moreno y «bolillo» [anglo] y pues la gente de uno pues, si no tenía aseguranza como el Señor Arturo, pues nada más le pagaban su trailita y no le pagaban nada de los daños de adentro. Hicieron buen trabajo para los que tenían seguro, los documentados, pero los que no tenían documentos pues sufrieron. Tal vez hubo gente que no sabía y la verdad se desanimaba porque te pedían seguro y si no tenias, no te ayudaban. Pero en el Red Cross, cuando yo estuve allí, sí a toda la gente atendíamos. Eran cositas que les daban, botellas de agua, pampers, todo eso. Fue buena ayuda para la gente.

AC: ¿Se acuerda de algunos otros detalles de la inundación? Los dias, fechas, o conoció gente?

J: La única familia era la familia de Don Arturo. Yo los conocía así de vista, nos saludabamos.

AC: ¿A donde?

J: Por ejemplo cuando íbamos a los bailes donde iban ellos, o en veces en el mall o en Wal-Mart los mirábamos.

AC: ¿Antes de la inundación?

J: Sí, antes, pero cuando de veras hicimos amistades que nos visitabamos fue durante esos días cuando ellos estaban con Antonio. Como yo estaba con Antonio, a veces iba para allí y entonces estaban ellos allí. Ya nos conocimos más y ahora hacemos carnitas asadas y nos juntamos con ellos. Ellos fueron los únicos que concí. Cuando estabamos en la escuela también vimos mucha gente así, Latinos que conocíamos por vista así en la iglesia.

AC: ¿Siempre habla de la inundación con sus amigos o familiares?

J: La verdad casi no, no más con Antonio. Yo casi no me junto con nadie. De aquí pa, mi casa. Con Antonio sí. A veces cuando estamos allí, recordamos por ejemplo cuando andábamos yo y el, sacando varios carros con la troca.

AC: ¿De gente que conocían?

J: No, no más así que se les quedaban los carros atascados o que se les apagaba porque se mojaba el motor. Los sacabamos yo y Antonio. No más con él, o con mi hermana a veces conversamos.

AC: ¿Cree que usted, y la gente que usted conoce, están en una situación mejor o peor desde la inundación?

J: Pues igual yo pienso. Ya llegó a ser normal.

AC: ¿Hay algunas cosas que le traen emociones intensas?

J: No, no hay mucho, pues gracias a Dios, mi familia no sufrió.

AC: ¿Cómo ha cambiado su perspectiva sobre la vida, la comunidad y las agencias del gobierno desde la inundación?

J: Ya cuando dicen que es temporada de huracán, yo tengo mi First Aid Kit, tengo mi «flashlight» [linterna], mi radio. Tengo todo preparado y como estoy en las reservas, tengo una caja de MREs [comidas ya preparadas]. Son esas cosas que se comen, como cositas café. Tengo una caja de esas. Toma uno más en serio porque uno ya sabe que ya pasó. Lo viviste, y ya pasó y varias gentes se murieron en esa tragedia. Toma uno más en serio cuando dicen que hay un huracán. Sabes que estás preparado y pues que hay que salir en veces. Para la otra yo major me voy a Wilson. Uno se siente también más a gusto de las aseguranzas. Ahora ya me aseguro que tenga aseguranza buena para la casa y todo.

AC: ¿Cómo cree que ha cambiado la comunidad después de la inundación?

J: Pues yo pienso que la gente, igual que yo, ya vieron y lo vivieron y ya toman todo más en serio y creen que puede pasar otra vez. Igualmente con sus trailas o sus casitas, ya sacaron «flood insurance» [seguro de inundación]. También varios Mexicanos o Hispanos tienen sus trailitas y pues no tienen aseguranza, las que compran así baratas de dos o tres mil dólares y las pagan en efectivo. Hay algunos con los que he hablado y les digo que vayan con All State o donde tengan aseguranza de vehículo y digan también que quieren aseguranza para el traile.

AC: ¿Entonces usted cree que todo ya regresó a ser normal en la comunidad?

J: Pues sí, pero algunos parqueaderos, por ejemplo allá con Don Arturo, antes estaba lleno y ahora casi no hay muchas trailas. También ya ve el Pine Crest que estaba aquí, esa también se echó a perder y hasta ahorita no se ha abierto. Allí también había mucha gente Hispana. Los negocios yo pienso que sí ya regresaron a ser normal. Los parqueaderos de trailes que estaban cerca de los ríos o algo pienso que no se regresa todo a normal.

AC: ¿De su punto de vista, ya que usted fue voluntario en la Cruz Roja, cree usteed que todos fueron tratados igual durante ese tiempo?

197

J: Yo con FEMA no fui, pero con Red Cross, los dias que estuve allí, como dos o tres dias estuve de «voluntear», sí, sì trataron a la gente parejo. Los que llegaban allí los atendían. Yo miraba que llegaba gente Hispana, Morenos y Americanos. Quién sabe adentro, la persona que les tocaba, porque agarraban un carrito y el voluntario los llevaba por las lineas y les daba un poquito de todo. Les decian que escogieran. Algunos sí miraba que solo les hechaban las cosas, pero la mayoría de la gente agarraban las cosas. Pero sí, los trataban igual.

AC: ¿Alguna otra cosa que usted observó de las personas que usted ayudó? Me comentó Antonio que había un señor que vivía por la casa de él. ...

J: Oh sí, Bill. Fue en los dias cuando estabamos allí con Antonio. Era un señor ya de edad. Nos fuimos y pasó el «Fire Department» [Bomboros] y nos dijeron que teníamos que evacuar. A la gente que miraban en la calle, pues se bajaban y les decian que tenían que salir. Luego al rato pasó el Sheriff, unos de la ciudad y todos se salieron. Entonces yo le pregunté a Antonio de su vecino y el dijo que no sabía. Ya nos íbamos y Antonio me dijo que fuera yo a ver si todavia estaba allí, y sí, todavía estaba. Yo le dije que nos teniamos que ir pero el no quería. Yo le insistía que el Fire Department dijo que teníamos que irons y él no quería. De último lo convencí. No quería dejar su casa porque era todo lo que tenía.

AC: ¿No tenía familia?

J: Tenía un hermano pero creo que su hermano vive por Bethel, y creo que tiene como dos hermanas pero estaba viviendo solo. De último lo convencí y me preguntó qué se podía llevar y yo le dije que ropa para dos dias y unas cobijas. Es muy buena gente. Entonces fuí y lo saqué y me llevé su ropa y tenía dos «flashlights» [linternas] y los llevamos. Aseguró sus puertas y nos fuimos para la Wellcome Middle School. Donde yo iba, pues me lo llevaba. Yo como que me junté a él un poco. Como que aprecié más a mis abuelitos porque miraba que se pegaba a mi. Como no tenía a nadie, se pegaba a mi. Cuando estabamos allí en Wellcome Middle School, se quedaba conmigo allí a un lado. Es un señor muy humilde, muy tranquilo, medio timido y platicábamos. Me platicó toda su historia de él y su esposa y más me le acerqué a él y entonces de allí cuando estuvimos en la escuela nos fuimos para Wilson con mis papas y me lo llevé también. No lo quise dejar allí. Le dije que iba a ir a Wilson y que si quería ir y dijo que sí porque no conocía a nadie y no se quería quedar solo. Yo le dije que yo lo saqué y yo lo iba a llevar pa' su casa. Ya nos quedamos en Wilson como por dos dias y mi mamá le presto la lavadora y lavaba su ropita allí como por dos dias. Entonces ya cuando cruzamos para acá, regresamos y todavía estaba el agua alta y él se quería regresar y yo le decía que no.

AC: ¿Entró agua en la traila de él?

J: Es una casita. No, no le entró. Ni a la de Antonio. Nada mas llegó como a la última grada. … Yo me metí para atrás y como tenía gatitos y se quedaron en el «porch», les habíamos dejado comida cuando nos fuimos. Entonces regresamos y ya no tenían comida y nos metimos y les echamos comida. El se quería quedar pero yo le dije que todavía no, que hasta que nos digan que sí.

AC: ¿Eso fue después que regresaron de Wilson?

J: Sí. Entonces fuimos pa'atras pa'la escuela. Nos fuimos a Wellcome Middle School. Entonces estuvimos como otros dos dias y fue cuando nos regresamos a la casa y también fui y lo dejé a él. El agua todavía estaba alto pero ya había bajado un poquito. Antes iba seguido y le hechaba vueltas porque es diabético y tiene alta presión. Cuando andaba conmigo pues traía sus jaritos de pastillas y se las tomaba.

AC: ¿Siempre vive allí?

J: Siempre vive allí. Últimamente tiene como tres meses que no voy para allá. Yo pienso que está allí. Muy buena gente … es muy buena gente.

AC: ¿Alguna otra cosa que quiere añadir de sus experiencias?

J: Pues, solamente que yo pienso que la que sufrió más fue la comunidad hispana. En la Red Cross, como te digo, iban unos que no hablaban ingles.

AC: ¿Habían otros voluntarios bilingües aparte de usted?

J: Estaba yo, mi sobrinita, y una cuñada. Estabamos allí y mi cuñada fue más que yo. Cuando se bajó el agua empezamos aquí con la tienda y aquí me ocupé. Pues sí, había mas gente aparte de nosotros.

AC: Bueno pues, eso es todo. Muchas Gracias.

It was a very frustrating experience for me

Carol Christian

Carol Christian teaches Spanish in the Department of Foreign Languages and Literatures at East Carolina University.

My department received a call asking if the Spanish-speaking faculty would be willing to volunteer to help with the large number of Hispanics who were devastated by the flooding. When I went to the Red Cross office, I was told that I'd have to go through a three-hour training session to learn what questions to ask the Hispanic people. I also had to become familiar with the forms that would have to be filled out. The following day I had my training in the morning, then was assigned to sit between two Puerto Rican women to begin my work. The Red Cross had flown these women in from Puerto Rico to help. One woman sat at the table working on her *per diem* form for reimbursement. She didn't help even one person during the entire afternoon. The other woman helped a total of five people. She would allow me to look at the form that needed to be filled out while she asked all of the questions. I can understand her doing this at first to show me how the procedure is done. However, once I knew the ropes I think I should have been able to help people on my own. This never happened. I was not allowed to do anything more than sit between these two women, while the one only worried about her *per diem,* and the other worked at a snail's pace.

It was a very frustrating experience for me. Here I was, an intelligent, Spanish-speaking professional, and I was not allowed to do anything on my own to help the many people who sat in the Red Cross center hour after hour. At the end of the day, I decided that I would not go back. It was a waste of my time and energy. I discovered that several of my colleagues had the same experience when they offered to volunteer.

I appreciate that the Red Cross had a very big job to do. It was also apparent that there was an incredible amount of red tape that the flood victims had to go through in order to get basic necessities. The Red Cross missed the mark by not utilizing local talent better. Once the federal people appeared on the scene, they seemed to take over and not pay heed to the local Red Cross volunteers.

Sighing

Sharon O'Neill

I knew a Greek lady that told me
that a sigh was a bad omen
that when you sigh,
you let the demons into your home
and your luck would be bad.
I suppose that comes from
the idea that
wanting what you have not got
may cause you to lose
what you already do have.
The whole "grass is always greener" thing
or "Thou shalt not covet."
It all comes back around to appreciation
for what you do have.
But, as I look around now,
I wonder
what do I have?
I thought I lost everything
just weeks ago
only to come back
and find everything
just where we left it,
dirty dishes in the sink,
moldy laundry in the washer,
the kids' homework half done on the table.
My life was still here
through the flood
that could have taken it all away
and I find myself sighing
because now I have to clean up,
muck out the freezer
of spoiled food,
try to get rid of that stench,
and go through the mail.
I finally got my mail,
and it's postmarked
Sept. 13, almost a month ago.

And the bills are late now.
Nothing has really changed.
Life goes on, bills come due.
I can't afford to be lazy.
I need to appreciate what I have
and what I could have lost.
What would I have lost, really?
My children were safe,
everything else can go to hell
as far as I am concerned.
At these moments I am struck by
an overwhelming feeling of guilt
and I suddenly want to
give it all away
to someone that did lose everything
because it's just stuff,
reminders of my past,
all too visible affirmation
that I am here
and going nowhere fast.
And I sigh
and dream of the grass
on the other side,
grass that isn't littered
with other people's lives,
and wonder if it really is an omen,
this sighing thing.

October 4, 1999

Section IV: A HOUSE TO LIVE IN FULL OF STUFF

Discarded flood-ruined household contents.

Photo by Phyllis Adams.

Letter to her son Cobie

Jenée Brewer
Pitt County Writing Workshop

Jenée Brewer teaches autistic children at Stocks Elementary School in Tarboro. At the time of the flood she was teaching second grade. She currently lives in Bethel.

MY DEAREST COBIE,

I am writing you this letter to tell you what happened to you, your dad, your house and me when you were four months old. When you are old enough to read this letter and appreciate it, I hope it means something to you in your life.

The weather had been real bad and we were feeling the effects from hurricane Floyd. It rained so much it seemed as if it had been raining forever. All of the trees kept swaying back and forth because of the wind.

My school had already closed for Thursday because of the bad weather. We still had power and we just kept watching the news and weather all night on the TV. I had packed up stuff to take down into the basement if a tornado came through. I laid you down beside the packed-up stuff to go to the basement and your daddy and I joked with each other saying, "Everything's now ready to go down there, even Cobie!" You were so good, it was almost as if you sensed how scared and unsure your dad and I were and knew that you needed to be good.

We all slept through the night and we woke up around 7 AM, which is when you woke up most every morning. When we first woke up we looked outside and there was a lot of water standing in the front yard but even more in the back yard. We kept watching the water in the back yard because it kept getting deeper and deeper. At around 9 AM all of the fields in the back yard were completely underwater. Your daddy went outside and moved all of the dogs into the barn because their pen was going underwater.

At around 10 AM, the water started to come up in the back yard really high and was completely covering the cement pad in front of the garage. Water was now up to the back door. The water was moving so fast and the wind was blowing so hard, we felt like we were at the river. I had some landscaping timbers around the shrubs on the side of the house and in front of the house; the water just pushed them right out of the way and they floated away. Your dad's friend Alford had given you a play slide to play with outside and we still don't know what happened to that to this very day. Everything in the garage that was on the floor was just floating around outside and in the garage. We couldn't see the road in front of our house. It looked like all you could see was water forever and more water just kept coming. Your dad put on his hip waders and walked out to the railroad tracks which at this point was the highest part that wasn't completely underwater. Several people in cars were trying to come down Hwy. 64 and many had to stop before they got to our house because the water was so deep and moving so fast. Chris James came by on one of his big tractors and it was the only thing to make it through the deep water.

Nobody could believe this was happening, especially not here because there wasn't a river around anywhere. I wanted to take a picture of you and the water so you would be able to show people later on how small you were when this happened. I was so scared and unsure of what was going to happen. Little did we know what would happen next.

Around 11 AM, we heard a loud gushing water sound coming from the basement. We ran down to see what it was. Water was pouring in under the house extremely fast. It was filling up the basement very quickly. The basement is about ten feet deep, and it was a matter of ten-fifteen minutes and the basement was full of water. I kept asking your dad what was going to happen and he didn't know either. He thought that the water might stop rising when it reached a certain level in the basement. Well, it didn't. The ductwork under the house began to fill up with water. The water started to splash up over the vents in the floor. I started crying because I was so scared and didn't know what to do or how to stop the water. Your dad was so calm. He took me by the arm and said, "Jenée, I know you feel like crying but we don't have time to get upset right now. We have just a little bit of time to go around the house and get up everything you see from your knee down." I was so grateful that he could use his experience of growing up at the river and preparing for hurricanes and apply it to us now that we were being flooded.

I watched Todd and began to do what he was doing. I put you in your bouncy seat in the kitchen and started to help your dad. In the bedrooms we pulled out the bottom drawers to dressers and put them on the bed. In the bathrooms we put everything in the bottom cabinets on the counters. In your room we threw everything on the floor in your crib. The kitchen was done the same way as the bathrooms; everything from the bottom was thrown on the counters. We used the dining room chairs to raise the couches and then piled everything in the den onto the couches. We did the same in the dining room, filling the dining room table full of stuff from the bottom cabinets. You really don't realize how much you have below knee level in your house until someone tells you to go around and pick it up. Todd used big pots and big bowls, both turned upside down, to prop the refrigerator, washing machine and dryer on. I would have never thought about doing that. He made sure that the sides that had the motors were propped up and out of the water.

Todd told me to pack up enough stuff for us to stay away about a day. So I packed up bottles, diapers, a few clothes and bathroom items. I did remember to grab you a few toys to play with. I also grabbed our wedding pictures and your baby pictures. We were throwing the items in the car very fast and the water was continuing to rise in the house. As we pulled away, you could hear the muffler on my jeep in the water sounding much like a boat in the water. When we got to the railroad tracks, which were not underwater yet, your dad looked at me and said, "Did you pack us any shoes?" We both had to laugh a little. He left the two of us in the jeep and walked back in the house and got our shoes. When we left we had no idea what we would come back to, or if we would have anything when we came back. I knew not to ask your dad a lot of questions because he didn't know either and we were both very unsure of the situation. We had everything that could not be replaced in the car and that was all that mattered.

We drove to Clint James's house and camped out there for a while listening to all the reports of what had happened in Greenville with the Tar River and its flooding. Clint and Todd went back to the house and took Clint's little boat. They drove to the flooding water, then switched to the boat to ride in up to the house. They needed to get all of the rabbit dogs, so they loaded them up on the boat and got them out. They took them to someone else's house to stay for a while.

We left Clint's house and went to my uncle Frank's house and spent the night with him. My aunt Ann had gone to stay with my cousin Sarah, so she wasn't there. My cousin Alex and one of his friends that he worked with were there, and that is when we learned about what had happened in Princeville. I kept thinking about the children and how scared they must be, knowing how scared I was as an adult.

The next day we went back to the house to get more stuff since we now knew we were going to be out for a while. You stayed with Clint's wife, and your daddy and I went with Clint on the boat again to get into the house and see what had happened. This time we only could drive to the Latham Road because the water had risen so much. We put the boat in there and rode back to the house. When we went inside there was about fifteen inches of water standing all around. We were wading in water walking all through the house. Anything we forgot to pick up before we left was just floating around the house. When we stepped on the carpet, it bubbled up and made a big squishing sound as we walked on it. Your dad always tries to look for the positive in every situation. He was joking with Clint saying, "Get off my carpet, stop making it bubble up." I was surprised that I didn't start crying. I guess I realized how lucky we were and how it could have been so much worse. Your dad had already started to explain to me how we were going to fix each thing.

After packing up more stuff, we went to Greenville and stayed with Grandma Mary. She was so happy to see us and so glad that we were all safe. Your dad stayed there for one day and I stayed for two days. We had to use the ferry system to get home and around the Tar River. When your dad got home, everything had been moved out of our house since the water had receded. Clint, Chris and Neal and the guys that work for them had come in and packed our entire house up and moved it to Todd's warehouse in Bethel. When your dad got home he was able to rip up the carpet and start fans inside to start the drying out process. I came home the next day and got us settled in my Granny Ruth's old house, which nobody was staying in. I believe it was God's doing that the power had not been turned off in the house and that the last renter had just moved out. I told your dad that Granny Ruth was still looking out for me even down from Heaven.

I worked hard along with Dot, your babysitter, to make Granny Ruth's house seem like home for us since we were going to be staying there for a while. We stayed there for six months. You learned to crawl in that house, eat baby food, had your first Halloween and Christmas there and even saw your first snow there. Oh, how lucky we were to have that house to go to while we were repairing ours! We moved back in to our house in February.

Many things happened as a result of the flood. Your dad and I saw how important friends and family are in a time of a crisis. Your dad and I grew stronger as a couple. I learned to be more flexible and I learned to trust God more. You were supposed to be baptized the weekend of the flood and we had to cancel it. You were baptized at a later date and I am so grateful for that change. Your church got a new minister in January and the Reverend Simpson made your baptism so special, which would not have happened had he not been a part of our church. He talked about the power of water and the dynamic effect it has on our lives and the ability it has to change our lives.

I hope that you really think about what is in this letter when you read it and know how much your dad and I love you. Remember what happened and apply the lessons learned from it to your own life, as you become your own person with your own family. Remember that no matter what happens to your surroundings, nothing is as important as your family, friends and your church. Don't ever take any of them for granted as you go through life.

Love,
Mama

It would be impossible to imagine

Julie Howard
Pitt County Writing Workshop

IT WOULD BE IMPOSSIBLE TO IMAGINE THAT THERE COULD BE SO MUCH WATER. I remember that it all started on a Wednesday. I was sitting in another workshop on how to raise writing test scores and everybody was wondering if we would get out early. Hurricane Floyd was approaching. I wasn't worried. We'd been through hurricanes before, Dennis just the other week. I planned to leave, get a few groceries, stop by to see my friend Sarah, then head home.

Finally the announcement came that we would get out at 1:00, and when we did I went to lunch at Hamm's with a few other teachers, just like there was nothing going on. I got the groceries and visited with Sarah until almost 5:00 when I figured I'd better go home. I still didn't know if we should leave or stay. We had always stayed during the hurricanes before, but Gail's offer for us to come over didn't seem like a bad idea. It wouldn't hurt to spend the night at her house. As I was driving home it began to rain really hard and the wind picked up. I was surprised to see my husband Russell's truck in the driveway. He was already home, early.

I came in and asked if we should leave. He said he guessed so, that the sheriff's deputy had come by with a bullhorn announcing that everyone should get out. That seemed strange. It had never happened before during any storm. I remember feeling a little more nervous suddenly, but I still wasn't really worried. I packed enough clothes for a couple of days, some towels, our food, and cat food. Russell emptied the litter box, and we loaded up the car and got Rascal, our cat, in her carrying box. Russell pulled his truck into the garage just in case, so that if any trees fell it would be safe. That seems funny now.

I remember thinking that everything would be OK, that even if the water came up a whole lot it would just rise up the hill, roll over through the front yard, and not get in the house. So we left. By now it was close to 7 PM and we really shouldn't have been on the road. The rain was pouring down in sheets. It was almost impossible to see. It took forever to get to Farmville. We found the turn to Gail's house and as we came around the corner into the subdivision I slammed on the brakes. The place where we needed to turn right, where the two roads met, was underwater. You couldn't really tell how deep it was. It looked bad. I didn't know what to do, but I knew we had to get there. It wasn't like we could turn back. Russell said to go for it, not to stop, so I started ahead. Just as we got in the middle and started to turn right the car began to slow down but I just kept pushing the accelerator and we made it through.

When we got to Gail's we got soaked getting all of our stuff in the house. Gail had a room ready upstairs, so we brought in our things, cat included, and put them up there. It was almost like being at a hotel. Once the cat was settled we came downstairs, ate supper, watched some television and eventually went to bed. All very normal. I remember praying before I went to sleep that God would watch over our house and keep it safe. I woke up several times during the night. Russell slept like a log as always.

Every time I woke up the rain was pelting against the windows and the wind was howling. I was nervous but not really too scared. And every time I woke up I would just say another prayer that our house would be safe. Finally I awoke and it was daylight enough to go outside and see what had happened. I got dressed and went downstairs.

Gail was already up. Her kitchen ceiling had started leaking in the night and there were towels and water everywhere. She had already surveyed the damage—a tree down, some shutters off, nothing too big. We walked out her front door to the porch to see the street that runs in front of her house, the river I should say. I couldn't resist. I had to go out and stand in it. It came up over my ankles and seemed to have a current. I got too freaked out and went back inside. There was no electricity, but that was to be expected.

We ate something and then just sat around—Russell napping, Meredith and Brendan (Gail's children) in and out, Gail and I talking and working on schoolwork. No fear, it was over. We had a radio with batteries and tried to hook it up but the antenna was broken and we really couldn't get anything. Eventually the water went down in front of the house but the end that was flooded where we first came in was still underwater. We just wanted to get home to be sure that everything was OK. Gail had a four-wheel-drive Jeep Cherokee so she offered to drive us home. Brendan wanted to go too.

We four-wheeled through the muddy empty lot across the street from Gail's and finally made it to the road. It's hard to remember all the turning around we did trying to get from Farmville to Greenville, the driving through water, hoping and praying we would make it. We got to Belvoir and the whole school was surrounded by water. It looked like an island. We didn't think we could make it on Hwy. 33 so we turned around. We tried several ways to get to Stokes Road. I remember when we crossed the bridge on Old River Road and the water was just gushing across and we weren't sure we would make it through. We did though, and finally turned left onto Stokes Road. We had seen so much water already, flooding on the roads. I was more nervous, but as we turned I could see that the road was dry. A ray of hope.

We drove down and around the first curve and that's when the nightmare truly began. The road, the curve before our house, was underwater and we couldn't even see any more. I just remember thinking that I had to know, I had to see the house and I had to know how bad it was.

We decided to wade through the water to get to the house. Gail and Brendan would wait for us. That was a risk, considering all the water we had gone through on the way. So Russell and I stepped into the water. I remember that it was hard to walk, shoes squishing, pushing against the water, walking through the current. Yes, current running across the road. It got deeper and deeper until it was over my waist. We passed a car floating on the side of the road—the water was to the top of the windshield. I don't think we were talking, I just kept thinking, *Oh my God*. It was really unbelievable.

I don't know how far we walked. I would guess it was about a mile. We came around the second corner and there was another ray of hope. The water was getting shallower and the road in front of our driveway was dry. I thought, *Everything is going to be OK*. But I was wrong.

As we came up on our land I could see water everywhere except the road. The front of our land was wooded with the home being on the highest part of the lot, so I couldn't see the trailer. But I could see the driveway through the woods, completely underwater. People were standing on the road right in front of our house. They all had something to say, stories about overnight, snakes, neighbors. I remember them talking but not really what they were saying. The guy across the street told Russell he could use his boat to go to the house. So we got in and paddled up our driveway. We came around the corner of the woods and saw the house.

The water was halfway up in the garage and at the floor of the house. Our biggest tree had fallen and covered the front of our home. I was pretty close to hysterical, crying, saying, "Oh my God." It seemed to be all I could think. Russell paddled around back to a tree beside the garage. I held on to the tree and he jumped out of the boat to go inside. The current of the river was so strong. I had both of my hands wrapped around the tree. The water was at his chest. He came out and said his truck was floating. The truck he had just painted a month ago. The garage he had just finished building in April. The pool table he had wanted all his life and had since May.

Then we paddled to our back deck and docked the boat on the steps. It's pretty funny to dock a boat at your house. Russell swam around to the front door, crawled through the downed tree, and came through the house to open the back door. I stepped inside and it was like nothing was going on. There was no water in the house. Everything was normal. I didn't know what to do. I was crying and on the verge of hysterics. Russell said to put everything up as high as we could, in the tops of the closets, and gather whatever we could carry.

The first thing I got was the box that had every paper you might need in it. Next I got the pictures of my daddy and all the things I'd saved from when he died. I got a few other pictures too and the bags that had all the letters and cards that Russell and I had given each other over the years. When you're faced with possibly only being able to save what you can carry, it is a daunting task to choose what to take and what to take a chance on, what to leave behind.

I remember walking into the back room and picking up my box of disks that had everything I had ever created for school, along with all of my work from my master's program on them. I had it in my hand and then I put it down thinking that Russell would think it was a silly thing to bring. In hindsight I'm sure he wouldn't have, but I put it up on top of the shelf thinking it would be safe. Russell gathered some clothes. I don't remember what else we took but I know we had two big garbage bags full. Everything we could fit was in the tops of the closets. We even took our couch and chair and put them on top of our bed thinking that if the water came in they would be safe up there. Still *if*, not *when*.

As we went out the back door the water was just beginning to seep in. It was lapping at the threshold like the river laps at the shore. We put the bags in the boat, paddled back to the road, got out, and began walking back to where we'd left Gail and Brendan. It was late afternoon, the sun was getting lower in the sky, and it was so quiet. Though I hadn't thought about it on the way in, I was worried about snakes now as we waded down the road. I said aloud over and over, "Please don't let me see a snake, please don't let me see a snake." It was obvious that the water was higher than before. Russell went ahead of me. I think he thought he could get to dry land first and then come back to get the bag from me. He kept shouting, "Are you all right?" I would say, "Yes, just keep going." I remember thinking it was like I was in a movie, like I was walking down the Nile. At one point a helicopter flew over. It was all surreal. Finally we reached the dry road, several hours after we first left.

Fortunately Gail was still there, though she had backed the Jeep up quite a ways as the water was rising. She was just about to leave. Brendan had been very anxious with the water getting closer. We got back into the Jeep and returned to Gail's house. I remember I cried all the way. I remember that I still had hope even then that it might not get any higher, that it would stop at the floor and then begin to back down. I remember calling the insurance companies for the trailer and for Russell's truck. One of us came up with the idea of taking a boat in the next morning to try to get some of our stuff—the TV, our clothes, my computer. Anything we could save was better than the nothing that we had now.

Friday morning we got up early and drove to Russell's friend Danny's house. Danny could get a boat and he offered to help. Russell had a truck that his boss let him use, so we loaded up the boat, some oars, and headed back towards Stokes Road. Every way we tried to get there was blocked but we kept trying and trying and finally got through.

As soon as we turned on to the road I knew it was bad. Houses on the left side of the road that had no water anywhere near them Thursday evening now had water at their floors like ours had yesterday. Still undeterred, we parked the truck next to two or three others that were parked, unoccupied, with boat trailers. Danny and Russell unloaded the boat and paddled towards the house. Russell wouldn't let me go. I had made a list of stuff to try to get, things that I really wanted, like those computer disks. I knew he would do his best. I stayed with the truck, waiting and waiting and waiting, having no idea what was coming.

Danny and Russell returned but there was nothing in the boat. They had never even made it all the way to the house. The current of the river was so strong that they couldn't get back in there. Hope lost again. Then we heard the humming of motor boats. It was David who used to live a few houses over from us. His parents and brother still lived back there, and they had been in to see what they could get. There was very little in their boats. Everything was already ruined. David's mom had saved her bird but his brother's dogs were dead, tied up in the back yard. There were unbelievable descriptions about how high the water was now—chest high inside the houses. It was a solemn moment. Then David offered to take Russell in his boat to see what he could save from our home. Again, I, of course, was not allowed to go, which I see now was really for the best.

Danny, David, and Russell took the boat and headed away from us down the river that used to be a road. I only know the next part of the story as told by Russell. The current was very strong so it was difficult to get to the house, and when they did, I had given Russell the wrong key (yes, we had actually locked the door) so he had to break a window and swim in. The water was chest high in the house and everything was floating. Russell said snakes were swimming in the trailer with him and climbing up the walls outside of the garage. David steered the boat to the living room window and Danny and David held on to the window to keep the current from dragging them away while Russell swam around inside gathering armfuls of our stuff and dumping it out the window into the boat. A lot of our things were still dry because we had put them in the tops of the closets. What a blessing.

Eventually they came back out with a boatload of stuff. I was so glad to see it, it really didn't matter what it was. It was good to have something. I remember feeling guilty because he had gotten so much of our stuff with someone else's boat and they came out with next to nothing. They said they were going back in. They had heard a dog barking and were going to try to save it and get one more load of our stuff. Off they went. The water was still rising. Once I even had to move the truck because it was getting too close to the tires.

This trip took much longer than the first time. I remember people driving down to where we were, curious, wanting to see the water. I remember other people with boats pulling up and going in to see what they could save. I remember David's dad getting worried and thinking about going in after them. Finally they came around the curve into our sight. They couldn't find the dog. It wasn't barking anymore. Russell had gotten some more of our things. We loaded everything up, thanked David (although we could never thank him enough), and headed back to Farmville.

We got to Gail's and laid everything out in her driveway in the afternoon sun so it could dry and we could go through it and box it up. I remember washing everything in a wheelbarrow at the end of her driveway in Pine Sol because on TV there was so much talk already about the mold and germs and dead things in the water. We worked until dark. We had almost all of our clothes, most of the pictures, the monitor, hard drive, and printer to my computer, my bluebirds. It was really amazing what Russell got out. We cleaned it up outside, ran some through the dishwasher, washed all the clothes, boxed it up and put it in our room upstairs at Gail's house. It was maybe five boxes without the clothes. This was all that was left of our home.

There was no need to go back until the water got out. Gail offered to let us to stay with her. She was an angel. We were waiting once again. There was a lot of waiting. Waiting for the water to stop rising, waiting for the insurance companies to call and decide what they were going to do, waiting for FEMA, waiting in the Red Cross line only to be told that they didn't think we needed anything, waiting at the grocery store, waiting for any idea of how to begin to put our lives back together, waiting. I knew already that I would never live there again, not in that house and certainly not anywhere near that piece of land if I could help it.

I remember it was like a war zone, helicopters constantly flying back and forth, back and forth. Russell was in Greenville for something one day and came home and told us how a truck pulled up with water in the Harris Teeter parking lot and people were like madmen trying to get over there. It was panic. It was unreal. No one knew how to deal with it or what was coming next. Russell went back to work the following Monday. School was closed, of course, so I was at home with Gail. We settled in to learning to live in someone else's home. Things were pretty normal there.

By Friday the electricity was back on. We went to the grocery store, and sat around watching "Flood TV." It was all that was on, which was OK because it was all we wanted to see. We watched it over and over, the same scenes, new scenes, predictions about when the river would crest, how high it was now. I think it helped to begin to process the whole thing. I remember being anxious all the time, wondering, having no idea where to start to put things back together. There were rumors of buyout. It was our hope that we would be one of the ones and they would buy it and we could move away.

The next two weeks come to my memory as a mass of different things. Eventually I went back to work, to a classroom where half of my children were affected and seven of them had lost everything just like me. I would drive to Stokes Road often, waiting for the water to back out so we could go and see what was left, what it looked like. I hadn't seen it since that first day. After the water started receding I think it took about two weeks before we could get in. I know it was awhile because we were the first to be flooded.

I remember the first day the water was off of the road so I could drive down there. I stopped in front of our driveway, which you couldn't really see anymore. I knew where it was because the mailbox was still standing. I walked back and forth and looked through the woods to try to see. The trailer was still there, and the garage was still standing. I remember that Russell thought we could go back, get another trailer, save the garage. I remember that I knew I was never going to do that but he had to hold on to it a lot longer than I did, probably because he built the garage himself—so much time and effort to see it washed away. I came home (well, to Gail's) and reported that the water was out. I remember that it was a Thursday because we couldn't decide whether to take off on Friday to go in or wait until Saturday. Some people had already been back in their flooded homes, so all over the TV were the warnings about the mold, about the bacteria, about how it could kill you, about how you couldn't get it out. So I knew there wasn't going to be but so much we could save.

On Saturday we went. Danny went with us again. I remember standing at the road putting on gloves and a mask. David was there again, along with other neighbors who were saying how they had never been told we were in the 100-year flood plain. We had been told when we bought our land that it meant it flooded once every 100 years. We never knew it could do this. David described how bad it was, about the mold on everything, how it was all ruined. I looked at Danny and told him he didn't have to go, that it was our stuff and that we were going, but he didn't have to go. And he didn't. He stayed with the truck and Russell and I headed down what used to be our driveway.

It's difficult to describe what we saw. There was all kinds of stuff down our driveway that didn't belong to us—furniture, toys, underpinning, a shed, a stereo speaker. We came upon the house. You could really see how big the tree was that had fallen on the front. Again, more of people's lives washed up in our front yard: steps, a play kitchen. No grass or plants, just gray looking dirt. Our back deck was up in the trees in the woods beside our house. You could see a path through the woods that must have come from a tornado cutting through, trees snapped. Russell opened the back door and found a crate to use as a step. He didn't want me to go in but I had to go. I had to see it.

The first thing I remember is the smell. It was a horrible smell. I've never smelled anything like it but it was burned into my nose for months. There was black mold growing on everything, overtaking the walls. There was dirt, a grayish brown film everywhere. Muck. Nothing was in its place. I guess it had all floated around. Everything in the back room was in one big heap in the middle. The floor was warped; the ceiling fans were warped. There was a dark brown waterline about eight inches from the ceiling all the way through the house where the water had crested.

Before we went in I had hopes that there might be something left that was salvageable. Once I saw it there was nothing that I wanted. I mean I wanted it, but I was scared to take it, scared of what might be growing on it or in it. We walked through the house taking it all in, all the ruin: the couch and chair, my grandmother's antique dresser and nightstand, the afghan my grandmother made, the disks, ten drawers of school files collected over the years, all of my graduate school work, the box of books that were mine when I was little that I had brought from Mama's—none of it worth bringing out. It had been sitting in that water for weeks and then drying and molding since then.

I would pick things up, things I really wanted, only to shake my head and put them back down. The only things we took that day were glass casserole dishes, silverware, pots and pans, dishes, things that you knew you could get the mold off of and not worry about. I remember bringing some things outside onto the ground, things I thought I was taking, and then looking at them and saying, "It's just not worth it." Russell was worse than I was. He wanted to bring out more stuff. He wasn't as scared about the mold. I had to keep saying, "No," and he ended up going back later and bringing out some tools, more than I would have liked him to get. It was so hard to let it go, so hard to leave all our things, even though they were ruined.

I remember joking about the things up in the trees, about all the "new stuff" we had. I took pictures of it all, the land, the woods, the house. I know it sounds morbid but I had to have a record, I had to be able to call it up, how bad it really was. I had to be able to show people and make them understand. Because they didn't. Even though it was all over the television, when I talked to relatives even two hours away they had no concept of what we were going through. It was unimaginable.

We left that day but went back several more times. It was hard to stay away. It was our home, and when you stayed away from it long enough you began to convince yourself that there might be something there, something you missed, something that was OK to bring out. Each time I would look back through, looking for something else I could save. I remember I did find one more thing. The last time I went in I went through a very high cabinet and way at the back was a Christmas afghan. It was still in the plastic and hadn't been wet at all. I don't know how I had missed it before. I took it with me and that was the last time I went into the trailer. I looked in the back door a couple of more times but I couldn't stomach it and there was no reason to be in there anyway.

Even after we had moved on and were in the new house I would still ride down there sometimes after school and just sit in the driveway and think about how unreal the whole thing was. Then I would turn around and drive away. I just had to go there sometimes.

After it first happened I thought we would be able to get it back together relatively quickly. We were fortunate to have insurance so we had enough to pay off what we owed on the house and have a little left over to put down on something else. In the beginning I really thought we would stay with Gail for a few weeks and then move into a new house.

As time wore on I began to realize that I had no idea when it was going to be over, no idea when the insurance money would come, no idea where we were going to go. So after about three weeks I knew we should find somewhere to rent so we could begin to collect some stuff again and have our own (though not really) home.

I started looking at apartments. We hadn't rented in years, and I couldn't believe how much they wanted for something scary. I was talking about it at school a couple of days after we went back and Jackie mentioned that her husband had a house in Ayden that he rented. It wasn't the best neighborhood, but it was a house, at a reasonable price, with no lease, and a place to start putting things back together. So that was our next stop.

Some women from church and Gail came over and we cleaned the whole house in one night and then we moved in. We bought a bed (not really a bed but the mattress and box springs), washer, dryer, vacuum, and TV. Jackie's family and our friends pretty much gave us everything else: microwave, dishes, bed linens, towels, shower curtains, rugs, couch, chair, two kitchen tables and chairs. We who were flooded six weeks before now had a house to live in full of stuff, albeit not our "old" stuff. It was stuff nonetheless and it was an amazing feeling to have a home once again even though we knew it wasn't permanent.

We still had our jobs, we didn't owe anything on the old property, and we had a small down payment. We were in fine shape compared to many, many, many people. I found it hard to complain. I still had the stuff we had saved from the flood boxed up. I remember taking everything out of the boxes one day, just looking through it, and crying because there were things in there that I didn't even remember that we had—things that I thought had been lost, like the autobiography I wrote in eighth grade.

The next big thing was getting the house. We started looking right away, even before we left Gail's, but everything was either too high or too run down. We didn't want to settle for something we didn't like just to have a house. Finally I went to a realtor for help. We set up several houses to go and look at one Sunday. Now we had been looking for a while, but this was everything available in Greenville in our price range that we might possibly want. It was pick one of these or wait until something new came on the market.

On the way to her office we drove by a cute brick house in Winterville with a "For Sale" sign in the yard, a house we hadn't seen in the listings. Karen, our realtor, called and we went to look at it first. I knew as soon as we stepped through the door that this was the one. Russell liked it too. We looked at all the rest of the houses anyway, then came back to look at the first one once again, and offered them what they wanted for it that night. We were on our way to being homeowners again. We closed on the house December 30, 1999, a little over three months after the flood. It was really a miracle.

The next hurdle was the buyout. We knew we were in it and we knew they were going to buy us out but how long it was going to take and what they were going to offer were still mysteries. It took until November of 2000 to be settled, and we were number seven on the prioritized list of damaged homes. I'm sure some people are still waiting. We were so thankful to sell it to the county so that no one would ever have to live there again.

We went back there one last time, after the county had demolished it. It was all gone, the trailer, the garage, the mess. It was like a chunk of our life was bulldozed down and hauled away. But it was closure. The only thing left was the concrete slab—the garage floor. It was so strange.

As I stood there I remembered the very first time we had come to the lot, when we were thinking of buying it. Then the only part of it that was cleared was where we were standing right now. There wasn't even a driveway yet. I remembered how excited we were to own our own land, how we loved the trees and being in the country, how we worked and worked to get the grass to grow, how we planted flowers and bushes, the hammocks that we hung, the bird bath in the front yard, the plans we had for building a house there. It was just so sad.

But through it all there were so many things to be thankful for. We weren't there when the tree fell on the house or the water began to come up. We didn't have to wake up and feel the water in our bed or be airlifted out or sit on our roof or spend the night in a shelter. We didn't lose anyone in our family or our pet. We didn't have a mortgage that we couldn't pay. We didn't lose our business or place of employment. We had a place to live. We had some insurance. We had good friends. We had each other.

When I think back over the whole experience now, over two years later, the main thing that comes to my mind is that God is so faithful. Through it all He was there, moving obstacles, straightening paths, making a way where there seemed to be none, working miracles. There were several very personal trials that we walked through during the same time. The flood was just the beginning. My marriage is restored, my new home is beautiful, and I have a six-month-old son that I might never have had if I hadn't learned to get my priorities straight. I would never wish it on anyone. It was by far the most trying time of my life. But I wouldn't trade seeing the hand of God move for anything.

Two things still trigger the memories of the flood for me. One of them is the smell of Pine Sol. Not just pine cleaner but the real stuff. I can't stand it. It turns my stomach. That comes from all the bottles of it we used to clean the things we got out of our home after the flood. I hope I never have to smell real Pine Sol again. The other thing that triggers the memories is several days of rain right in a row. For a long time after the flood I would be anxious and nervous any time it rained. It was a subconscious fear, I guess. Now I sometimes feel strange when there are days and days of rain, one after another. I guess all the water makes me think of it again.

Lessons from Floyd

Jill McClanahan
Pitt County Writing Workshop

AS SOON AS I ARRIVED AT MY PARENTS' HOUSE IN BURLINGTON, NORTH CAROLINA, I started crying. I don't remember why. I guess the shock of it all was beginning to surface. I recognized my feelings as the same ache I felt when someone I was close to had passed away. Everything around me seemed surreal; my surroundings and conversations were draped with some sort of fog that would not lift. My body felt so heavy and numb, but all I wanted to do was talk about it. I remember thinking that if I talked about it, maybe the events would seem more real. Floyd had hit on Wednesday and now it was Saturday. Unfortunately, many people weren't aware that a flood was devastating my hometown, and surrounding area. The news was just beginning to spread.

I told my parents about going from grocery store to grocery store in Winterville and Greenville looking for milk, bread, ice and charcoal. Lines were long and supplies were limited. The flooding river had destroyed many of the bridges leading into Greenville. This made it difficult for delivery trucks to get supplies into grocery stores. The storm had also knocked out electricity in our area and it would be difficult for us to keep things cold and cooked. The water was continuing to rise in the Tar River and our utility substation was at risk of being damaged. With these difficulties bearing down, I finally ended up standing in line for three hours at Sam's Club bakery. A friend put our names on a waiting list and indicated to the baker the type of bread we wanted. As we stood in line, I had difficulty internalizing these recent events.

To pass the time, I turned around and tried to count the number of people in line behind me. I had only been in line fifteen minutes and the line stretched from the bakery, past the deli and beyond the vegetable section. I couldn't see past the tall shelves from that section, so I lost count. I counted 60 people to that point. While I counted, I noticed something that disturbed me even more. The people standing in line were very quiet. Everyone seemed subdued. Looking closer, I thought it appeared the light was drowned out of their eyes, as if their very souls had drained into the streets with the rising water. I knew I was standing in line with others who had nothing to go home to. Their belongings were taken with the flood. They had survived and now they would have to learn to live again.

I also told my parents how earlier that day we were getting together with neighbors to cook our meat on the grill so it wouldn't spoil. That morning my husband Mike and our neighbors cooked a mammoth amount of eggs and sausage. We spent most of our time that morning on our deck in the back yard listening to our battery-powered radio for weather updates and hearing the helicopters pass overhead. This was actually the first day since Floyd hit that we were able to be outside with the sun shining. From our back yard in Winterville, you wouldn't have known that anything had happened. Our yard was drenched with water, but since our home was new and had been built on what was once a tobacco field, there were no large trees to cause damage or leave debris. We were fortunate. However, just a few blocks away an entirely different story was unfolding.

Our neighborhood has a small area built in a flood zone. A hard rain will usually cause the small creek nearby to swell and spill water into the back yards of a few of the homes there. Today these homes were surrounded by what looked like a river. I had taken an early morning run to survey my neighborhood and take note of the wind damage caused by the hurricane. While on my run I noticed many houses with shingles missing on their roofs, soaked front yards and a few items of trash that had been blown into the street. I was surprised at how good everything looked.

As I rounded the curb and descended into the lower part of our neighborhood, I could hear the sound of people talking—a lot of people—but I couldn't see where the voices were coming from. I continued running toward the sounds I heard and as I got close, I could hear static and echoed voices coming from a radio or walkie-talkie. There was a familiar beeping sound that I was able to identify as I approached the last house on the curb. The sound came from an ambulance, and a few police cars lined the street. A crowd of people stood on the street with their backs to me, and I found it difficult to make out what they were watching.

As I approached the back of the crowd, I gained sight of what was holding the crowd's attention. This group of people stood at the edge of what looked like a creek bank. Just beyond I could see that the small creek had overflowed and the inclined street I stood on was acting as a shoreline. The homes located in a small cul-de-sac built near this creek were flooded and families were trapped in the second floor of their homes. It was difficult for me to believe what I was seeing. The brown murky water had formed a river just a couple of blocks from my own home. It flowed as far as I could see to my left into the next neighborhood. Shocked, I watched as families climbed out of their windows, legs first, to get into a small rescue boat which delivered them quickly to the dry area where I stood. Their pants legs were soaked and they looked frightened and exhausted. I heard one of the flood victims say to someone else as he walked past me that his family had moved furniture to the upstairs during most of the night. He had no idea the water would rise as high as it had. Silent, I stood at the edge of the water and felt helpless and guilty. I wanted to do something to help, but I didn't know what to do.

Sitting on my parents' couch, I continued to cry as I relayed the events of the day. My parents sat stunned and amazed. In preparation for the hurricane, they expected wind damage but not a flood. No one expected a flood. I couldn't imagine that it could have been any worse than what I had seen earlier that day.

But as the day went on, I learned that areas like Greenville, Rocky Mount, Tarboro and Princeville were far worse. I spent a lot of time on the phone trying to make contact with co-teachers and friends to see how they had fared. Mike was keeping me up to date on the situation in Winterville, where things seemed to be under control. The worst report I received was that Princeville, a town which is home to many students in our elementary school in Tarboro, had been completely flooded. All residents in that area had been evacuated and most were scattered throughout the region in shelters. At that point in time people were uncertain where their family members and friends were located. All I could think about was how helpless and guilty I felt. I told my dad that I should be back in that area helping in some way. I didn't want to feel like I had deserted my family and friends by taking refuge with my parents, even though Mike had insisted I take the kids to Burlington where the situation was more stable while he kept an eye on our home.

I think the comment about feeling helpless and having the need to help out in Greenville spurred my dad into action. The next day, Sunday, my dad was scheduled to work. At that time he worked with a small textile company in Burlington. That particular day, dad returned unusually early from work and asked me to go to the store. Dad had been burdened by the disaster taking place in my hometown and he had shared our previous night's conversation with his friends and co-workers that day. He said his co-workers had taken up a small collection of $36 and the money was to be used to buy water and bread. Dad said that as soon as we could get the bread and water loaded in his truck we would take it back to Winterville and deliver it to family and friends.

I was excited. I immediately took my stepson Lance with me to the store. We were able to purchase fourteen loaves of bread and twenty-three gallons of water with the money. Lance and I were very careful to count and recount the items to make sure we had enough money to cover the cost. I held on to the receipt so Dad would have evidence that we had used the money for the intended purpose.

Dad and I loaded the bread and water into his truck and we both recounted to make sure we had everything: fourteen loaves of bread and twenty-three gallons of water. He seemed pleased that we were able to buy as much as we did. Dad got his small cooler from the garage and put in a half gallon of water and two twelve-ounce cokes from his refrigerator. He placed the items inside the cooler and mentioned we could use the water and drinks for ourselves if needed. After stopping for three bags of ice, we had packed our cooler to capacity and we were on our way.

We arrived in Greenville some three hours later and drove to my house. I provided my husband with two loaves of bread, two gallons of water and one bag of ice. Mike insisted that was all he needed but he was concerned that his father might need some supplies. Prior to the disaster, Mike's father had been very concerned about the hurricane's intensity. He and his wife had chosen to leave the area and stay in a hotel toward the western part of the state. He returned when he realized the storm had subsided, but he was unaware of the rising water, hazardous driving conditions and food situation. Mike, my dad and I decided we would pay them a visit and see if we could supply them with any bread and water. We were aware that Mike's father would be providing shelter for some of his wife's family members who had lost their home near the coast due to the hurricane.

Before leaving for my father-in-law's house, my dad got my attention as he stood near the bed of his truck. He asked me how much bread and water Lance and I purchased at the store in Burlington. I told him fourteen loaves of bread and twenty-three gallons of water. I mentioned that this was the amount we had counted before we left his house. He had a strange look on his face and told me to count the water and see how many gallons we had. I counted the water. I had to count again because I thought I might have miscounted the first time. Each time I counted the water I kept counting twenty-nine gallons. I was confused. Dad stared at me for a time and then said, "Check and see how much bread we have." I counted twenty loaves of bread. Dad and I counted and recounted.

I couldn't make any sense of how we could start out with fourteen loaves of bread and twenty-three gallons of water, distribute two loaves of bread and two gallons of water to Mike, and still come up with twenty loaves of bread and twenty-nine gallons of water. I immediately pulled the receipt from my purse and took it to dad. He looked at it and shook his head. The receipt confirmed our initial count of fourteen loaves of bread and twenty-three gallons of water purchased with $36. Neither of us could explain nor comprehend what was happening. Mike even joked about the idea of throwing two dollars into the back of the truck to see if it would multiply. We laughed but deep inside we felt that something strange was taking place.

My father-in-law was so thankful to receive the bread, water and two bags of ice we delivered to him. He knew the extra supplies would help out since they had others who would be staying with them awhile. We were also concerned about Mike's brother and his wife. Mike's brother had been busy throughout the entire hurricane due to his work with the Greenville Parks and Recreation Department. His wife was a nurse and was required to work at the hospital around the clock during the onset of the hurricane. We were worried that they may not have had time to prepare for the water and bread shortage. We left two loaves of bread and two gallons of water for them on their doorstep, since no one was home when we arrived at their home. As we left their home, Dad, Mike and I continued to talk about what was up with having more bread and water than we had started with, but we could not come up with a logical solution.

We drove to downtown Greenville to deliver the "mysteriously multiplying" items to a drop-off point we had heard would be set up by the National Guard. When we arrived, we were told that things were not organized well enough to leave our stuff, so we might have to wait awhile. As we sat in the parking lot across the street from the humvees and olive green Army vehicles, we took notice of several cars pulling up behind us. Carloads of people were stopping to ask the National Guard if they would be able to get bread and water from this area. The National Guard soldier informed the crowd that supplies had not arrived and he couldn't tell them when it would be there. My dad told the soldier that we had bread and water in our truck and asked if we could distribute what we had to the crowd. He gave the OK and my dad walked behind the truck to tell the people that we had bread and water and they could take what they needed. They offered to pay but dad said it wasn't necessary.

Dad, Mike and I jumped out of the truck and began passing out the water and bread. It was amazing to see how unselfish these people were. They were looking behind and around them as they took the supplies, to make sure that others were getting what they needed. Within minutes, everyone seemed to have what they'd needed. They offered us blessings and left in their cars.

Only one person remained. She was a young mother holding a small infant in her arms. She walked up to my dad and asked if he had any water left. Dad looked at me and asked if I would check the front of the truck. Disappointed, I looked at the back and saw only the cooler; I was so saddened to realize that we were unable to provide for everyone. I looked in the front of the truck and knew we didn't have any water there. I could see the look of desperation on her face and I felt her panic.

Suddenly, I remembered the half gallon of water Dad had put into the cooler for us to drink. I reached into the cooler and showed her the amount of water and the two Cokes. She said all she needed was the half gallon of water to make formula for her baby. She was so relieved and happy. She said it would be just enough. She didn't need the Cokes. She just wanted the water. There was also a bag of ice left in the cooler. I offered her that and she took it also. She was so grateful. When she left, everyone else had disappeared. All that remained in the back of the truck was Dad's cooler with two Cokes. I was amazed that the crowd we had just helped was able to leave with the items they came looking for.

Dad and I left Mike in Greenville as he requested and returned to Burlington. We had a large, hot meal with our family that night. Dad said the blessing over the food and asked for God's blessings on the ones suffering through the flood. The experiences of the day had opened my eyes to how fortunate and lucky I am. My children, mother and mother-in-law listened carefully as Dad and I retold the events of how the water and bread mysteriously multiplied after we had distributed the bread and water to Mike, along with three bags of ice between Mike and his dad.

While we were talking, my mother-in-law interrupted to ask how many bags of ice we had purchased. I told her three bags, because that was all the cooler could hold. I told her I had given two bags to my father-in-law, and one bag to Mike.

Then dad and I realized what she was asking. I stared at Dad and tears filled his eyes. The bag of ice we had given the young mother shouldn't have been there. That was all the confirmation I needed to know that God's love was at work that day. God's love was at work in all the people who rose to the challenge and gave help to those who were desperate during the Floyd disaster.

Since that day, my dad will never be the same. Today, he travels all over and tells the story of how fourteen loaves of bread and twenty-three gallons of water and one bag of ice made a difference in his life and hopefully the lives of others who hear this story. I know, for me, I will never take for granted my home, my health and my family. My perspectives on my needs have changed. It is amazing how one day I thought I'd never live without those tailor-made heavy green jacquard drapes to match my new sofa, and the next day I and all the people living around me would sell all we have for a drink of water.

Tragedy does not favor class. When material possessions are washed away and we are left with only what we wear on our backs, we are all the same. Our needs become the same and our wants become the same. Floyd taught me that a disaster can draw out the true humanity and compassion in all of us. In times like these, we have the opportunity to learn to work together, to listen and think of others before ourselves. I hope I never experience a natural disaster again in my lifetime, but I am grateful to have walked away with a deeper appreciation for others and their needs, a knowledge of the love of God, and a desire to re-evaluate my daily priorities. May I never forget these lessons.

Tell the truth

Anthony Donnell Dudley
Grifton Writing Workshops

THE DEVASTATION OF THE FLOOD BROUGHT PEOPLE CLOSER TOGETHER. TELL THE truth, when the water came, didn't everyone feel more pulled together as a family? I know we love our family. You didn't have any lights, couldn't drink the water, couldn't eat. House and cars floating down your streets in your used-to-be back yards. All the emotions and all.

I could never ever imagine living at my high school for almost a whole month. But I am much grateful for my high school. All the hard-earned years at my high school came back to me again. These are the halls where I used to get out of the class, go to my locker. I used to go through these halls when I was out here in 1992-1996.

The night I got my diploma, I said to myself, "I am free. I served my years in this high school and I'm not coming back." But this proved me wrong. Now I love my high school because it was where I took my showers, where my family and friends were. It is where I got my meals from. What I am saying is, it is and was my home. I can't imagine, never in a million years, that I would stay in my high school as a home. That is the funniest thing because I realized that even when I got my diploma and I walked across that stage, I took for granted that I'd never go to school again. What's funny, though, is it didn't need me after I got my diploma, I needed it. Thinking of that at night at the shelter, that was the funniest thing that happened to me during the flood. I don't know what else to say.

Some people talk around each other about the "flood of the century." But I'm going to talk about my experiences that I had after the flood left and the media, president and the organizations around based on the government's help. So let me start to begin to tell you I was not pleased at all. It seems all I worked hard for went down the drain and no one helped me. So the government said it would help us. It's true it helped most of the ones that didn't need it at all. Who can explain that? I can. If FEMA had taken the time to see how people was abusing the generosity of the organizations, making them bad. People from another county or town come down and take the things you need for their own purposes. The clothes or food that you need. Some others come down every day taking and taking and taking. They didn't even need it. They saw a free opportunity to get and they took it.

How can the president not stop it? Let's admit it—if he can't control that, how can he control the whole country? FEMA, Red Cross, SBA—should have checked out the backgrounds of the person or something. I've known people most of my life down here. They lost everything, like me, but received nothing. I lived down here almost my whole entire life and I never seen nothing to beat it. What is the problem with our officials and government and president?

✳ ✳ ✳

That water messed everything up

Interview with William Mansfield
William Mansfield with Earl and Mary Teel

Julie Fay with Mary and Earl Teel, Grifton Writing Workshop.

Photo courtesy of the North Carolina Humanities Council.

Earl Teel was born in Pitt County in 1933, and his wife Mary was born in Greene County in 1939. At the time of the flood, the Teels lived in a small community called Tick Bite in Lenoir County near Grifton.

WILLIAM MANSFIELD: What kind of preparations did you make before the storm came?

EARL TEEL: Well, I tied down everything that was loose, you know, took swing sets down where they wouldn't blow and done everything normally you would do. Got up water and got gas for the gas grill. We had canned goods, bread and stuff like that, milk, flashlight, transistor radio. What I usually do, you know. My brother-in-law and his wife came to our house and spent the night with us during the hurricane. And the next day about dinnertime, they went home. We fared good during the hurricane. Just a tree blowed down against the house—that was about all the damage we had except stuff blowed in the yard. But what we got was that water. That water messed everything up.

MARY TEEL: I said I wished that tree had of "boomp" in the top of the house, then we would have had some insurance.

WM: So the insurance didn't cover the flood?

MT: I think we got eight hundred dollars for the tree falling in the clothesline.

ET: It tore the doghouse up and the clothesline. And the TV antenna I had just bought.

MT: But we got up the next morning because a couple of trees had fell out of the woods behind our house, just kind of hit the edge of the house. So, they got out with chain saws and cut the trees off of the edge of the house so they could get to the air conditioning and check it out. And that's what we were all doing. If we had known the flood was coming, we'd have been getting out.

ET: But we didn't know the flood was coming. And I had the radio on and they never announced nothing on the radio.

MT: Or we didn't hear it. I was going to sweep the yard and clean up the debris.

ET: And then the Volunteer Fire Department came down there from Grifton and they told us that they had come over there to tell everybody to leave, that the National Guard was coming in to take them out. I didn't think that the flood was going to be that bad, and I talked to my neighbor and he said he wasn't going to leave. And it was a decision you had to make. And they said that five feet of water was coming. I told my wife, I said, "What we'll do, we'll leave on my pickup because if we went with the National Guard we wouldn't have no transportation to get around with." We'd have been stuck over there with no way to get around.

I had a car phone and so I called my first cousin and asked him could we come over and spend the night with them and they said we could. Because I thought we'd be back the next day. So we packed up enough stuff to spend the night, you know, something like a change of clothes and something to sleep in. And I took my other stuff, you know, my guitars and my employment papers and all that stuff and put them in the boot of the car because the garage was built flood level and five feet of water wouldn't have bothered them. We went on over to my cousin's house and spent the night.

And the next day my cousin said, "Don't you want to go down there and see?" I decided I would, so we got out and rode down there. And a neighbor that lived down the road from me was down there with his boat and he took me and George and my uncle in there. And instead of five foot of water, there was about seven foot of water in there. I mean you can't even walk on the road, it would be over your head. People's trucks drowned out and stalled in the road, and people was running motor boats over the top of them trucks and ain't touching them. That water was that deep in places.

MT: That was about lunchtime on Friday.

ET: Then they come in and said we had to leave there. That surprised me, that the water kept on rising.

WM: So you got flooded out of your house and flooded out of your cousin's house?

ET: Told people to leave on account of it was crossing the road so deep that you wouldn't be able to get out if you didn't get out. So we had to get out again.

MT: That was on Saturday.

ET: And it still was rising. So it was pretty wild.

WM: Where did you go after that?

ET: We went to my daughter's house in Kinston and we stayed there, what?

MT: From Saturday after the flood until in November when we got the little FEMA trailer.

ET: They set it up out there in the front yard at the old house that was flooded. And hooked it up. And we stayed there. Because after the water went down where I could get in and get the house cleaned out, the first thing I done then is started working on the house. I took all the electrical settings out. I took all the breakers out. And I hooked wiring up and got everything fixed. I had the electricity turned on and I could go ahead and do things then. I could run saws. And then I got the water working. And then when FEMA come in, all they had to do was hook onto my water and my electricity. I already had that done, so that made it a little faster. They were slow, but I wont.

WM: They hooked the water and electricity up to the trailer?

ET: From the old house.

WM: But you have moved into your new house?

ET: Yeah.

WM: Is the trailer still there?

MT: No. They come got it when we moved to the other house.

WM: Did it feel kind of strange living in the trailer with your house right behind you?

MT: It sure did. It wasn't a good feeling. But I'd rather have been there than in one of these little settlements where they got the FEMA trailers. We had a choice, but I had rather been at my own place. It was strange, being there like that because you were right there at the house and you saw it constantly. So it was strange.

WM: Do you mourn it much?

MT: At times. Because I could walk through it sometimes and I would just cry. Because it brought back so many memories of raising our three children

227

there. We'd been there, would have been thirty-two years the 28th of this past March. It bothered me sometimes. But not to a point I couldn't stay there. Right now I miss it. I mean, this other new home—I know it's my home, but still it's not home.

ET: Home, you feel it.

MT: Home to me was out there all these years. I know in my heart it's not my home now, but still there's a little place back there that it's still home.

WM: You know it in your head, but in your heart you're still back in Tick Bite.

MT: Right. Right. Right. Right. When I go out there I don't want to leave. But I know I have to.

WM: How about you, Mr. Teel? How is it for you?

ET: It didn't bother me that way. I knew from the Friday after the flood when the water was there, I knew then that it was over and that I wouldn't never live there no more, not unless I done something to it. So I accepted the fact that it was gone and it didn't bother me like it did my wife. Because like I say, it was gone and you know it was gone. There's no need of looking behind. You got to look forward.

MT: He's accepted it a whole lot better than I have.

ET: Well, I've never had no brothers and no sisters. I was the onliest child. So I learned at an early age to depend on myself, you know, used to being alone. So it don't bother me to be alone and things don't bother me like they do some people. I get worried like everybody else and I get bothered, but stuff don't affect me like it does some people. I don't get close to things like some people get close to dogs and cats. I treat them good and all, but when one dies you get another one. You know, it's a fact of life. I don't know whether I'm a little hard-hearted or not.

WM: But you're still bound to feel some sadness about that?

ET: Well, you probably do at times. Sometimes, you know, you say, "Well, I got so and so." And then you say, "No, the flood got it." I got some stuff out there I'm trying to clean up and fix, like lawn mowers and stuff like that. And I think, "Well, I used to have this over here." And I'll turn around, and then I'll realize that I ain't got it no more. I was coming from my uncle's house the other night. He lives down the road from me. And just before I got to my place, where I had in my mind the whole time to turn in, I said, "I don't live there no more. So I've got to go somewhere else."

WM: So your new house is not where the old one was?

MT: It's out here in Forest Acres. It's just right out of Grifton a little. In fact, it's in the city.

WM: Well, does it get to the point where you just need to talk to somebody about it?

MT: I went over here to this man, he was from Chapel Hill. I was doing good, and I just talked to him. I had a problem—and I still do have a problem—with sleeping. I wasn't a big sleeper before the flood, but since the flood I've had times I didn't sleep at all. Now my doctor prescribed medicine for me. And so when I went to talk to this doctor from Chapel Hill and I told him what I was doing. He decided I was already on medication if I needed it. But I hadn't been back because I was handling it pretty good.

WM: And were you all good listeners to folks when they were worried about the flood? Did anybody share their troubles with you?

MT: The girl across the road from us—she's my cousin—she has had a horrible time. In fact, her and her husband both. And seems like they just can't get over it or something. And they're planning on repairing their house. Their house didn't get flooded as bad as ours. Their side of the road was higher. But she has really had a hard time. We've all—you know, the ones that live right around there—have kind of met with one another and talked about our problems and things.

WM: Before the flood or after the flood?

MT: Since the flood. Everybody worked before the flood. And I used to work so I didn't see my neighbors. We didn't visit and talk to one another like that. But everybody was home after the flood so we saw each other more and talked about things. People in our neighborhood that never really had things to do with each other, they've just all been different. But since the flood, everybody just has visited more—and are more concerned, you know. We would be out there cleaning up, you know, and everybody would come by and stop and talk. And it just brought everybody more together. I mean, sharing things with one another, and helping one another. They all shared love and concern and were helpful.

ET: It was like people come together to help one another. Like the guy that lives down the road from us, he took his boat and he tied it out to the end of the road and anybody that wanted to go in and out he took them in for nothing. And he didn't save anything except the clothes he had on his body, you know, but he was willing to take people in and out on his boat. He done it the whole time that the water stood down there, I would say close to three weeks. And he didn't charge for the gas. Of course, when I went in, I gave him some money for gas because I knew that it costs money to run a boat. Before the flood people would work and everybody was in a hurry to get there and it was a fast pace. But when the flood came, it slowed everybody down. They had time to speak to you. They had time to do a lot of things.

They couldn't go nowhere. That's one thing about the flood. It didn't single out the poor people. It didn't single out the rich people or the middle-class people. It got everybody.

MT: Everybody. Everybody was equal.

ET: It wasn't like a tornado that hit here and jumped over and hit down the road. As it went, it took everything. It didn't matter who you were or where you come from.

WM: Do you feel like that's continued? Or do you think things are going back to the way they were?

MT: Well, they're not exactly the same as they were to start with, because most people have gone back to work and got so busy fixing what they had and doing things that they just hadn't had time like they did to start with. But a lot of it has continued. Even people out of Grifton would come out and stop and talk to you. And that meant a lot. And there was one episode—there was a patrolman here from Aberdeen. He was stationed out guarding the road from people coming in and out off Hwy. 11.

ET: Keeping looters from going in.

MT: He just meant so much to us, you know. He was a Christian man, and he talked to you. And he just talked about everything, you know, and just helped ease your mind. And he was a special person to me; at Christmas he sent us a Christmas card and he enclosed a hundred dollar check. So he kind of kept in contact with us, you know. He was a special person. And I'd always kind of had a fear of patrolmen.

WM: The officials who came in like the National Guard and the Highway Patrol and stuff, what kind of experience was that?

ET: Well, it looked like a war zone—like you see in movies and newsreels and on TV—where they would close places where there was fighting and where there was a curfew. It was just about like a war zone. You couldn't go in and you couldn't go out at certain times. Everything was locked.

MT: Even on a boat at certain times.

ET: And I guess it was for your own benefit, for your safety. And another thing for people taking things, you know. And then, the water was contaminated, and it wasn't good on your health to be in that water. So it was something that had to be done. But you never thought it would happen in your neighborhood, where you wouldn't have the freedom to do what you wanted to do. They had to do it for the safety because a lot of people will take chances. I guess you can't trust everybody to do the right thing. Not all the time.

WM: Do you think you'll stay in touch with that community now that you've moved?

MT: I think so. There's a lot of people down there I really care about. So I will keep in contact with them. And the girl across the road just about cried because we were moving. She said she couldn't hardly stand it out there now because there's nobody right there now. She worked in Kinston, and she's so bad she hasn't worked since the flood.

ET: In my opinion it would have helped her if she had went back to work. Because I think that's what helped me. I really ain't had time to set down and do nothing. I'd go all day and then at night I would have to go buy building materials. I'd be at Lowe's till it closed up, and then I could be back home. Just continual, you know, something you had to do. You worked till bedtime, and you really didn't have time to think about it.

MT: That's why I wanted this little trailer, more normal living, you know, than it was staying with somebody.

ET: I think a fellow's better off if he's doing something. The way I come along you had to do everything. You changed the oil in your own car. You washed your car. You patched the window if it broke. If you put a hole in the floor, you fixed that. You fixed everything around your house. If your watch went bad, you fixed that. You fixed everything. Because old folks didn't have no money to have nobody to do it, so I come up that way. It might be because I'm not educated and don't know no better. I'll tackle anything that I own. If it tears up, I work on it. You know, simple things like changing the oil, filters and stuff like that, I do that.

WM: So you think that because you came up the hard way, that made it easier for you to deal with all the mess of the flood?

ET: I think so. When I grew up, what little bit I went to school, when I come home, you had to get in the firewood, you had to feed the mules, you had to feed the hogs. You had things to do and everybody done their part, you know.

WM: Do you think you're living simpler lives now?

MT: Well, in some ways but we still kind of do the same things, you know.

ET: It's getting closer to living about like we were. The only thing now, I'm in debt where I wasn't in debt. I had got out of debt, and I had to go back in debt. So I got that to think about, you know, being in debt now. And I joke about it, and I tell people that I've got to work till I get 96 because I've got a thirty-year loan. I had planned, you know. I had got so I could take off from work and not have to work as hard as I used to because I had my stuff paid for and with my Social Security and working a little bit, I could do things I wanted to do. Whereas now I got to be more careful because I got to pay that loan back.

MT: Because we've got a house payment where we didn't have.

ET: But I'm hoping that something will come up and FEMA will buy me out of my old place. Even if they don't, whenever I get a breather I'm going to go in there and try to fix it up and if I can't sell it, I'll rent it out. Somebody'll rent it. So I got two options. If I rent it, I could take the money and pay off the mortgage I got. And then if they pay me off, I could pay off the mortgage. That would get me out of debt again. I feel like a man my age don't need to be in debt. Of course nobody knows, but as you get older the chances are against you. You don't know how long you're going to work. You can get disabled so fast. Things can happen and you get where you can't work. And if you get where you can't work, then you wouldn't be able to pay your loan back.

WM: What do you think about the government and FEMA and all that sort of stuff? Do you think they did a good job, or do you think they could have done better?

ET: I think they done the best they could. But I think there's room for a lot of improvement in it—to pay more attention and listen to the people more. And it seems to me that a lot of it was going by what they thought or what they thought it ought to be instead of listening to what people are telling them and saying. And being sure they get it right. Because they weren't communicating with the people in my opinion. They were seeing the people, but they yet never looking beyond. Like computers—I don't know much about them, but I think I know enough that you've got to know what you're doing when you're putting the stuff in. It'll do what you tell it. You're in command. I think a lot of people—I don't know whether they work too fast or don't pay attention to what they're doing or something—but they're always putting in wrong things. And it's going to come out wrong. You give a man information, and if it's put in the computer right it's supposed to come out right. But a lot of this stuff didn't come out right. The people didn't get the right understanding that put it in, or either they didn't pay attention to what the people were saying. I don't know which it was. A lot of confusion, you know. People didn't have the right information.

WM: That's a very good point. Where did you go to get the information and to give the information? Did you just talk to them on the phone? Were there big meetings?

MT: Meetings, and we also went down in Kinston on Queen Street. Turned in all our reports like filing for all the stuff.

ET: They had a building that they rented.

WM: What were the meetings like?

ET: I never went to any.

MT: I went to one. Well, we did come over here to the Baptist Church to one. And I learned a little bit from it, but I didn't learn a whole lot. Everybody was just giving their opinion on what was going on and how they thought FEMA was supposed to be one way, where FEMA wasn't doing what they had been led to believe they were going to do.

WM: These were people like you all who had been flooded out?

ET: Yeah. And they had one representative to answer your questions. So, it was basically what he said, you know. But that's another thing. What they said one time, they would change. By the time two weeks went by, it was different. And the rules and the regulations of it would change so much. That's another thing, it's a lot of confusion. Of course, people wont mean and I don't think they done it for spite or intentionally. I think that it was done through not enough communications amongst them.

WM: This was a meeting where people could voice their opinions and frustrations to the right officials?

MT: The one I went to out here to Contentnea School—me and my daughter went one night to a meeting out there—and I liked the way they done it. They met in the auditorium and they introduced each person. And then they introduced the person for each thing, like inspectors or whatever. Then they all met in the cafeteria, had tables where each person was assigned to, and you could go to that person and talk face to face with that person instead of in a big crowd. You were there one to one to talk and ask them things.

WM: So they had representatives who would cover different problems and they told you who they were, and then you could go and speak with them and ask questions. And that seemed to work pretty well?

MT: Yeah, that was a whole lot better, but that's the only two I went to.

WM: Did the adjustors or the FEMA people ever come and talk to you individually, come to where you were staying or meet you at your home?

MT: They met us at our house.

WM: What was that like?

MT: The only ones I met was the last one and the first one. But we've had so many to come.

ET: They would come out and talk to you and take a list of what you lost. And they would tell you what FEMA would do for you. They would explain to you that it wont gonna give you this and that, but it would help you with your basic needs, you know. Like one woman told me that they would allow you one television because you needed to watch the news, and they would allow you something like one bed, and one refrigerator—a basic refrigerator—and I think a stove. And that was about it, you know.

MT: What little bit we got from FEMA, they say you can't buy anything for a house—no furniture, no nothing. Because when they sent you the check, they specified "housing only," so you couldn't buy anything except what they had told you that you could use it for. Because the first check we got, before I done anything with that check I got on the telephone and I called the headquarters. I said, "Tell me really what can be accomplished with this check." And he said, "Nothing but housing. You can pay rent for a place to stay, or you can put it on repairs and things like that." I said, "What about furniture? When you lose everything you had furniture-wise." I said, "I mean you need something to start with." He said, "No, ma'am. You cannot spend one penny of it for nothing personal." But see, they misled you on things. A lot of stuff.

ET: I don't think they really done it intentionally. I think it was just caught up in the web or something.

MT: But I tell you, the last ones that come to our house, they would not even stick their head into that house to re-evaluate the house. They would not stick their head in that house because it was very poison to your system.

WM: Did that make you wish you hadn't gone in the house?

ET: We all turned around and washed it down with Clorox. After we washed it down and everything and aired it out, I didn't have the mold to grow on the two by fours like I have seen in some houses. But now our top is molding because I didn't tear out the ceiling. I didn't tear the top sheet rock out. I tore all the side out but I didn't get the top, and it's starting to mold.

WM: Will you go back in and tear it out?

ET: I don't know, really.

MT: Plus if someone else did it they'd have to raise it up.

ET: I went over there and I got a permit to build it back. And then they said that you had to have it elevated before you could build it back. I mean you had to have a surveyor run a elevation on it to get it above flood level. They say I have to do that now. But I said there wont no use to do that if they were going to buy it. If they don't buy it out, I'm going to have to do something with it. I'm going to have to fix it up, try to sell it or rent it out or something. So I'm going to have to have one run. But I said I wasn't going to because I didn't want to spend the money if they were going to buy it out and tear it down, you know. You never know what they're going to do with it.

WM: Are you still in contact with them?

MT: The last we heard we were still on the top priority to buy out.

ET: But they said they didn't know when, that kind of thing, ought to be in five years. I'll have another hurricane before then.

MT: Well, last meeting I went to, the county told us if two hurricanes come back to back like happened with Floyd there was a strong possibility that it would happen the same way and worse. So that's why I didn't want to go back and put my money that we had borrowed back down there. I told him, I said, "If we're gonna have to borrow money and pay it back," I said, "I am going to put it somewhere else." Now where we live they say at the inspector's office it's a hundred year flood zone.

ET: But what I believe is that when you go to Raleigh, it's building like wildfire. They're paving everything. There's concrete, asphalt, everywhere. The rain comes in Raleigh, it falls on that. It can't soak in the ground. It's got to run right here. And also these people that's gone out up there and built these mansions, they have dammed up and built them a place for water sports and stuff. They're going to turn that water loose. Before it tears up a five hundred thousand, seven or eight hundred thousand dollar home, they're going to turn that water out. Well, that water ain't got nowhere to go but down here. Because they're paving, they're building. Just like Greenville, you know, it's building up, we're paving everything. There's nowhere for water to seep.

And the creeks and the rivers ain't been cleaned out in my lifetime, I don't think, like the tree tops took out and stuff like that. They don't clean rivers out no more. They used to—well, it's been years ago—but they used to bring fertilizer and supplies up Contentnea Creek on barges all the way to Snow Hill from New Bern because the railroad was over here. And just think about that creek now; you can't even run a boat down the waterways. You know, they used to bring it down here to Grifton. And all that stuff is against you. The water ain't got nowhere to go. And if the wind blows and backs the water out of the sound, and a hurricane comes, you're going to be getting water from Raleigh and you're going to be getting water from the sound. And you're going to be caught right in the middle of it. And it could happen before five hundred more years.

MT: When they had the Shad Festival here just recently, in the book it told how many years ago that Grifton was ocean, was covered with water. I mean all around, you know.

ET: Yeah, it was ocean one time, all this place. How long has Mr. Bryson been dead?

MT: I don't know, honey.

ET: He was a captain on one of the boats that used to come down here. He died, I guess it's been thirty years ago, or twenty years ago. He was real old when he died, and he would tell stories to the kids about when he was captain on the boat that come down. So, you know, I guess it's been a hundred years now.

MT: I know we'd been out there just about thirty-two years and we never had water like that.

WM: Has your church been real helpful?

MT: Yes, they have helped us. There was seventeen or eighteen families in our church affected by the flood. We go to Free Will Baptist here in Grifton. Our church took up money and distributed it evenly amongst everybody. Plus we had oodles and oodles of food and clothes and things that was donated. Plus the Baptist people here in Grifton, I just can't praise them enough because they have been a tremendous help.

WM: Has their aid been a little more focused than the federal aid or government aid? More direct and on target?

MT: We had so many come down there. Church groups, Red Cross, Salvation Army. Even little Cub Scouts.

ET: Social Service. They would come down and bring cold drinks, coffee and some hot food. These people here, they come on the scene and they know what's going on … they just jump in and go to work. They're here. And they're available. And they know what's going on. Where FEMA's got people working here, but everything's got to be approved and go through Atlanta. FEMA has got to go through so much red tape. The only thing I say is that there was a lot of confusion. There was a lot of mistakes. You would fill out the papers and you'd get everything right, and then you'd get word from someone that something didn't go right. And you had to go back again. And I guess it was because it was so big, and—now this is my opinion —that people was hired that wont experienced and they put them right to work. They didn't know everything they probably should have known about it, which wasn't their fault but it made a lot of confusion with the people that was flooded because they needed help. And they were getting mad and frustrated when they had to do things over.

MT: Constantly having to go back. When you needed to be doing something else, you were having to run back over there constantly.

ET: In other words, you couldn't do nothing because you stayed on the road all the time. You was like a supervisor. You couldn't actually do no work, but you had to keep everything going in line, you know. And you'd wind up spending all day and not get nothing done. And it just took so long. A lot of people didn't have no money. And a lot of people live from pay check to pay check.

Everybody, you know, in this country, ain't got bank accounts. They live one pay check to another pay check. And them kind of people was hurting because it took so long to get something to them. Had to buy flood insurance to get on FEMA. Never had flood insurance before, but now it's nothing but a hull we had to go get flood insurance on it now.

MT: We got one letter one time that told us that our house was fixed, OK to live in. And there was a condemned sign on the house. I mean, this come from FEMA. Livable. It was livable.

ET: And I realized that what they said. A lot of people didn't realize it, but FEMA said they were there to help people. They didn't say they were going to help you get back like you were. And a lot of people had a misunderstanding. FEMA was just going to help you with basic needs. But a lot of people thought FEMA was going to do more than they done. But you know, I listened to start with and I heard what they said. They said they were just going to help people. And helping people don't mean they're going to get you back just like you was before. But you had to listen to what the President said real close. He didn't really promise you a whole lot. If you set down and listened to his speech real good, he said, "We gonna help everybody if it's there." See, he said, "If the money's there." But the money might not be there. I comprehended that thing after a day or two. I kept saying it over and over, and I realized what he was saying. He really didn't say he was going to give you nothing. We had to put in for a loan to rebuild our house. And then we had to modify the loan to use the money to buy another house. The SBA loan finally came through, but it was such a long drawed-out thing. We had to go all the way to Goldsboro, which I didn't see no need of that but we went. We got the loan and the man gave us a check for seven thousand dollars to do the yard work, landscaping, at the old house where we was flooded. Who cares anything about a yard when you ain't got nowhere to live? And you couldn't spend that money for nothing else. You had to keep it in the bank. The only thing you could spend it for was landscaping. I was thankful to get a low interest loan but, you know, it was just so long.

MT: It's just been a mixed-up mess.

ET: It would just get you so frustrated, you know. You said, "Well, I don't guess I'm going to get nothing." Then next day or two, you hear something, you know, "Well, we're going to get it." So I guess it was like I said, they just hired people off of the street or something. Another thing—one person would say, "You can do this and do that." And then another person, "No, you can't do this and do that. You've got to do this and that." So there ain't nobody really in charge. Everybody's in charge, you know, but come down to it, they ain't nobody in charge. But I guess in the long run it all come out for me to get this loan.

MT: We got a state grant but we can't use it. We got the check first, and I went and deposited it. I said, "On this check it says you've got to cash it in 60 days," and I said, "we've had this check for a month." I said, "Now what are we supposed to do with this money?"

ET: I was scared somebody was going to steal it, you know.

MT: They said, "Keep it or either deposit it in the bank." So I went and put it in the bank. It's supposed to be where you could pay it on your loan and things.

ET: And I would be glad to do that because that would lower how much you have to pay back. It would cut down on the interest, you know.

WM: Somebody said how one of the things that made the flood worse is if it had been a fire, everything would have been burned up and you wouldn't have seen it.

MT: Right. That's the way I felt. Because if a fire had just wiped it out, you wouldn't have had to go back and look at all your stuff. Because a fire would have burned it up. As it was, we had to drag all of our possessions of forty-five years out and see it piled up beside the road. So I think a fire wouldn't have hurt me half as bad. That's my opinion. The thing that really hit me the worst was the first time I went into my house afterwards. When we could drive the truck back in there, my husband took me. And when I opened the door and just looked in the house it was a shock, a bad shock. Because it was like a tornado had gone through and everything was piled up in piles. I mean, it was just horrible.

WM: You said something about how you had laughter in you and the wife didn't?

ET: Well, I like jokes and comedy and stuff like that. I think that's what hoped [*helped*] me get through the flood. Even though I lost everything I never thought of it as that. Because I had been raised on a farm. My daddy, part of his life he was a tenant farmer and what they used to call a share-cropper. We didn't have radios. We didn't have refrigerators. And we had outside bathrooms and toilets, you know. I know what tough times are. So when I lost everything, it was like it was when I was starving in the beginning. So I had been there. So, you know, it wasn't as bad, I guess, as for some people that never had been there and had to go there. This flood put everybody in the same predicament. They didn't have nothing. Nowhere to stay and nothing to eat, nothing to cook it on. Didn't have anything. But like I say, I had been almost there before, so I felt like that hoped me too. People that's never been where they had nothing, it would be harder on them than it would be on somebody that has known and then lost it again. In the beginning, didn't have nothing. Because when we got married, I didn't have anything. We had one another and that was it. I borrowed money to get married on. And we lived with my parents for about a year. We finally moved off in what they used to call a "shotgun house"—if you know what that was—and we lived in that about a year. And then we moved to Grifton and we lived there and finally bought the house we lived in, in Grifton. Then we sold it and built a house outside of Grifton.

MT: In Tick Bite.

ET: Yeah. And we lived a lot of years without any living room furniture. We had a big room and a kitchen, you know, but we had a empty living room. We finally got able to buy us some furniture. Right now we've got a bed. We ain't got nothing in one bedroom but a bed. That's the one we're sleeping on. There was one homemade table I made, you know, being a carpenter type, fix-it man, handyman. I made some tables and stuff like that. And I made a gun cabinet. And that's the only thing that survived three weeks in the water, was what I made. All the furniture I bought, it tore it up. It come to pieces. But that stuff I made, it was all right. I took Clorox and washed all that stuff down, and it looks almost like it ain't been in a flood. The stuff you buy, a lot of it's made from a photograph of wood printed onto a piece of flake board and that ain't gonna last in water. And you pay a high price for it, some of it.

WM: What's the funniest thing that happened to you during or after the flood?

ET: What surprised me was all the wildlife down the road. There was spots where you could stand on, and there was spots you couldn't because the water was on them. But you could look down the road, and it looked like herds of deer coming out of that water, going to higher land. Stuff I've never seen. Amazing how they survived, you know. My son had a dog that was staying at my house. I didn't know nothing else to do with the dog—I couldn't take him nowhere because they wouldn't let you carry animals to the shelters. And I couldn't take it to my cousin's house. And I didn't know the water was going to come that high, so I turned him loose. Because I knowed if he was tied he couldn't get away and he couldn't fend for hisself. So I turned him loose. And when I came back on Friday, I looked for him and I didn't see him. And so it was on Sunday, I stopped and talked with people that was standing around and asked them had they seen this dog? He looked kind of like one of these old bull dogs used to, long time ago. Had a spot on the side of his head, you know, and he was a friendly, good-natured dog. He never barked, except at a cat—he hated cats.

   And I finally got to a man that told us, said, "Yeah, I saw that dog," said, "He was a good-natured dog." And said, "He came up here and run around." And said, "The people from the Animal Shelter was picking up animals, and I believe they got him." So me and my son went to the Animal Shelter and they said that they didn't have him, but there was some animals carried to the fairground in Lenoir County. They had set up a temporary place to put the animals over there. So my son lives over that way and he was going home that night but the water was so bad over the road you couldn't cross Kinston. You had to go around. He had to take a long route on account of the water. But anyway, he come back up to the fairground and the dog was there.

MT: They hauled him out on a boat. His picture was in the paper. He was in the Kinston paper.

ET: He made the Kinston paper. They didn't know whose dog it was. You could tell it was him. So I told everybody the dog made the paper.

WM: You said you were thinking about doing some songs about the flood?

ET: Well, I got something going around in my head, and I had thought about the beginning and the chorus. That chorus would be like:
"There's no light in the window tonight.
The old house that used to be home is dark now.
My old neighborhood is dark and cold and scary."
Or something like that. And then the starting of it would be something like:
"September the 16th, 1999,
The flood of '99"
. . . and so on.

WM: What kind of story did you have?

ET: Well, what I was thinking about, the story would be that your neighborhood where you used to live is gone. There's no one around at night. It's dark. There's no light in the window. And there's no family around the table—that kind of thing.

Section V: **BACK TO SCHOOL**

Belvoir Elementary School under water.

Photo courtesy of Ana Cowó.

Sharon O'Neill

Slowly drying out,
children finally at school
half their friends are gone.

Bus travels the route
once taken by the river
no one to pick up.

Houses marked condemned,
orange X's and the date
tell the time of death.

Living on the floor,
days without destination,
hope in a hot meal.

The questions, pictures,
nightmares play constantly
in their fragile young minds.

Talking in hushed tones,
crying together, holding
until the fear goes away.

Children left silent
adrift in the aftermath
need hope to cling to.

Never stop talking,
cry all you want, I'll cry too!
We can heal from this.

October 4, 1999

Back to school

Jill McClanahan
Pitt County Writing Workshop

At the time of the flood Jill McClanahan was a second grade teacher at Stocks Elementary School in Edgecombe County. McClanahan was then living in Winterville, Pitt County. She and her family now live in Greensboro.

MY CAR POOL BUDDIES AND I WERE FINALLY ABLE TO TAKE HWY. 33 TO REACH our school in Tarboro. It had been almost a month since we had been to work. We drove slowly, like a carnival car on a track, to get a close look at the damage done by the flood. All along the sides of the highway we could identify how high the water reached by what looked like brittle, mud-caked leaves and branches from the mid-part of each tree down, for miles along the road. Plastic grocery bags, flip-flops, shoes, and clumps of grass were sifted only part of the way through the holes in chain link fences where the flood waters had tried to leave them behind. A lounge chair sat precariously on a branch of a high pine as if someone had used the tree as an observation post.

The smell of rank water was everywhere. Often during our ride we would pull our shirts over our noses or try to fix the air conditioner in our car so we wouldn't have to smell the odor. The smell reminded me of a time when I had left my

X-marked flooded house.

Photo by Neil Moore.

aquarium on at school, during the summer, and the filter stopped working. The water in the tank became stagnant and killed the aquarium plants. The stink was filthy and turned my stomach, the same as it did that day. In front of all the houses, heaps of materials which had been stripped from the flooded homes were piled high. Sheet rock, dining-room chairs, stuffed animals, mattresses, floor boards, insulation, pictures—everything in a brown, wet, stinking dome. Windows were missing from blackened windowpanes. Huge orange X's covered the front doors indicating that the house had been checked by someone and everyone had been evacuated. A wide brown streak along every house and trailer was left as evidence of what had come and gone. Everything from Greenville to Tarboro on 33 looked dead and smelled like death.

On this first drive back, we were awed at what we were seeing. We continued shaking our heads and talking as we rode along pointing to this and that, making comments about the large bodies of water still left in many of the yards, counting the number of trees down in one yard and the size of the tree's roots that were exposed. Everything that had been so familiar on our trek to school each day looked like something out of a disaster film. My descriptions could never do it justice.

There was once a place along this road where we would take our students on a field trip. The owner had llamas, pigs, ducks, ostriches, peacocks, emus, rabbits, geese and several other animals. Our children loved to visit the farm located in the back yard of this home each year to learn about the different animals. It was sad to find out the majority of these animals were killed by the flood. Just a couple of months before, my daughter and I had raised two ducks and we had brought them to this farm to live. I scanned the front yard where a pond was located. I was happy to see our ducks swimming in the pond as we passed.

When we arrived at school, our principal had arranged for our entire staff to meet together and share our experiences from the flood. So many of our staff had lost their homes and were having to live with families and friends, or had to take up residence in Rocky Mount until things got back to normal. We hugged one another and listened to the stories of those who had experienced the worst parts of the flood. We cried as we heard story after story. We were all relieved to realize everyone was able to make it back and there were no casualties on our staff.

We were to spend the next few days trying to get things straight before the children came back to school. We were also allowed time to go to the shelters and look for any of our students who had not been accounted for. Immediately after the flood hit, many of us had called our students' homes to check on them after hearing about the flooding in Princeville and Tarboro. My friends, co-workers and I volunteered in the Tarboro's Sheriff's Department to call Red Cross shelters in order to contact family members who were looking for each other. That first day back, our staff went from one shelter to another, checking names on the Red Cross lists. When we found a student and family, we would sit and talk with them about their experiences and try to find out if they knew where other people could be found. We visited the FEMA trailers being set up in Rocky Mount to find some of our students. After several phone calls and visits, I was able to locate all of my students. I discovered four of my families had been living in shelters for the past few weeks until they could find a better place to stay.

When the day came for students to return, we had counselors on site to talk to them. I spent days talking over what had happened with my students. In an effort to purge sorrow and distress, we created our own big books in which the students would draw pictures and write about what had happened to them. The pictures would often show families on rooftops waiting to be airlifted into a helicopter, or families riding in a boat with lifejackets. Brown crayon scribbles represented the violent water, with stuffed toys, trash and other debris floating along the top. Many of the people in the pictures had a conversation bubble over their heads calling, "Help me. Flood!" We also made up songs about the flood. We sang about what we did during the flood and how happy we were to be back at school with one another. Students would write personal narratives and tell stories about the helicopters, snakes, and washed-up coffins so many of them had seen.

I can remember our principal telling us at that first staff meeting after the flood that we would have to dig in our heels and find a source of patience to deal with many of our students. She was right. Even after a few weeks back, a few of my students would break down and cry over anything. Some students who were reading on grade level or performing above grade level before the flood showed signs of mental fatigue and exhaustion. Most everyone's mind was somewhere else during instruction. When it would sprinkle or rain, it was very difficult to hold the group's attention. I would often have to close my blinds and read a book to them, or I would make up stories to keep our minds off the rain. These were bonding times I never took for granted. It reminded me of cuddling up close to my mom during a thunderstorm and listening to her create a suspenseful story so I wouldn't be afraid of the lightening and thunder. The sound of her voice was soothing, and I hoped that these times provided that kind of comfort for them as well.

For us teachers during this time, homework became a non-issue. I was aware that many of the students had parents who could not provide them with the tools and time needed to help them with the work. Instructional books and reading books the students had taken home had been lost in the flood. Some were living in cramped quarters of a shelter, while others were sharing homes with two or three other families. It became important to give them academic and emotional support at school and avoid the pressure of homework. I think that must have been the only positive result from the flood for many of the children at that time.

Supplies came to our school from all over the nation. Other elementary schools from Virginia to California had adopted different schools affected by the flood within Edgecombe County. At our school, Stocks Elementary, we received thousands of books, pencils, crayons, markers, notebooks, toys, clothes, anything the children needed for school or personal items to help them feel like their lives were getting back to normal. Our multi-purpose room, which we used as a gymnasium for physical education, remained packed with supplies for weeks and weeks. These supplies were intended for our staff members and students' families who needed to replenish their personal belongings. People were constantly in and out of that room getting pillows, curtains, baby formula, clothes and sometimes donated furniture.

Another elementary school in our county had been completely destroyed by the flood. Our school's playground became their new school. Several trailers were placed side by side in perfect white rows to be used for classrooms for the remainder of the school year. Ironically, we rarely came in contact with these teachers after they moved onto our schoolyard. Another school in the district would cook their lunch and shuttle it to our cafeteria where the teachers would pick it up and carry it back to their classrooms. The set-up seemed so confining and inconvenient for them.

As Stocks teachers, we could only imagine how strained the Princeville teachers and administration must have felt. So many of their students were devastated by the flood. It was bad enough they had no home to return to but they did not even have a school. For us at Stocks, we were able to pretend that things were somewhat back to normal because the students were able to return to a familiar place. For Princeville students and staff, no place felt normal or familiar. It wouldn't for a long time.

Almost two years have passed since the flood of the century in North Carolina. Princeville students and staff have moved back into their school. New and improved roads and bridges stand where they were once washed out. The trees, grass, and crops look stronger and more alive than ever. Everything is green. Houses along the stretch to Tarboro have been rebuilt, restored or removed. Personally, there are areas where I think the landscape looks more attractive than it did before the flood. Many of the once dilapidated homes are either gone or have been fixed with FEMA funds. However, there still remain a few reminders of the flood. There is one in particular that catches my attention every day. It is a large sign posted at the intersection of Old Sparta. The sign reads: "Flooded by Floyd, Denied by FEMA, Ignored by the Government, the forgotten town of Old Sparta." It is a reminder that many have not recovered from what happened two years ago. Many are still waiting for financial help, emotional help, or spiritual help to help them heal. I hope they find it soon.

Just last week while hanging out at the beach, a few of my teacher friends and I spent most of our time indoors due to the rains from tropical storm Alice. While we were talking, we reminisced on the flood. We laughed when we mentioned how we measured time by B.F. and A.F.: Before Floyd and After Floyd. We talked about how the first tornado drill after Floyd caused the students to go "ballistic." Some of the students were crying and moaning because they thought we should evacuate the building in case it got flooded. Jennifer Bullard, a Pre-K teacher, said one of her students shared the story of how "Martians" had picked her up in a helicopter and saved her from the flood.

Emily, a kindergarten teacher, reminded us of the couple who got married in the flooded Tarboro Episcopal Church in rolled-up overalls. The bride's father was unable to get into town, so he gave her away over a cell phone. The story was covered in Raleigh's *News and Observer*. Emily MacDonald also mentioned she was so scared when she was awakened in the middle of the night by lights shining outside her house and people calling out over loudspeakers, "Get out of your house; water is coming!" She said she grabbed her baby and nothing else, no diapers, no nothing. Her husband heated bottles on a gas grill because they had no electricity where they were staying. As soon as they could, they visited the lot they had just purchased to see if it had flooded. She said if it had, they had decided they would never build there. It was fine; today they have a nice, new house there.

Terry Parker, another kindergarten teacher, told us about how she piled all of her belongings on "tater" buckets as high as she could to keep the water from reaching them. She prayed, "Jesus, you just helped me get this new house and I know you'll help me keep it!" Today she is still living in her home.

These memories will remain a part of my life and my students' lives forever. We are always talking about them and referring to the time after the flood. For instance, at the beginning of this school year, while working on a unit of study about our town Tarboro, my students worked together to create a large map of their town. On part of the map, the students had a wide blue area painted in to represent the water that had covered the area of their town. They included a landing pad near the Sheriff's Department for the helicopters used by the National Guard during that time. I asked them why they had done this and they said that this was something that had happened in their town and it was important to remember. I agreed with them and encouraged them to finish it the way they wanted. When the map was complete, we talked about what was on it. From our conversations, I realized the water had washed away some of their innocence and security, but it also provided them with new insights and understanding. Today, we all continue to heal. Unfortunately, our county still has one school housed in trailers. We all hope they will begin classes in their new classrooms this year.

Where We Live

A poem written by Stocks Elementary School students
with Mrs. McClanahan and Mrs. Harrison

In Tarboro, I live in the country,
it is very far
from one place to another,
you have to drive a car.

In Tarboro, I live in the town,
where there is many a store.
The streets are sometimes crowded.
My best friend lives next door.

I have a big house in
my neighborhood,
it is called Blount Bridgers.
Here there is art work that is good!

Near Park Avenue there's the commons,
there are statues, cannons and fun things to do.
I once saw a clown there
when a fair happened to come through.

Last year, our town was flooded.
Hurricane Floyd made a mess,
Many families lost their houses,
Six children in my class have a new address.

I live near the hospital
with a flower store nearby.
There's a fire station near my church,
you can hear the sirens cry.

On Anaconda Road there are factories,
a sheriff's department and a railroad track,
from there you'll find Highway 64
to go to Rocky Mount and back.

Tarboro is a special place.
with countryside beyond the town.
The people here are friendlier,
than any other place around.

It was very odd

Interview with William Mansfield
William Mansfield with Chad and Tammy Bullock and Phyllis Adams

WILLIAM MANSFIELD: Chad, how long were you out of school?

CHAD BULLOCK: Two weeks.

WM: What was it like when you went back?

CB: Everybody was talking about the flood. I mean, everybody wanting to know how everybody else came through the flood and what happened. It was very odd.

WM: Did you lose a lot of stuff?

CB: Yeah, I lost the majority of all I had. A lot of my friends didn't get flooded. I was pretty much the only one of my friends that really got flooded. I mean, I lost everything except for a few clothes. That's about all I saved. And CDs.

WM: When you told your friends that you lost everything, how did they react?

CB: Well, you know, "I was glad it wasn't me," and, "Feel sorry for you." And that's about it. I know I had it bad, but I know there's a lot of other people that had it worse than me. People had to live, big families, in tight places for a long period of time. And I was lucky that my granddad took us in.

WM: Did the school do anything special?

CB: They had some meetings where you could just sit down and talk about it, and I'm not the type of person who just likes to sit down and talk about stuff like that. But I didn't really go to any of them. And the school also helped get supplies. They gave book bags and all the school supplies. If you'd lost school books, they just replaced them, you know, you didn't have to pay for them or anything.

TAMMY BULLOCK: I know the psychologist called and she wanted to come out and meet me because they had given Chad a test and they said he showed some signs of …

CB: Post Traumatic Stress Disorder.

PHYLLIS ADAMS: That's what we all had. I feel real bad for Chad being sixteen, You were fifteen years old at that time? You turned sixteen right afterwards. And for him to be that age and go through a flood. And you know here I am older and I'm supposed to be able to handle it better, but I think he's handled the flood better than I have.

World Order

Katharine Blackburn
AFTUR Committee

All my life
now begins
with dis- or un-.

Even half of
the tin roof
over the martin
house is dislocated;
blown away,
I think, by Bertha
in 1998.

My family
is dislocated . . .
broken bones
all over the
family cemetery.

Dispossessed without
anything, but only
temporarily
dispossessed.
Expecting our
rise to the next
level of
unbelievable slowness,
in the aftermath
of hurricane Floyd
and the flood
of the century.

If you could
imagine a recipe,
buy all the
ingredients, mix,
level, sift, add,
pour, and wait
for this special
cake to bake for
two years, you
might begin to
imagine what
I'm talking
about.

You have to
attend the cake.
Problems arise
that you must
deal with.
You have no
time; the cake
steals all
your time.

After a few
weeks you
begin to care
less about your
cake. And
still you imagine its
perfection. Its
new wholeness,
what you want.

Why should the
simple recipe
take you high
take you low
take your life?

If you imagine
the cake on
a crystal
pedestal
you are
too late.

For the anthropologists
have been digging
around your
kitchen door
and found you
mummified
wearing an apron;
wielding only
a wooden spoon.

Epilogue: *IT'S OVER*

Betty Howes, Grifton Writing Workshops.

Photo by Jean-Henri White, courtesy of *The Daily Reflector,* Greenville.

When is the disaster over?

Betty Howes
Grifton Writing Workshops

EARLY ON WE TRIED TO SURVIVE IN OUR NEIGHBORHOOD. WE HAD THE ONLY generator in the neighborhood and all meals were communal. Two days after the flood I became aware that the water backup was very widespread. Rescue squad, fire department, and police were working around the clock.

Our neighbors and I started pulling food out of the freezers to make soup for those volunteers. I still wasn't aware of the homes flooded.

Sunday I went to the Ayden-Grifton shelter to look for some of our elderly neighbors. This was a driving force for me to help. That night we were doing sandwiches at school for flood victims. About 7 o'clock two National Guard men arrived from Fayetteville with a big generator so that we'd have power at the relief center. We had seen no outsider since the flood until then.

Shortly after the guard arrived, a group of men from Memorial Baptist Church in Greenville arrived with ice coolers filled with hot stew.

For two weeks volunteers served three meals a day and tried to supply basic necessities—clothes, toilet tissue, etc. We broke the lock on the lunchroom storage room so we could continue to feed.

After about two weeks the distribution center moved to the Tucker building. There was a steady stream of victims in line all the time for food and clothes. The Mennonite ladies were there faithfully. Other volunteers worked too. For three weeks the Charlotte Hornets sent a chef and a cooking crew for meals. Volunteers helped serve.

Two weeks after the flood, people went back to work and to school. The volunteer corps shrunk. People were still needing basic things for living and a place to live. There was a constant hunt for those. Then there were the long lines for FEMA, government money, Grifton flood relief, anything to survive.

Now it's six months after the flood. Is the disaster over? No! No! No! Hands still need to be held, hugs still needed. Saying, "I'm sorry you're confused. I'm confused too."

Where can I go to get my house rebuilt? Do I have to raise it? How many permits do I need? Can you imagine going to make a cake and not having cake pans? Mr. Sylvester wanted to repair his car but first he has to find his tools and clean them.

I've learned a lot I didn't want to know.

Suzy has $500/month income—Supplemental Security Income [SSI] and Social Security. She'd lived in public housing and wishes to rent a trailer for $250 a month. The problem is she pays $250 for "dying insurance" for herself and seven others including young grandchildren. NC Insurance Commissioner, where are you?

Ruth lived with her son and three young grandsons in a doublewide home with no insurance. The son died with pneumonia in February. The sixty-seven-year-old grandma is raising the three boys. The oldest is very traumatized from losing his father, his home, and from displacement into an apartment in another town. Ruth will move back to Grifton to an unfurnished new doublewide. How will they exist on $400 a month? The mother, who pays no attention to the kids, has legal custody. She has not even gotten a Medicaid card for the kids.

Sam is a proud man, his family used to have money and is land depleted now. The Health Department won't let him stay in his house because the septic tank doesn't work since the flood. He can't replace the septic system because the ground won't perk. Water and electricity have been turned off. He stays with friends in the daytime and goes back to a dark home with no water at night. He also lost his car and has had to borrow one to go to agencies for recovery. He just asked for help about six months after the flood. He is a minister and stated that he used to help others and now he has to ask for help. Social Services is paying for a room in another place. Here, we got clothes and some small amount of money from a private stash for him. He's not able to work and has just two weeks ago applied for disability. Meantime, he has to live.

James finally got permission to rebuild his house. He got all permits for rebuilding, electrical, and plumbing. It's time for another inspection and the ceilings are two inches too low. The sub-floor and walls are finished, but he can't get a new occupancy permit. After my husband called our county commissioner to complain that this was an unfair penalty, a new inspection has been done. It seems all rooms are OK except the bedroom where the ceiling is still two inches too low. And this house is at least fifty years old.

Some people are stuck and can't move ahead. Others have made less than wise decisions. Social workers are needed. Some are so overwhelmed they're thinking about suicide. The trauma goes on. Some people who managed until now are falling apart. I give them a hug and they're trembling. There is a small group of volunteers still going. The National Conference of Black Mayors has a major rebuilding effort going.

I've felt overwhelmed lots of times, but a minister guided me to the realization that my husband and I have chosen this recovery role. The relief phase was short; the recovery phase is many times longer. How can we communicate to others that the recovery period is just a much needed as the relief phase?

Katharine Blackburn
Pitt County Writing Workshop

At the time of the Floyd flood Katharine Blackburn was a resident of Belvoir, NC. She currently lives with her husband Bob Rausch in a house Bob built in Beaufort.

June 14, 2000

She returns. There's her old rocking chair, missing the left arm and rocker, next to it the big cement container she bought at Little's Nursery. That spring she filled it with beautiful pink geraniums, the color her mother had best liked them. She nursed those flowers all through to that September. There was the pot, all empty, on its side; the geraniums just sucked out of there, vanished, like part of the porch.

Now she knew everything: Epidemics, fires, torture, dying in trenches, tidal waves, earthquakes, the holocaust, lies from God. And still she prays for logic to show her the stages and steps she must complete to establish order.

But disorder is all around her, all around like ten acres of wilted schefflera, all needing water, their leaves cleaned and polished. One leaf at a time; a billion leaves.

She is overcome.

June 20, 2000

She backs her Jeep out of the place she knew. She has a momentary question about her neighbors, but she knows they are safe. Weren't they just at the road clapping when Bob and the two dogs came out in a boat and a canoe? The water line of the flooding is high and she imagines all that will die of the flora and fauna. She imagines nothing will survive or come back. Knowing nothing can survive gives her the feeling it's all right to let go, give up, and not spend her energy. She has questions about the flood; does God have an answer for her?

God waits and does not answer all the questions about the damage of the flood; He does not give us a clue. How much harder do we need to search? He, like all of the authorities, keeps us uninformed and helpless. There does not seem to be a God or Jesus helping me. Maybe you with better connections can conjure him up for me.

December 1, 2000

Bob and I heard the motor of a boat around eleven Friday morning. We didn't know what the sound was at first. Who would expect this noise so close to our house? The boat pulled up to our front porch. The neighbors said, "You have to get out!" I recall a simultaneous feeling of such absolute doubt and absolute wonder. I was stunned. When I looked at Bob, I knew. We were given a few moments to pack some clothes. At this time, all of our cats (nine of them) were in the house. We set out as many containers of food, water, and litters as we had. The cats might be all right, but what about Max and Ike? We began negotiating with our neighbors about taking the dogs with us. Thank God they agreed to the plan or we never would have left! Max went on the bass boat with John and Sam and Bob. Ike and I got into our Wenonah canoe and left. Each slight movement Ike made threatened to capsize us. We motored down our driveway through the woods, current, hidden snakes and easement to a dry place next to the huge holly tree. The rest of our neighbors were waiting. Their crying and applause greeted us.

July 4, 2001

Tomorrow we sign papers giving my home to the government, so they can demolish it. We will get a check and I thought that would alleviate everything but now I reconsider that I am giving up my home. We have been moving things out of our Belvoir house for a couple of weeks because you must have taken all you want before they will close. I am crying a lot because my life feels knotted, winded and going off in directions I have no control over.

Will I ever be joyous again?

March 26, 2002

I like to spend my days in my pajamas decaying. Lately I've been looking back at the flood and all it changed. If there had been no flood … Rosie, Romeo, Mom, Bob and I, my flowers and my 32-year-old phone number, etc.

Bob is recovering, rebuilding; I am not.

Two and a half years since, my eyes still see raging water, snakes, destruction and a path created by underwater mailboxes.

April 15, 2002

Bob and I bought a used lawn mower today, a 1981 Yazoo. Bob is out there now and I smell that grass mowing smell, sweet, defined, a fragrance of order. I myself have planted a few containers today: basil, sage, lantana. I think they may flourish in the sun here.

I still spend time with myself and my loss of direction. One moment, I'm on the mend, the next sucked out of myself like that geranium on my old front porch. I believe that time heals all wounds and I would like to reveal to you those wounds. But in truth, I want to protect you from them now. Please feel safe, secure. Odds are you will never be flooded. Odds are I will never be flooded again.

We have hope.

We were not victims of Floyd

Betty Burlingham

I HAVE RECENTLY BEEN THINKING BACK THROUGH OUR TWENTY-TWO YEARS of life on our 465-acre ranch here in Eastern North Carolina. The reason for these thoughts is that we are preparing to move to a new country—to the island of Dominica in the Caribbean. The move is not tied to the flood but rather to a career change for my husband. We are currently selling our 200 acres of trees and using the proceeds to purchase a new ranch in Kansas. Our retirement home will be built there on the banks of another river, the Kansas River. We will be selling this farm and bringing to a close the North Carolina chapter of our lives. All of this calls for reflection.

Our lives at the Tar River Ranch have been touched with joy, excitement, amazement as well as violence, horror, and intrusion. The flood is a minor interruption in the big picture of life here. It pales in comparison with having our home broken into on several occasions, having two of three children shot at, finding a live hand grenade in the yard, opening the door in the middle of the night and finding a man with a running chain saw in one hand and a baseball bat in the other.

But perhaps I shouldn't compare a natural event with the unnatural acts perpetrated by our fellow humans.

As hurricanes go, Bertha and Fran are far more vivid to me than Dennis and Floyd. Our oldest son lost his "state fair" steer in Bertha when he got out on the road and was hit by a wrecker truck. During Fran, we lost my favorite 300+-year-old tree that shaded our house and provided a great place for the kids to play when they were little. The flood was very gentle. The waters rose slowly here. We had lots of time to get prepared. We measured the rate of water level change every hour or so and plotted it. We even predicted the crest and missed it by less than two inches. We moved all our equipment to our highest ground, then moved all our livestock—twenty-five cows and about 150 sheep. The last thing we did was put the furniture on blocks. We had ten inches of water in the house. We stayed here the whole time. It was really a very nice quiet family time. We fed the animals from a washed-up row boat; we rescued neighbors in a canoe. We even took the canoe all the way to the by-pass bridge on Hwy. 43, walked to the medical school and bought groceries at Food Lion.

It was a time of creative thinking and I do not remember it as being stressful until the National Guard moved in. At that point the water was down and we could drive to town. They gave us a hard time about getting back home on more than one occasion.

The real stress began after the house was condemned. It was so hard to get

257

information about what we needed to do. We never did move out of the house but it took seven weeks to get the electricity turned back on. That's what I remember the most—seven weeks without electricity. When November arrived, the weather was getting quite cold and I was trying to arrange to get a FEMA camper so the kids would have a warm place to study (we home school them). Many of our neighbors had gotten campers but I had to go over and over and over to the FEMA office at the East Mall Annex. I remember leaving there in tears on two occasions because we weren't granted a camper. Finally, I called the Raleigh office and the camper arrived in a couple of days.

We enjoyed having the camper. The FEMA employees who came once a month were all very courteous. As summer neared, we were told the government wanted to sell the campers. I asked them to give us a week's notice but that didn't happen. I was baling hay one day in June when I saw a truck hooking up to the camper. The kids and I really had to scramble to get our things emptied out before they hauled it away.

After the flood waters receded, we ran a pipe from the Greenville Utilities Commission water meter to the house. Of course, this was illegal, but we had no electricity and we needed water. We all remember those cold showers but we did stay clean. A couple of months later, the meter reader disconnected us but we had our new pump in place by then. We never did repair the house. In fact, in a real sense, we have just been camping here since then.

After the water receded, we removed the carpets and scraped up the linoleum. The sub-flooring is still the only flooring in the house today. We moved the kitchen appliances to the first floor of our feed mill building. We moved our dining room to the second floor of the mill. Our living room furniture had been moved to the mill's third floor before the flood so we were only left with the bed and dressers. Thus the house became the "bunk house." For the first year after the flood, I would cook our meals on the first floor (there was running water outside the building but none in it), take the food up to the second floor where we would eat, carry everything back down—then haul it all to the house where I still had a kitchen sink to wash dishes. Then the clean dishes had to be hauled back to the mill to start the whole process over again.

In December of 2000, we finally finished installing a sink on the second floor and moved the range and refrigerator up there onto a newly-tiled floor. That was the best "Christmas present" I ever had. We took the kitchen cabinets out of the house, repainted them, and installed them in my new kitchen. My husband began removing the paneling from the walls of the house to install it in the mill. Our bunk house has several "walls" that are bare studs but the new room in the mill looks great. So, our house is in two separate buildings. That is certainly inconvenient at times, especially in bad weather, and I do look forward to living in a "real house" in Dominica.

The flood took its toll on our land, washing out the soil. We've had to apply lime and more fertilizer and our grass productivity is just now returning to the pre-flood yields. Horse hay is our cash crop and we have had financial losses with it since the flood. Gifts left by Mother Nature include fire ants and new breeds of weeds we did not have before.

Cleanup was a major task. We had over 200 sets of trailer steps deposited around our pastures and countless bags of garbage, bottles, and cans. No one came back to claim anything except for a trash service which recovered some of their dumpsters. We disassembled the stairs and have recycled most of the lumber into other projects. We have spent many hours picking up trash, hauling old tires, etc., to the dump. There are still a few remains left in our pond.

Immediately after the flood, the quality of our lives improved because the people were gone. We enjoyed the rural life when we bought our farm. We did not expect urban development. When they left, we had peace once more. Honestly, the worst thing that has happened to our quality of life since is the return of the people. In the past year, our farm equipment has been damaged to the tune of several thousand dollars by 8- to 12-year-old unsupervised children. Gangs roam up and down the road once more. Sheriff sirens are a common sound.

We were not victims of Floyd. We were participants in that natural event. Floods happen. We experienced one of them. We've been through hurricanes, tornadoes, fires set by lightning, and a flood. This is all a part of life on the earth. We deal with it and we move on. It is nothing compared to the horrors inflicted upon man by his fellow man—remember September 11th.

I do think I will write a book about our lives in North Carolina to pass on to our children and descendents. The Floyd flood will definitely be included but it pales in comparison with many other experiences we have had here. We've had a great life here. Eastern North Carolina is an amazing place. You reap what you sow and we have had a very fertile season.

May 31, 2002

There's a dead end road to this journey

Gary R. Redding
Assistant Editor and AFTUR Committee

BORN IN THE SAME POVERTY AND RACISM JUST A FEW MILES UP THE ROAD FROM Princeville, but with a radically different view of resolving the human conflict of being black and poor, this twenty-one-year-old continues to be impressed and perplexed by the commandment of love, the self-discipline and the joy and moral craft of black Princeville.

Recently viewing the hostile and oppressive remnants of the area and listening to the dreams and hopeful resolutions in the words of an abandoned people, and indeed the haunting melody of one newly created song, *There's A Dead End Road To This Journey*, would make some want to scream in outrage and despair. Nowhere are the inner dynamics of race and exploitation more at work than in the psyche and the culture of present day Princeville.

The people interviewed seemed calm enough and more than thankful enough, but like Ralph Ellison's *Invisible Man*, the people of Princeville walk softly among the rubble and shattered lives after hurricane Floyd and the 1999 flood, strongly resembling dangerous *sleepwalkers*.

Former resident Clarence Jones graciously took the time to be my guide through the small rural enclave. A quiet gentle person, Jones relocated to my hometown of Tillery in Halifax County, NC, after hurricane Floyd and the great flood of 1999. Through all the upheaval and loss of his home, his automobile and all his material goods, the 40-year-old Jones has kept a positive attitude. He struggles to be an effective long-distance father to his four children from a former marriage, and to be a topnotch professional in his job as a correctional officer with Caledonia Prison in Tillery

"Do you remember details about the flood?" I asked as Jones drove us down the newly-paved, two-lane portion of Hwy. 258, the main drive through Princeville, and maneuvered the narrow paved streets of his old neighborhood.

"Actually, the flooding was September 16, '99. I'll never forget it. As far as actually being there because of my profession, I had to be at work in case we had to ship inmates to other institutions," the fifteen-year veteran correctional officer answered proudly. "I was actually there when the flood occurred. It was two weeks later before I was even able to get back to my home to see what damage I had sustained."

When Jones was finally able to get back into his neighborhood, he felt fortunate that he did not lose a family member. "Everything else was materialistic, and I knew I could recover from materialistic things. I didn't lose a family member and I'm grateful for that," remarked the former US Marine.

When I asked what triggers certain emotions about Princeville as he knew it, Jones took a deep breath and answered, "Actually, when you come into Princeville on 258, the Town Hall, and there was also a store/recreation center where every Friday night me and quite a few of my friends would hang out. It gave us a place to mingle with other friends. When I first come into Princeville on 258, yes, it does trigger memories."

Jones admits that during his six years in the US Marines where he helped give aid during other natural disasters, "I never saw anything like it. So when they named it 'the Flood of the Century,' they didn't underestimate it. And, I would also like to thank you for giving me this opportunity to speak out on it."

Johnny and Lois Clark were also appreciative that someone was allowing them to speak out about the tragedy of the flood of 1999. As husband and wife, they too lost everything in the flood. Their house, valued at $98,000, had to be torn down. "It was a year and some months before we were able to come back to our home," reported Mr. Clark. In spite of all the tragedy and the separation and "a whole lot of changes" they experienced, and not knowing if everybody in the family was all right, the Clarks are a bouncy, virtuous and magical couple. They are full of life and longing, and seem well equipped with the ability to help and sustain, and "to be a provider" for the well being of their daughter and her children and other extended family members who share their new home in Princeville.

They reminded me of a king and queen of great African ancestry. The two talked all over each other, finished each other's sentences, complementing one another, expressed wonder and marveled at being separated during the flood and then finding each other at a shelter. They seemed to be sensually and emotionally attuned to each other. No one pronounces the word *husband* with the warmth and feeling of Mrs. Clark. The twenty-five-year natives of Princeville gave every indication that they share a common fulfillment in their spirituality, in acquiring new territory and possessions, and in doing for others.

The old house had eight bedrooms and three full baths filled with relatives and grandchildren, and had a special room built just for the pleasure of the two of them.

"The last room he built [*onto the old house*] was our special room," said Mrs. Clark. "I mean he built it, I'm talking 'bout, he built it himself. He built it from scratch. It was our special room."

"It was a 16 x 16 room with a walk-in closet," Mr. Clark added.

They are proud of Princeville's history. "It's the oldest black town on the charter," recited Mr. Clark. "Princeville has a lot of history," he continued. "More lawyers, doctors, and a senator have come out of Princeville. I can show you the exact spot where Freedom Hill is, where the slaves were first freed."

In 1865, right after the Civil War, black slaves in Edgecombe County, North Carolina formed a small community they called "Freedom Hill," now known as Princeville. The community went through many stages of development, and suffered several floods because of the overflowing of the Tar River until a dike was built in 1965. The first permanent teacher, Robert S. Taylor, a native of Jamaica, also later served as a justice of the peace and served two terms in the North Carolina Senate.

When the town was incorporated, February 20, 1912, under a special act by the North Carolina General Assembly, the residents renamed "Freedom Hill" after one of its oldest members, Turner Prince, who died in 1912. Under this special act, Princeville became the oldest incorporated black town in America.

The existence of Princeville has always been threatened by racism, exploitation, the ramifications of "Jim Crow," and unfair economic strife.

Even though the Clarks maintain that they suffered no racism during the flood, listing help from white churches and the Moose Lodge, they admit suspicion about the motives of whites about their historic town. "White people pretend they don't want Princeville," explained Mr. Clark, "but they do in a way. They act sneaky with it. 'Cause they would love to steal the town. But we manage to hang on to it. We had some rough times trying to hang on to it. But we got it going. After the flood, we made a lot of progress. Lotta new houses being built."

The terror of the flood of 1999 still lives with Mrs. Clark. "Every time it rains, especially if it's real hard, I get scared to death. I don't know how to react." "I'm in good shape," said Mr. Clark. "Me, I have always been a provider. I like to have things. Lotta folks who didn't have anything before the flood, now have better things than they had before."

Mrs. Clark wrote a song about the flood, "because we all had been through so many trials and tribulations, gone through many changes since." This is just a little portion:

> Lord, I've been through the storms
> And I been through the rains
> I been through tossed and driven
> But I know, I know one day
> It will be over
> There's a dead end road to this journey.

May 31, 2002
Princeville, North Carolina

So much has changed for me

Sharon O'Neill
Assistant Editor and AFTUR Committee

SO MUCH HAS CHANGED FOR ME, FOR US, SINCE THE FLOOD THAT IT'S HARD FOR me to believe that it's only been three years. It seems like a lifetime ago, at least it did seem that way until I started working on this project again. When my now ex-husband left us shortly after the flood for work in Oklahoma I dealt with a lot on my own. I came to a place in my life where I realized that I was going to have to make my own future.

My kids and I still live in Belvoir, in the same house. I had lost my herb garden and all the plants put in before the flood, and afterwards I didn't want to spend any time outside for a long time. Last year, though, I had tomatoes, and this year I have some herbs in pots and I even put some flowers in and put up a birdfeeder. We are constantly fighting fire ants. They are vicious, getting worse every year. We are also finding the strangest weeds in our yard, but we do have volunteer plants that are welcome, like tiny oxeye daisies spreading across my lawn.

My kids are doing so much better now. Joseph is going into fifth grade and Jasmyn is going into fourth. They went to the new Northwest Elementary School this year that was built to help ease overcrowding at Belvoir and they loved it. They were both suffering symptoms of Post Traumatic Stress Disorder after the flood, and East Carolina University offered counseling sessions through the school system to them for free. My kids are growing to be very expressive, communicative and compassionate, and the tools they learned through counseling helped them a great deal through the divorce and this year after September 11.

I think that one thing that this made me face is how tenuous life is. My dad used to say, "Nothing is a sure thing but death and taxes," and now I think I know what he meant. I used to see things as all or nothing, either bad or good, but this has made me stop and search for the good aspects and, if I don't find them right away, I try to have patience and wait, for I know the good will show itself to me somehow.

Every day is a gift, each trouble a chance to learn. I'm still impatient—can't stand waiting in lines—but I'm not sure if that has anything to do with the lines we waited in during the flood. I think it has more to do with me not wanting to waste any more time. I want to live each moment with an eye on my purpose, with my goals firmly in place, ready to accept whatever comes my way.

It makes me very thankful and very humble to think of the amount of work that total strangers did for us. I remember driving to the airport in Raleigh about a week after the flood and realizing I was on the road with fire trucks and rescue vehicles from several different states as they were heading home.

One group that directly affected us, especially my kids, was the animal rescue volunteers (EARS) who set up a makeshift shelter in the life sciences building over at the hospital. When we could finally pick up our cat to bring him home, he was handed to us well fed and loved, with a new collar, a pet carrier and a bag of food. It was one thing that I know made a difference in my children's lives, to see how much these people cared for animals, that they risked their lives to rescue them.

This project also reminded me of how much work our own rescue personnel did—the volunteer firefighters, the Greenville Utilities Commission workers, the police, the county workers, many of whom had just lost their own homes. I was in tears a good deal of the time in those days, but much of the time it was from gratitude as I heard the stories of how hard they were working to save the substation, to keep people fed during those first ten days. I can't imagine how exhausted they must have been or how they got through it themselves.

I don't know if they were ever thanked, but I would just like to thank them now.

June 21, 2002
Belvoir, North Carolina

The flood of the century

Anthony Donnell Dudley
Ayden-Grifton Emergency Shelter
September 24, 1999

MANY PEOPLE KNOW THAT THE LORD FLOODED THE WHOLE, ENTIRE EARTH AT one point in time. Well, this is now. This is how the Flood of the Century is to me. This is a reminder that it is about time for the Lord to reclaim his precious beautiful Earth and its people. The Lord knows all and sees all. In my heart, I feel this flood is bringing people from different cultures and races together as a family. Our hearts go out to all of the people who lost their lives in the flood. I know our Lord has them with him.

This is a wake-up call to everyone to pull together as one big family. People around the world know the situation that the buildings, counties, animals and people are in. So does the Lord. You see, everyone and everything belongs to the Lord. This is his Earth and all of us are his creation. The Lord gave his Son for our sins. The Lord loves all of his creations. It is time for the people to help out one another. Now is the time.

Anthony Dudley at Grifton Writing Workshop.

Photo courtesy of the North Carolina Humanities Council.

It's over and that's it

Willa Peaden

I AM WRITING AGAIN ABOUT THE FLOOD AFTER ABOUT TWO YEARS. YES, I STILL remember all the details about the flood. It's a permanent picture in my mind, everything that happened from the day I had to leave home until thirteen days later when I could get back. The mice had taken over and all my forty laying hens here dead.

I don't mind talking about it all. My brothers and sisters still can't imagine that much water being here. It hasn't bothered me as far as sleeping or relationships but I never had high blood pressure before, now I have to take medicine all the time for it.

I am aware that it was not all Floyd that caused all the water to descend on us, but that is in the past now and I don't think it will ever happen again.

I didn't lose my house but I had a lot of losses. My family helped me a lot. I got some help and am very thankful for that, but not enough. As for the way the officials handled the money, it was not fair. Some got a lot, more than they needed, and some got a little or nothing. Now they say they have millions of dollars left over and don't know what to do with it? They should just go ahead and give it to the ones who didn't get enough or none.

I'm not bitter because it's over and that's it.

April 2002
Belvoir, NC

Appendices

This chronology combines information from several sources including: ECU's Joyner Library Special Collections Hurricane Floyd chronology on their web page at http://www.lib.ecu.edu/spclcoll/chronology.htm; Richard Moore and Jay Barnes, eds., Faces from the Flood: Hurricane Floyd Remembered *(Chapel Hill: The University of North Carolina Press, 2004); and John R. Maiolo et al., eds.,* Facing Our Future: Hurricane Floyd and Recovery in the Coastal Plain *(Coastal Carolina Press, 2001).*

Saturday, September 4

Tropical Storm Dennis comes ashore near Cape Lookout, bringing heavy rainfall to eastern North Carolina

Thursday, September 16

Hurricane Floyd makes landfall near Cape Fear, NC, around 3 AM and moves north to Virginia; around 4 AM winds are 86 mph; massive rains causing flash floods that result in most of the 52 deaths resulting from Floyd

First death in Eastern North Carolina from the flood is a worker from Dupont on the outskirts of Kinston who drowns when his car enters several feet of water on NC 11

Local towns begin to establish a dusk-dawn curfew that lasts through October 1 in flooded areas

Storm waters begin to recede in many parts of Pitt County

By 7 PM floodwaters begin to rise in Rocky Mount and evacuation begins

Friday, September 17

Midnight - 3 AM evacuation of residents of Rocky Mount continues

By 3 AM Tarboro and Princeville are flooding, residents evacuated

By 3 AM floodwaters are rising in Belvoir area; some residents evacuated by helicopter; other residents congregate at Belvoir Volunteer Fire Department; NC Forestry Service and local residents begin rescue efforts

Nearly 1500 people are evacuated by helicopter; the Tar River crests in Rocky Mount at 32-35 feet

70-75% of roads in Lenoir County are impassable; Pitt County road to Stokes impassable; evacuations begin in the Clarks Neck/Tranters Creek area near Grimesland Bridge Road

U.S. Coast Guard rescues approximately 300 people stranded on rooftops in Dunbar, NC

Grifton sewage treatment stations surrounded by water

Pink Hill without power and using generators to operate sewage plant

Snow Hill evacuated; dam breached at Contentnea Creek flooding the downtown area of Kinston; curfew ordered until Saturday 7 AM

Trenton evacuated by 6 PM

Eastern Pines had power through the day but not through the night

Saturday, September 18

Flooding moves east

Massive aerial rescues take place; U.S. Coast Guard helicopters from the CG Air Station in Elizabeth City fly more than 273 hours of rescue missions in the Tarboro area using six Coast Guard aircraft

Contentnea Creek at Grifton floods residences

General curfew in Kinston lifted, but 8 AM - 7 PM curfew still in effect for flooded areas

As flood waters rise, refugees in Belvoir move from Fire Department to Gum Swamp Free Will Baptist Church

Nearly 2000 evacuated from Wilson County; approximately 250 residents evacuated from low lying areas in Grifton; 1200 people evacuated in Snow Hill

Scuffelton and Hookerton under water.

Sunday, September 19

Carolina Power and Light reports 6,000 homes without power in Lenoir County; Carolina Electric Cooperative reports 14,500 homes without power

3 PM curfew in flooded areas

Rivermont in Lenoir County evacuated by 8 AM

Monday, September 20

President Bill Clinton visits Tarboro on his flood tour; Tar River crests in Tarboro at 41.51 feet

Duplin, Jones, Wilson, Pitt and Edgecombe Counties under extreme flooding; mandatory evacuation; mass feeding and sheltering of evacuees

Pitt County water plant is sandbagged and in danger of flooding.

Bell Arthur plant has many line breaks

Sheets of tobacco moved out of warehouses in Kinston

Telephone access restored in Eastern Pines

Tuesday, September 21

Tropical storm Harvey brings an additional three inches of rain to parts of eastern NC

City wastewater plants shut down in Kinston

Aid begins to reach Belvoir residents

Wednesday, September 22

Tar River crests in Greenville at 2 AM Wednesday morning at 29.72 feet

Thursday, September 23

Neuse River reaches 27.7 feet at 5 AM

Displaced residents of Rocky Mount begin moving into government provided trailers; the Arts Center, Playhouse Theater, Art Museum, Children's Theater and three electric substations destroyed; Sunset Avenue Water Treatment Plant remained out of service for approximately a month

Governor Hunt visits Kinston

Friday, September 24

Greenville airport closes due to flooding

Men's Ministries International of the Pentecostal Holiness Church serves free meals in Kinston from 6:30 AM to 6:30 PM until October 1

Neuse River at 26.9 feet; Kinston sets curfew in flooded areas indefinitely

Sunday, September 26

Floodwaters begin to recede in Princeville

New areas of Greenville flooded by Green Mill Run

Monday, September 27

East Carolina University in Greenville reopens for faculty and staff

American Red Cross works with Pitt County to consolidate and move temporary shelters from six schools to Boys and Girls Clubs in Ayden, Greenville and Grifton

Tar River down to 20.1 feet

Holloway Recreation Center residents in Kinston go back to collect clothes and other items not destroyed by the flood

Neuse River at 23.97 feet and dropping

Goldsboro has 6 more inches of rain

Tuesday, September 28

Additional rain falls over portions of eastern NC

Wednesday, September 29

The Reverend Jesse Jackson visits Princeville

East Carolina University students return to class

Neuse River in Kinston up to 24.1 feet after Monday's rain

Friday, October 1

Some areas of Greenville still under water; dusk to dawn curfew still in effect in Pitt County

Monday, October 4

Tar River in Greenville down to 16.38 feet

Tuesday, October 5

Governor Jim Hunt makes plea to Congress for emergency aid

Monday, October 18

Hurricane Irene brings additional rain to many counties in eastern NC

Monday, November 8

Final flood fatality in eastern North Carolina discovered in Nash County

PITT COUNTY WRITES:
STORIES FROM THE FLOOD

Offered to the community of Grifton by the North Carolina Humanities Council

Led by Julie Fay, published poet from East Carolina University's English Department.

NCHC invites you to attend Workshops tell and write stories and poems about personal and community experiences with the recent floods. Children and adults are welcome.

▶ Session 1: April 10, Grifton Depot, 6:30-9:30pm

▶ Session 2: April 17, Grifton Depot, 6:30-9:30pm

Please contact Mitchell Oakley at (252) 746-6261 to sign up or Emily Dings at the NCHC office at (336) 334-5704 for information or to sign up.

Pitt Community Writes: Stories from the Flood
Pitt Community College Workshop
Thursday, October 26, 2000
6:30-9:30pm

workshop leader:
Julie Fay

I.   Introduction

This evening, we are going to be talking about our experiences during the floods of
September 1999 and what has happened since then. Why? To record and witness these
extraordinary days, to remember, to understand ourselves better as well as our definition
of community, to learn.

We will be doing—as a group and on our own—a series of exercises that are aimed at
getting you to write things down—or tell them to someone who will write them down for
you. The most important thing to understand is that this is not a class, there is no such
thing as right or wrong here, you are not getting graded on what you do, not judged and
anything you say is valuable, You may find that writing some of your feelings down will
be very uncomfortable, may make you relive very unpleasant moments, grief, fear. You
may find in the end, however, that once you've written things down you understand your
feelings better and can move past them, get on with rebuilding and continuing your life
after Floyd.

II.   Who's here? Why?

III.   Fast writing

IV.   Exercises, writing suggestions

If these are of use to you. Use them; if not, discard them. Try doing some fast writing for
at least one half hour tonight. Try to focus your writing on flood related events and
issues. Start you fast writing with one of the following questions or suggestions. If you
get off the topic as you write, that's ok. Just keep writing wherever your mind takes you.

- What was the most surprising thing that happened to you during or after the flood?

- What was the funniest thing that happened to you during or after the flood?

- Tell a story about one of your neighbors, (you don't have to name the person)

- Did you get mad at any time during the floods? When and Why? What did you do about your anger? Do you still feel angry?

- What does the word community means to you? What was you neighborhood like before the flood?

- Describe you neighborhood after the flood?

- Describe Eastern North Carolina as a community before and after the flood.

- What happened to you the day before the flood? What were you doing> Where were you?

- What happened to you the day of the flood? Where were you? What did you see? Smell? Hear? What did you touch?

- Did the flood make you more aware of natural disasters in other parts of the world?

- What people did you meet as a result of the flood that you otherwise probably never would have met?

- Did you learn anything new about people that you'd never knew before?

- Did people surprise you or meet with your expectations in their response to the floods?

- What are your feelings about the officials whose job it was to help people with flood-related issues? FEMA? Red Cross? SBA? Your insurance company? Shelter officials? Church?

- Write a story as if you were someone other that yourself during the flood.

- Write a letter to your great-grandchild telling her about the events last fall.

- Write a letter to someone who will be in the a flood next year in another part of the world.

- Write a list of things to remember.

- Write a list of questions you have.

ROCKY MOUNT WRITES:
Stories From The Flood Workshops

SPONSORED BY:
North Carolina Humanities Council
Bridging The Gap
Rocky Mount Edgecombe CDC
Community Enrichment Organization
The Franklinton Center At Bricks
Visions Incorporated
NAACP
Northeastern NC Association Affairs of Black People

Workshop Facilitator:
Phillip Shabazz

About the facilitator:

Noted author, poet, educator, Phillip Shabazz has conducted workshops at over 200 public and private schools, colleges and universities, correctional facilities, cultural and community centers where as a result, he has edited volumes of student poetry. He is currently Artist-In-Residence in the Mary Lou Williams Center for Black Culture at Duke University.

These writing workshops will provide:

- An opportunity for citizens to write about their Hurricane Floyd experiences as a way of processing this devastating event.
- Create a historic family document in the participant's own works and feelings
- The opportunity to think reflectively and critically about how their experiences are connected to the lives of other people in the community

Dates and Locations:

August 10th	OIC Classroom	1st Floor	6:00-9:00 pm
August 17th	Edgecombe Comm College		6:00-9:00 pm
	Rocky Mount Campus	Room 163	
August 24th	Rocky Mount Edge CDC	Room 104	6:00-9:00 pm

Space in each workshop is limited to 25 participants. For additional information of registration, please call Latoria Davis at 446-2134.

The NC Humanities Council is based in Greensboro and affiliated with the National Endowment for the Humanities. For information on the council's flood history project or any of the group's other activities, call (336) 334-5236.

PITT COUNTY WRITES: STORIES FROM THE FLOOD

Offered to the community of Grifton and Belvoir by the North Carolina Humanities Council

Led by Julie Fay, published poet from East Carolina University's English Department.

NCHC invites you to attend Workshops tell and write stories and poems about personal and community experiences with the recent floods. Children and adults are welcome.

▶ Session 1: April 25, Belvoir Fire Station, 6:30-9:30pm

▶ Session 2: May 1, Belvoir Fire Station, 6:30-9:30pm

Please contact Pat and Eugene James at (252) 752-6336 to sign up or Emily Dings at the NCHC office at (336) 334-5704 for information or to sign up.

Contributors

Co-editors and Assistant Editors:
Julie Fay
Joyce Joines Newman
Harlan Joel Gradin
Ana Cowó
Sharon O'Neill
Gary Redding
Lois B. Watkins

Layout and Design:
Katherine Kubel
Brandie Knox-Kirkman

Visuals:
Susan Luddeke
Henry Stindt
Michele Hayslett
City of Greenville
The Daily Reflector, Greenville
Lois B. Watkins
Neil Moore
Joyce Joines Newman
N. C. Forestry Service
Phyllis Adams
Ana Cowó
N.C. Humanities Council
Jean-Henri White

Supporters:
Weyerhauser, Inc., Greenville, NC
Riverside Printing [formerly Walker-Ross Printers], Rocky Mount, NC

Rocky Mount, Tarboro and Princeville Contributors:
Philip Shabazz
Nellie Johnson Hunter
Melinda Belcher
Lois B. Watkins
Ida Boddie
Shirley Myrick

Mae Ricks
Sondra Williams
Juanita Wright
The Reverend Richard Joyner
C. Michael Shaw
Willie Harper
Lewis Turner
Linda Virgil
Angela Bryant
Clarence Jones
Johnny Clark
Lois Clark
Stocks Elementary Second Grade Students
    with Mrs. McClanahan and Mrs. Harrison

Belvoir Contributors:
Willa Peaden
Sharon O'Neill
Derrick Moore
Sandra Warren
William Mansfield
Phyllis Adams
Mike Adams
Doug Bullock
Tammy Bullock
Chad Bullock
Eddie James
Tammy Abeyounis-James
Mary James
Danielle Abeyounis
Kristen Abeyounis
William James
Benjamin James
Charles Tucker
Gene Tucker
Walter Allen
Ed Meeks
Robert Garrow
Ricky Gray
Sheila King
Mary King

Bruce Brady
Wendy Brady
Allen Smith
Pat James
Eugene James
Jenée Brewer
Julie Howard

Hispanic Section Contributors:
Norma
Victoria
Pilar
Wilber
Arturo
Jorge
Antonio

Pitt County Contributors:
Katharine Blackburn
Carol Christian
Jill McClanahan
Mike McClanahan
Betty Burlingham

List of Grifton Contributors:
Betty Howes
Earl Teel
Mary Teel
Anthony Donnell Dudley
Billy R. Sutton
Nadine Willis
Jonathan Willis
Ashley Nelson
Vanissa Nelson
Darelene Nelson
Johnnie B. Nelson
Representative Marian McLawhorn
Stephlee Simmons
Tracey D. Simmons
Janice Periquet